Rand McNally Guide to
The
MID-ATLANTIC
By Andrew Hepburn

RAND McNALLY & COMPANY
CHICAGO / NEW YORK / SAN FRANCISCO

F
106
H 4

Photo Credits.

The following sources have kindly given permission for the photographs appearing in this book, on the pages listed: Niagara Falls International News Bureau, 6; New York State Department of Commerce, 13, 16, 19, 20, 23, 25, 26, 28, 31, 34, 35, 36, 37; Corning, New York, Glass Center, 18; National Park Service, Department of the Interior, 30, 48, 95 (top and bottom); The Solomon R. Guggenheim Museum, 38; New York Stock Exchange, 44; Philadelphia Convention and Tourist Bureau, 50, 59; Pennsylvania Department of Commerce, 57, 63, 69, 75; American Airlines, 60; Pocono Mountains Vacation Bureau, 66; Hershey (Pennsylvania) Estates, 73; Chamber of Commerce of Pittsburgh, 77; Drake Museum, 79; Greater Erie Chamber of Commerce, 81; New Jersey Department of Conservation and Economic Development, 82, 87, 89, 92, 98; Trenton Chamber of Commerce, 88, 90; National Park Service, U.S. Dept. of the Interior, 95 (top); Thomas Alva Edison Foundation, 95 (bottom); W. P. Kent, 96; Delaware State Development Department, 99, 101, 103, 104; Henry Francis du Pont Winterthur Museum, 106, 107; Maryland Department of Economic Development, 110, 113, 120; Chamber of Commerce of Metropolitan Baltimore, 116; Maryland Port Authority, M. E. Warren, 118; Maryland Jockey Club, Jerry Frutkoff, 119; Baltimore Association of Commerce, M. E. Warren, 121; Trans World Airlines, 123; Earl Palmer, 131, 145; The Greenbriar, 134; West Virginia Department of Commerce, Gerald S. Ratliff, 136 (top and bottom); Colonial Studio, Richmond, 142; Virginia Department of Conservation and Economic Development, 146, 151, 154, 160, 166; Virginia Chamber of Commerce, 149; Virginia Conservation Commission, 152; Dementi Studio, Richmond, 153; Colonial Williamsburg, 156, 158; Photos by Marler Alexandria, 169; The Mount Vernon Ladies' Association, 170. Title page: David C. Kent.

59979

Contents.

How to Use
This Guide.

THIS GUIDE is a practical tool designed to help you discover, understand, and enjoy the scenic variety, historic cities, and charming villages of the seven Mid-Atlantic states. It will assist you in selecting a lodging for the night or in choosing a restaurant.

One of a growing series of Rand McNally travel guides, this guide links several elements in a practical, tested, easy-to-use pattern. These elements include: (1) a readable, informative, and accurate general text that describes many places worth seeing; (2) short features on subjects of interest in the area; (3) a series of maps keyed to the text, adapted especially for this guide; (4) fine photographs, with detailed captions; (5) detailed descriptions of the best accommodations and restaurants, arranged alphabetically by state and town; (6) a table of contents, with a summary of sections and features, and a detailed general index at the end of the guide.

To use the guide most effectively you'll need to understand each element and its relation to the others.

General Text and Photographs. The general text describes communities, historic and scenic places and regions, the character of the land and routes through it. The text describes recreational facilities and tells when each is open and the admission charges, if any. It gives enough history to make the character of the place understood, tells you how to get from one town to another and how far it is from the point previously described and whether the route is a fast expressway or a slower scenic highway. Photographs, each with an informative caption, supplement the text.

Accurate Maps. The maps for this guide, prepared by some of the best cartographers in the country, are simple enough to be easily used, yet detailed enough to provide all the information needed for a clear understanding of the region and the routes through it.

Each state or regional map shows geographical features and national or state parks. On each regional map appears a series of numbers. The numbers indicate major places of interest described in the text under boldface headings. In each numbered area are other places of interest, indicated on the map but not numbered. They are also indicated by boldface headings and are located in direction and distance from a numbered point of interest in the text.

Feature Supplements. Scattered through the general text are brief, informative essays supplementing the text but not directly related to it. These features appear in tinted blocks.

Accommodations and Restaurants. This very important section appears toward the end of the guide. It is a selective list of the best and most interesting hotels, motels, and restaurants in cities and towns covered in the text. Each entry gives detailed information on the establishment based on careful research. No fee has been charged proprietors for a listing, and each listing is as impartial and accurate as care and judgment can make it.

The border between the United States and Canada passes through the 176-foot high Horseshoe, one of the three cataracts that make up Niagara Falls.

NEW YORK.

LARGEST MID-ATLANTIC state, and the only one that borders both the Great Lakes and the Atlantic Ocean, New York's range of topography and scenery is unmatched in the East. Although it is the second most populous state in the country, it has vast wilderness regions.

New York covers 49,576 square miles; it is 30th in size in the country. Vaguely triangular in shape, it extends about 300 miles north to south, 315 miles east to west. Neighboring states and countries include, on the north and northwest, beyond Lake Erie, Lake Ontario, and the St. Lawrence River, the Canadian provinces of Ontario and Quebec; on the east, Lake Champlain, Vermont, Massachusetts, and Connecticut; on the south, Long Island Sound and the Atlantic Ocean, and a land border with New

Jersey and Pennsylvania; and on the west, a very short land border with Pennsylvania.

New York's notable features include the thundering cataracts of Niagara Falls and the wide channel of the St. Lawrence River, shared with Canada; Lake Champlain, one of the largest lakes in the East; the Hudson River, one of the most beautiful of the nation's great rivers; the tremendous forest and mountain wilderness of the Adirondacks, which spread over about five million acres; the slender, glacier-carved Finger Lakes; the low, rugged Catskill Mountains; and Long Island, extending 125 miles from the southeast corner of the state, with superb ocean beaches.

The modern history of New York began in 1524, when an Italian mariner named Giovanni da Verrazano, command-

6

ing a French ship, sailed into New York bay. New York City honors him today with a tremendous bridge spanning the entrance to the bay.

In 1609 Samuel de Champlain, a French explorer, traveled south along the lake named for him, and Henry Hudson, an English sailor working for the Dutch, sailed up the great river that bears his name. In 1624 the Dutch established a fur trading post, called Fort Orange, just south of the present city of Albany. One year later they founded New Amsterdam, on Manhattan Island, at the mouth of the Hudson River. The Dutch settled all along the lower Hudson Valley, on Long Island and Staten Island. In 1664 the English took over and renamed New Amsterdam New York. For the next hundred years settlement continued steadily, impeded here and there by battles with hostile Indians and later with the French, who claimed much of the northern part of the area. New York grew from a village into an important city, ranking with Boston and Philadelphia.

During the Revolutionary War almost one-third of all engagements were fought on New York soil. Washington led his army through a chain of defeats across Long Island, up Manhattan Island into Harlem, to White Plains, and finally into New Jersey. But there were decisive American victories. Ethan Allen and his Green Mountain Boys took Fort Ticonderoga away from a surprised British garrison, and at Saratoga the British general Burgoyne was roundly defeated in two engagements that marked a turning point of the war.

The war over, General Washington took leave of his troops in a New York City tavern, and in 1789 he took the oath of office as president on the steps of Federal Hall on Wall Street. For a few years New York City was the nation's capital.

New York began to grow. By 1810 it had almost one million people. Twenty years later there were almost twice that number. The opening of the Erie Canal in 1825 gave New York a waterway link to the Great Lakes, reducing the cost of hauling a ton of freight from Buffalo to New York from $120 to $14. The Erie Canal established the destiny of New York City as a great seaport and the gateway to the New World for a steadily increasing stream of immigrants.

Today New York's manufacturing industries exceed those of all other states in the number of establishments, the number of employees, and the value of the products. New York leads all other states in clothing manufacture, printing and publishing, instrument making, paper and paper products, and in many other categories. New York makes nearly 70 percent of the nation's photographic equipment, prints more than half of the magazines published, and makes half of all gloves manufactured.

Though industry and manufacture far outrank farming in New York, by a ratio of almost 20 to one, nearly 18 million acres are farmland, with about 150,000 acres in orchards and vineyards. New York ranks second in the country, surpassed only by Wisconsin, in dairying. Only Vermont makes more maple syrup and only Washington harvests more apples. Long Island is noted for potatoes and poultry, particularly ducks.

The most important highway in New York is the New York State Thruway, extending from New York City north to Albany, then west to Buffalo and southwest along Lake Erie to Pennsylvania. It is the longest toll road in the country, nearly 500 miles. From Albany Interstate 87 continues north through the Adirondack Mountains to the border of Canada. Through the center of the state Interstate 81 extends north and south from the St. Lawrence River through Syracuse to Binghamton and the border of Pennsylvania. New York 17 leads northwest from New York City through the Catskill Mountains to Binghamton.

Points of interest in New York are indicated by number on the maps on pages 8-9 and 10-11, and described in associated text, starting in the southwest corner with

1. CHAUTAUQUA, population 500, in summer about 10,000, on the west bank of Chautauqua Lake, about 15 miles south of Lake Erie. The village is renowned for the

Chautauqua Institution, founded almost 100 years ago as a center for education, recreation, and religion. The summer school, directed by Syracuse University, has a busy schedule of opera, drama, and symphony, and lectures by leaders in the fields of music, politics, education, and religion. On the grounds are an amphitheater, a campanile, and Palestine Park, developed around an enormous relief map of the Holy Land, used in teaching Bible history. Visitors spend most of their leisure time at

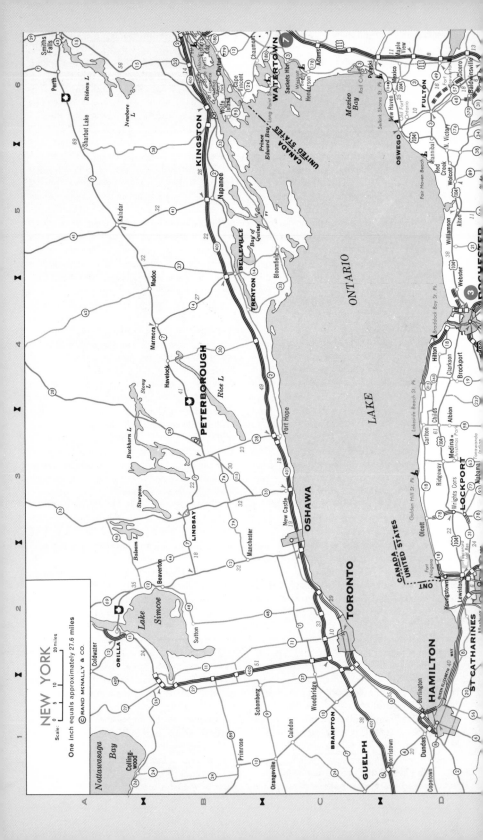

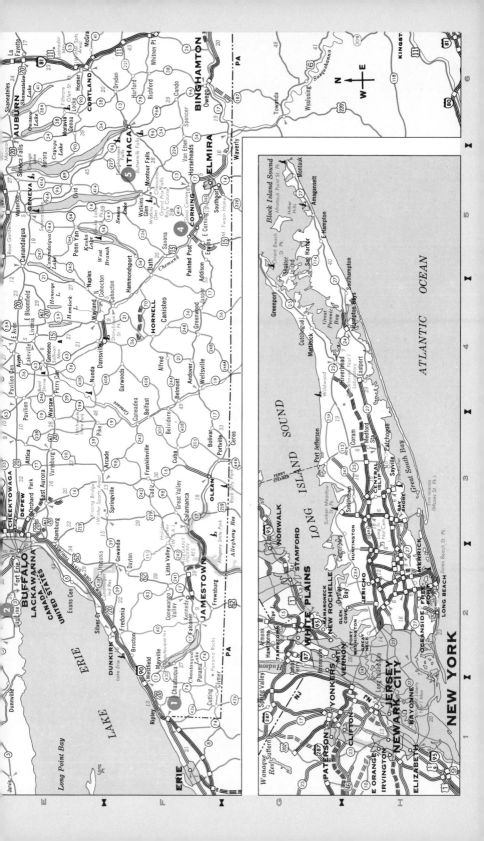

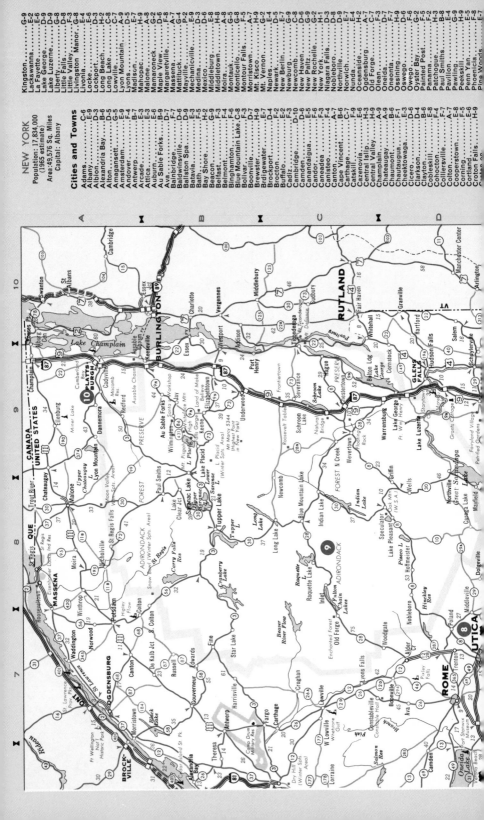

NEW YORK

Population: 17,834,000
(1965 estimate)
Area: 49,576 Sq. Miles
Capital: Albany

Cities and Towns

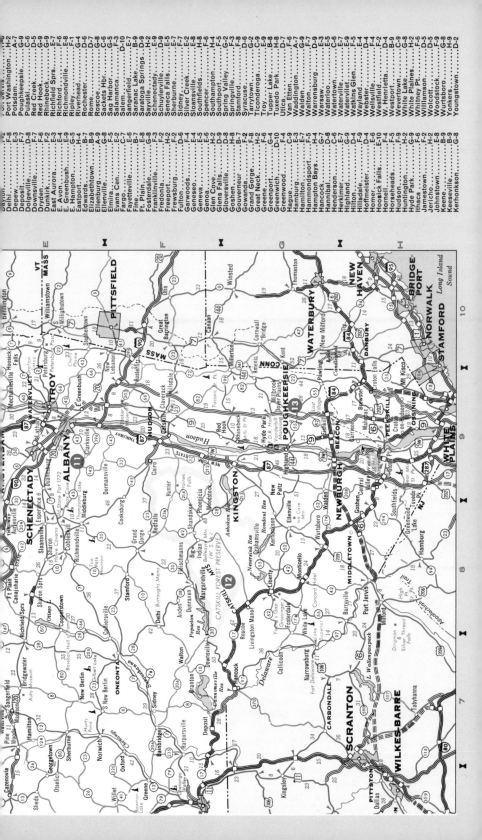

NEW YORK FACTS

Name. For the Duke of York and Albany.

Nickname. Empire State.

Area. 49,576 square miles, 30th in the United States.

Population. 18,210,000, 1969 estimate, second in the United States (after California).

Admitted as a state. 1788, 11th among the 13 colonies.

Capital. Albany.

Largest city. New York, 8,000,000, largest in nation.

State tree. Sugar maple.

State flower. Rose.

State bird. Bluebird.

Industry. Leads the nation in total industrial production; first in apparel, printing, publishing, photographic equipment, ocean shipping and foreign trade, banking, security marketing; important in paper, wine, electric power.

Agriculture. Clover (first in nation), maple syrup, dairy products, vegetables, grapes.

Odds and Ends. Is the world and national financial capital, United Nations headquarters, and the birthplace of four presidents; has the nation's longest internal waterway, the largest ocean port, and the most extensive mountain and wilderness area of the Mid-Atlantic states.

Lake Chautauqua, 18 miles long, from one to three miles wide. Besides offering water sports, boating, and swimming, the lake is famed for muskellunge, one of New York's finest game fish, growing to 50 pounds.

From the south end of Lake Chautauqua and the city of Jamestown, New York 17 extends east about 25 miles to the village of Salamanca, at the north end of

Allegany State Park, largest state park in New York, with more than 60,000 forested acres, and elevations of from 1,300 to more than 2,300 feet. Allegheny Lake extends along the west side of the park for 25 miles; it offers boating and fishing. The park has over 50 miles of paved roads, hundreds of miles of trails, ski slopes, camping and picnicking facilities. It adjoins huge Allegheny National Forest in Pennsylvania.

From the Chautauqua region, New York 17 leads northwest to a junction with the New York State Thruway (Interstate 90), which closely flanks the shore of Lake Erie. From the junction it is about 60 miles northwest to New York's western metropolis:

2. BUFFALO, population 450,000, New York's second largest city, core of a metropolitan district of more than 1.3 million people. The world's largest center for the milling and shipping of wheat, Buffalo is also one of the country's largest railway centers. Its port handles more than 15 million tons of cargo each year from both Great Lakes and oceangoing ships. Buffalo is a center for diversified manufacture, with the emphasis on iron and steel.

In 1679 the French explorer La Salle built a tiny ship called the *Griffon* with timber cut from Buffalo forests. The *Griffon* was the first vessel built by white men to navigate the Great Lakes. In 1758 French settlers established a village at the mouth of Buffalo Creek, which the British destroyed the following year. Buffalo began to grow around 1799, when a survey was made for the Holland Land Company, and a town, planned after the new capital at Washington, D.C., was laid out, with main streets radiating from a central square. Buffalo's streets still follow that pattern. During the War of 1812 Buffalo, with a population of about 500, was burned by the British, but was quickly rebuilt. In 1816 the *Walk-on-the-Water,* first steamboat to operate on the Great Lakes, was launched at Buffalo.

In 1825 an event occurred that determined most of Buffalo's future growth. It was the completion of the Erie Canal, which gave Buffalo a direct water link with New York City. Within months warehouses were bulging with eastbound farm produce and westbound manufactured goods. Hundreds of immigrants on their way west arrived almost daily. By 1832 Buffalo had a population of 10,000 and was growing fast.

Two Buffalo citizens became presidents: Millard Fillmore, the 13th, and Grover Cleveland, the 22nd and 24th. President William McKinley, while attending Buffalo's Pan-American Exposition, was assassinated there in 1901, and there Theodore Roosevelt took the oath of office to succeed him.

Routes To and Through. The city pattern of Buffalo is controlled by its location, at the east end of Lake Erie and the south end of the Niagara River. Main streets radiate from central Niagara Square. The New York State Thruway (Interstate 90) skirts the eastern edge of the city. Interstate 190 diverges east along the shore of Lake Erie, continuing north through the Niagara Falls area. From Interstate 190, just north of the city's center, the Canadian express highway, Queen Elizabeth Way, linked to Buffalo by the Peace Bridge, diverges northwest into Canada.

Points of Interest—Downtown.

Niagara Square, a landscaped park in the heart of the downtown area. At its center is the impressive McKinley Monument, an obelisk rising above a series of fountain pools, erected to the memory of the assassinated president. On the west side of the square is

City Hall, with a central tower rising 32 stories, above 14-story flanking wings. Inside are murals and statues relating to Buffalo's history. At the main entrance are statues of the two Buffalo presidents, Millard Fillmore and Grover Cleveland. About two miles northwest of Niagara Square, with an entrance at Porter Ave., is

The Front, a handsomely landscaped 50-acre park along the shore of Lake Erie. In the central plaza is a statue of Oliver Hazard Perry, hero of the 1813 Battle of Lake Erie. Perry defeated a British fleet near Sandusky, Ohio, and became famous for his victory announcement: "We have met the enemy and they are ours." At the north end of The Front is the

Peace Bridge, built in 1927, commemorating 100 years of peace between Can-

Buffalo's waterfront has been a focal point for the shipping of food ever since the completion of the Erie Canal. Here are a few of the city's many huge grain elevators.

ada and the United States, spanning the Niagara River, linking Buffalo with Fort Erie, Canada. (Toll 25¢.)

Points of Interest—North and East.

The best route for a concentrated tour of Buffalo's sights and historic places is

Delaware Ave., extending north from Niagara Square. The Buffalo Club, at 388 Delaware Ave., now a private club, was the setting for an emergency meeting of the cabinet while President McKinley lay dying in another mansion, at 1168 Delaware Ave. At Gates Circle, Lincoln Parkway leads north from Delaware Ave. to

Delaware Park, laid out in 1870 by Frederick Law Olmsted, the architect of Central Park in New York City. The 350-acre park has a lake for summer boating and winter ice-skating, a golf course, tennis courts, and bridle paths. On the western side of the park is the

Albright-Knox Art Gallery, 1285 Elmwood Ave., an impressive marble building housing extensive collections of art, from prehistoric to modern. Notable features include a sculpture court and a Mirrored Room, lined with mirrors, with all furniture made of mirrors. The gallery is open free, Monday through Saturday, 10 a.m. to 5 p.m.; Wednesday to 10 p.m.; Sunday, noon to 6 p.m. Nearby is the

Buffalo and Erie County Historical Society, Elmwood St. and Nottingham Ct., with exhibits of pottery, glass, costumes, pioneer tools, period rooms and shops, and a re-creation of a typical 1870 Buffalo street. Open free, Monday through Saturday, 10 a.m. to 5 p.m.; Sunday, 2 p.m. to 5 p.m. From the Albright-Knox Art Gallery, a park drive leads northeast to the

Buffalo Zoo. More than 1,000 animals are displayed in barless and cageless habitat areas. Open free daily, April through October, 8 a.m. to 7 p.m.; rest of the year until 5 p.m. From the southeast gate of Delaware Park, Humboldt Parkway leads south to Humboldt Park and the

Buffalo Museum of Science, with a series of exhibits, many of them animated, illus-

trating scientific processes. Open free, Monday through Saturday, 10 a.m. to 5 p.m.; Wednesday to 10 p.m; Sunday, 1:30 p.m. to 5:30 p.m.

From Buffalo the Niagara River, split into two channels by Grand Island, flows north with increasing turbulence. About 15 miles from downtown Buffalo the two channels unite in surging rapids that reach a spectacular climax at

Niagara Falls, shared by the United States and Canada. East of the river are the American Falls and the United States city of Niagara Falls (population 90,000). West of the river are the Horseshoe Falls and the Canadian city of Niagara Falls, Ontario (population 56,000).

Since 1678, when Father Louis Hennepin, a French priest, stood spellbound at the gorge of the Niagara River and made a sketch of the falls, Niagara Falls has been luring visitors. In modern times man has been able to conquer and use the falls. The Welland Ship Canal, which bypasses the falls, accommodates the largest Great Lakes ships. Vast hydroelectric installations on both sides of the river have tapped the power resources of the falls and the rapids.

To understand and appreciate Niagara Falls, both as a spectacle and a force, you need to know what they are. The falls are part of the Niagara River, which is not a true river, but a 34-mile channel linking Lake Erie to the south with Lake Ontario to the north. The waters flowing from Lake Erie to Lake Ontario drop more than 300 feet. The most dramatic aspect of that descent is Niagara Falls, a plunge of about 160 feet. Horseshoe Falls carries 94 percent of the river's flow, with a curving rim of about 3,000 feet (hence the name). The smaller American Falls, a little farther downstream, is 1,000 feet wide.

In June 1969, American Falls was turned off, by an extraordinary feat of engineering, to reduce the rate of erosion at the lip of the falls, which might have eventually converted the falls into a rapids. The water was diverted to Horseshoe Falls or to hydroelectric pipelines. The falls was turned on again in November 1969.

Points of interest on the American side of the river include

Grand Island, reached from Buffalo by Interstate 190, which cuts through the cen-

NIAGARA FALLS

NIAGARA FALLS, which the United States shares with Canada, is both a unique spectacle and a resource of enormous economic value. It attracts more visitors than any other natural feature of the North American continent. Its flow of well over 200,000 cubic feet per second produces the greatest amount of electric power in the western hemisphere.

Millions of years ago, glaciers blanketed the region around the falls and gouged out the basins of the Great Lakes. At the end of the Ice Age, when the blanket of ice melted, the lakes were brimming with water. Since Lake Ontario was more than 300 feet lower than Lake Erie, a surging torrent was created. This was the beginning of Niagara Falls.

The falls got their name from an Indian word meaning "thunder of waters." The first report on the falls by a white man was made in 1678 by Father Louis Hennepin. The place where he stood to sketch the falls is a favorite viewing point today.

The French, between 1678 and 1759, controlled the portage around the falls, built two forts to protect it. The British gained control in 1759. One of the forts, now restored, is a major tourist attraction.

The first person to do anything about putting the enormous power of the falls to work was Augustus Porter. Early in the 19th century he bought land around the falls, built a grist-mill, and became master of the portage. For a time he did well in milling and portage fees. But the completion of the Erie Canal in 1825 put him out of business.

The first generator went into operation in 1881. Power resources were steadily developed, reaching their peak in 1961.

Millions of visitors come to see Niagara Falls every year. For some reason the falls have an immense appeal to honeymooners. All sorts of tourist facilities are available: scenic shore boulevards, viewing towers, boat rides around the base of the falls, catwalks underneath, and bridges spanning the gorge and river.

The falls have always been a challenge to fools, daredevils, and publicity seekers. People have crossed the falls on a tightrope. Others have attempted to shoot the rapids and go over the falls in barrels and custom-built boats. Some succeeded, many did not. Steve Brody, who became famous by jumping off the Brooklyn Bridge, went over the falls in a rubber suit in 1889 and lived to tell about it.

The latest episode in the history of Niagara Falls was an engineering project to divert water from the American Falls so the crumbling rim could be shored up. This was done to check the erosion that has been going on for thousands of years. If the project is successful, in a few years the American Falls will be restored to their former splendor. If it fails, the falls will eventually disappear, leaving only surging rapids.

ter of the island. West River Parkway diverges from the express highway, providing a scenic drive along the west side of the island and linking two state parks. From the northern end of Grand Island Interstate 190 crosses to Niagara Falls, New York, to link with the Robert Moses Parkway, which closely follows the river, providing spectacular views of the upper rapids, the falls, and the lower rapids through the gorge of the river.

Niagara Reservation State Park, foot of Falls St., which includes Prospect Point, at the brink of the American Falls. Prospect Point Tower, rising 282 feet above the river, provides fine views of the falls and the gorge. (Admission: adults 25¢, children under 8 free.) A Viewmobile offers a 30-minute miniature train ride from Prospect Point to Goat Island and back with stopovers at several viewpoints, daily, mid-May to mid-October. (Fare: adults 60¢, children 30¢, under 5 free.) One of the best viewpoints for both falls is

Goat Island, separating the American and the Canadian falls, a wooded 70-acre park with drives, walks, and picnic areas. From Goat Island, elevators operate to the river level, where wooden bridges lead to the Cave of the Winds and to stunning but moist views of the American Falls below. From the Niagara Reservation Robert Moses Parkway continues north along the rim of the Niagara gorge to

Whirlpool State Park, a 125-acre park from which trails and steps lead to the base of the cliff for a close-up view of the swirling water and the great whirlpool, more than 1,750 feet wide, 126 feet deep. About two miles north of Whirlpool State Park is

Power Vista, four and a half miles north of the falls, at 5777 Lewiston Rd. (US 104), with an observation and information building for the chief Niagara Power Project. It offers fine views of the gorge and the huge power plants along both sides of the river and has audiovisual explanations of the project. A mural by Thomas Hart Benton shows the discovery of the falls by Father Hennepin.

A place of high historic and scenic interest is 15 miles north of the falls, just outside the village of Youngstown:

In Letchworth State Park are 17 miles of the Genesee River Gorge, sometimes called the Grand Canyon of the East, with sheer cliffs 600 feet high.

Old Fort Niagara, a National Historic Landmark within Fort Niagara State Park. Built by the French in 1726 on the site of an earlier one built by La Salle in 1678, the fort was a strategic point on the western fur trade route. Seized by the British during the French and Indian War, it was taken over by the Americans in 1796 and recaptured by the British during the War of 1812. In a scenic setting at the mouth of the Niagara River, overlooking Lake Ontario, the restored fort is crowded with interesting relics: 52 mounted cannon, a drawbridge, and a fortified French castle furnished in Louis XV style. Open daily during summer, 9 a.m. to 8:45 p.m.; winter until 4:30 p.m. (Admission: adults 60¢, children under 12 free.)

About 50 miles east of Buffalo, US 20A crosses the Genesee River, which flows through

Letchworth State Park, a 14,000-acre tract extending about 17 miles on both sides of the river, preserving a dramatically scenic gorge with cliff walls rising to 600 feet. In the gorge the river drops over three waterfalls. The park, with facilities open May through October, has accommodations, swimming pools, camp, trailer, and picnic sites, and a historical museum.

About 70 miles east of downtown Buffalo by the New York State Thruway is New York's third largest city:

3. ROCHESTER, population 295,000, on the Genesee River and the New York Barge Canal, which replaced the old Erie Canal. From a settlement established in 1789 around a gristmill on the edge of a swamp, Rochester has grown to a notably handsome and prosperous city, one of the most important industrial centers in the East. It is a world center for optical and photographic equipment, and is preeminent in electronics and instruments. Its most celebrated industry is the Eastman Kodak Co., world's largest maker of cameras and photographic equipment. Other important Rochester-based companies include Xerox, Bausch and Lomb, General Dynamics, and Taylor Instruments.

Routes To and Through. The main route of the New York State Thruway (Interstate 90) skirts the southern suburbs of Rochester. An extension from it, Interstate 490, leads to the city, links with two loop express routes: east-west US 104 and north-south New York 47.

Points of special interest in Rochester are widely scattered. In the downtown area is the new

Civic Center, adjoining the War Memorial Auditorium, seating 10,000. Just south is one of Rochester's historic houses:

Campbell-Whittlesey House, S. Fitzhugh and Troup Sts., built in 1835, a fine example of Greek Revival design. The house has been restored and furnished in the style of the canal days and has notable examples of French, American, and Empire furniture and decor. Open Tuesday through Saturday, 10 a.m. to 5 p.m.; Sunday after 2 p.m. (Admission: adults 50¢, students 25¢, children 6-14 10¢.) One of Rochester's most popular civic features, well worth seeing, is the new

Midtown Plaza, between Main and Broad Sts., about four blocks east of the river, with 20 shops and two department stores flanking an enclosed, air-conditioned, landscaped plaza, over an underground garage. A few blocks east of the central business district is the

Museum and Science Center, 657 East Ave., with exhibits relating to natural history, anthropology, and pioneer life, with habitat groups, dioramas, and period rooms. An adjoining garden is devoted to roses and herbs. Open free, Monday through Saturday, 9 a.m. to 5 p.m.; Sunday, in September through May, 2 p.m. to 5 p.m. The garden is open daily in summer, 9 a.m. to 9 p.m. About three blocks east is Rochester's most famous dwelling, now a museum, the

George Eastman House, 900 East Ave., a splendid mansion with landscaped grounds, built in 1906 by the founder of the Eastman Kodak Co. and willed by him to the University of Rochester. The 49-room Georgian mansion is now a museum of the history of photography. Open free daily, 10 a.m. to 5 p.m.

South of the central business district is

University of Rochester, with a landscaped campus of 150 acres, overlooking the river, on River Blvd. at Elmwood Ave. The massive, handsome buildings are of Georgian design. The university has seven colleges and schools and about 8,000 students. Just north of the university is

Highland Park, Highland Ave., a small park famous for lilacs. During the May Lilac Festival more than 500 varieties are in bloom. South of the university is

Genesee Valley Park, main entrance at Elmwood Ave. and River Blvd., on both sides of the Genesee River, with two golf courses, swimming pools, and an ice-skating rink. The river and the New York Barge Canal intersect in the park.

Most visitors to Rochester want to see

Kodak Park, about four miles north of the center of town, at 200 Ridge Rd. W. (US 104). The largest camera and photographic supplies factory in the world, Kodak Park has more than 80 buildings scattered over 400 acres. The Eastman Memorial, a circular plaza on the bank of the river, has a pedestal in the center with an urn holding the ashes of George Eastman's body.

Free tours of the vast plant are conducted Monday through Friday at 9:30 a.m. and 1:30 p.m.

About 20 miles southeast of Rochester on New York 31 is

Palmyra, population 3,500, where Joseph Smith, founder of the Mormon religion, lived as a boy. The most interesting exhibit is

Hill Cumorah, four miles south on New York 21, where 18-year-old Joseph Smith claimed he received the golden plates from the Angel Moroni. Smith's translation of the plates resulted in the Book of Mormon. The hill, now a Mormon shrine, is the setting for a Mormon Pageant held in late July each year. A statue of the Angel Moroni on top of a 40-foot-high pillar is at the crest of the hill. Nearby is the

Jackson and Perkins Rose Garden, nine miles east of Palmyra on New York 31, in the town of Newark. The garden, on S. Main St., has the world's largest display of growing roses: more than 35,000 bushes. Open free during summer.

From Rochester, US 15 leads south and southeast through the hills and lakes at the western edge of the Finger Lakes region about 80 miles to

Major attractions in Corning, New York, are the Steuben Glass Factory, where skilled glassblowers and artists work, and the company museum.

4. CORNING, population 16,500, a city almost wholly devoted to making glass since 1868, when a Brooklyn glass company moved to the area and grew into the Corning Glass Works. The company now has plants scattered throughout the country and abroad making everything from Christmas tree ornaments and light bulbs to the finest optical glass. Executive headquarters of the company and several of its divisions are in Corning, including the highly publicized Steuben Glass Factory, where glass and crystal are converted to unique art forms by renowned craftsmen. At Corning the company maintains the

Corning Glass Center, on Centerway, both a company showcase and a museum devoted to the history of glass from about 1500 B.C. to the present. The most notable exhibit is a slightly flawed duplicate of the 200-inch mirror disk cast for the Palomar

Mountain Observatory in California. One can tour the adjoining Steuben Glass Factory and watch skilled glassblowers and artists at work. The center is open free daily, but closed Monday November through May.

Also in Corning is the

Rockwell Gallery of Western Art, 22-23 W. Market St., in the Rockwell Department Store, with a notable collection of Western paintings and bronzes, antique guns and toys, and the world's largest collection of Carder Steuben glass. Open free Monday through Saturday, 10 a.m. to 5:30 p.m.; Friday to 9 p.m.

From Corning US 15 leads northwest about 20 miles to a junction with New York 54 at the village of Bath. Six miles northeast on New York 54 is

Hammondsport, population 1,200, at the tip of slender Lake Keuka, one of the Finger Lakes, stretching 20 miles north, in a region of rolling wooded hills. The village is the center of New York's extensive vineyard and winemaking region, with wineries all around and slopes patched with vineyards. Wineries that welcome visitors include: Gold Seal Vineyards, noted for champagne, four miles north on New York 54A; Taylor Wine Co. and Pleasant Valley Wine Co. (Great Western), about two miles south on Old Bath-Hammondsport Hwy. Conducted tours weekdays, morning and afternoon, about 30 minutes. Near Hammondsport is the

Finger Lakes Wine Museum, about two miles north on Bully Hill Rd. The museum, housed in an old winery, displays old winemaking equipment and offers conducted tours of former wine cellars. Open June through October, Monday through Saturday, 9 a.m. to 11 a.m., 1 p.m. to 4:30 p.m. (Admission: adults 50¢, 12-18 25¢, children under 12 free.)

About 20 miles northeast of Corning on New York 414 is

Watkins Glen, population 2,800, noted for big salt mines and for sports car races held during the summer and fall. But the chief attraction is

Watkins Glen Gorge, in a 660-acre state park near the southern end of Seneca Lake, which stretches 35 miles north. The stream creating the gorge drops about 700 feet in less than two miles, with many rapids and 18 waterfalls along its course. Cliff walls rise 200 feet above the water. Stairs cut in the cliff sides make close-up sightseeing possible, or one can take a taxi to the top of the gorge and walk down. The park has a big swimming pool, bathhouse, picnic grounds, and tent and trailer sites.

Eighteen miles southeast of Corning on New York 17 is

Elmira, population 45,000, on the Chemung River, once the home of the country's greatest humorist, Mark Twain. The city is famed for pioneering in higher education for women, for penal reform, and for the sport of soaring in sailplanes. Points of interest include

Mark Twain Study, Park Pl. near Washington Ave., on the campus of Elmira College. Octagonal in shape, built to look like the pilothouse of a Mississippi River steamboat, the study was Mark Twain's workshop during the first years of his marriage. Open free, Monday through Saturday, 9 a.m. to 4:30 p.m., July and August; September through June by appointment only.

Elmira College, founded in 1855, has about 1,500 women students.

Woodlawn Cemetery, Walnut St., north end of town, has the grave of Mark Twain. Nearby is Woodlawn National Cemetery, with the graves of almost 3,000 Confederate prisoners of war who died in an Elmira Civil War prison camp.

American La France Plant, 100 E. La France St., which began making fire engines in 1834, is now the largest fire engine fac-

The Finger Lakes area of New York state furnishes many of this country's finest domestic wines. Here the wine is being aged in outdoor barrels.

In one of New York's more than 80 state parks is preserved the delicate, fairy-castle beauty of Watkins Glen Gorge, near the southern end of Seneca Lake.

tory in the world. Free tours June through September, weekdays, 10 a.m. to 2 p.m.

Harris Hill Soaring Site, eight miles northwest off New York 17E, is the best place in the country to watch soaring in sailplanes. The field offers sailplane rides and soaring lessons, and is the setting for several national soaring contests.

About 40 miles northeast of Corning by way of New York 17 and New York 13 is an industrial city that is also a famous educational center:

5. ITHACA, population 29,500, on Cayuga Lake, largest of the Finger Lakes, stretching north 40 miles between steep-sloped, wooded shores. The city is the center of an important salt-producing district. The Adding Machine Division of the National Cash Register Co. is located here, but the main point of interest is

Cornell University, with a splendid, 423-acre, handsomely landscaped campus at the crest of a high hill overlooking Lake Cayuga, on the southeast side of town. Cornell, with 14,000 students, is privately endowed but has some state-aided divisions, and maintains a full range of schools and colleges. Outstanding are the colleges of Engineering and Agriculture and the Hotel School. Student-conducted tours of the campus leave Willard Straight Hall at 11 a.m. and 2 p.m. weekdays during the academic year. Special campus features include a

Clock Tower, 173 feet high, of Romanesque design, with a 14-bell chime.

Anabel Taylor Hall, a World War II memorial, is an interfaith center with a revolving altar used by all faiths. A notable small garden adjoins it. Cornell's art collections are displayed in the Dickson Art Museum and in the Franklin Hall and Van Rensselaer galleries. There are waterfalls and several rugged gorges, one spanned by a foot bridge, on the campus. The **Laboratory of Ornithology,** three miles northeast of the main campus, at Sapsucker Woods, is a wooded, 180-acre bird sanctuary with a ten-acre pond. An observatory in the middle of the sanctuary, open weekdays 8:30 a.m. to 5 p.m., adjoins a library. There are hiking trails through the woods.

From Ithaca New York 96B and New York 96 lead southeast about 50 miles to

Binghamton, population 67,000, at the junction of the Chenango and Susquehanna rivers. Just north is Johnson City (population 20,400) and just west is Endicott (population 17,500). The three cities form a closely built industrial district with a wide diversity of manufacture including shoes, cameras, aircraft accessories, and plumbing fixtures. The Roberson Center for the Arts and Sciences in Binghamton, at 30 Front St., specializes in local history. There is a small zoo on Park Ave., open free daily, May through September.

From Ithaca, New York 13 leads northeast 25 miles to a junction with north-south Interstate 81. On Interstate 81, 35 miles north of the junction, is

6. **SYRACUSE,** population 210,000, fourth largest city in New York, at the southern end of Onondaga Lake. Syracuse is one of the oldest cities in the East. It is said that the Indian chief Hiawatha chose the shore of Onondaga Lake as the site of the capital of the Iroquois Confederacy. The first Euro-

peans in the area were Jesuit priests, who established a mission in 1656. American and English settlers arrived in 1788. All the early settlers came for the same reason— salt. For many years Syracuse supplied most of the salt used in the country. Huge plants now produce chemicals derived from salt; others turn out electrical equipment, automotive parts, and air-conditioning units.

The parallel north-south routes of Interstate 81 and US 11 lead through the city, intersect on the north edge with east-west Interstate 90, the New York State Thruway.

Although primarily an industrial city, Syracuse does have exhibits of interest for visitors. One is the

Canal Museum, Weighlock Bldg., corner of Erie Blvd. E. and Oswego Blvd., near the center of town. Canal operating equipment, models, buoys, and pictures are displayed, and there is a library devoted to canal history. Open free, Tuesday through Friday, 1 p.m. to 5 p.m.; Thursday to 9 p.m.; Saturday, 10 a.m. to 5 p.m.; Sunday, 2 p.m. to 6 p.m.

In the southern part of the city is

Syracuse University, University Ave. at University Pl., with a handsomely landscaped hilltop campus and about 20,000 students. The University is famous for its College of Forestry, which offers exhibits of landscape architecture and natural science. Other points of interest are the Lowe Art Center, the Rare Book Room of the main library, and the Mayfield Library, with a notable collection of books devoted to 19th-century English and American literature.

From the center of the city scenic Onondaga Lake Parkway (New York 57) leads northwest along the shore of the lake to Onondaga Lake Park. In the park is the Salt Museum, with relics of early salt extraction; the Jesuit Salt Well, discovered in 1654 by Father Simon Le Moyne; and a reconstruction of a French fort built in 1656. Open free daily, 8 a.m. to 8 p.m., and to 9 p.m. in summer.

From Syracuse the parallel routes of US 11 and Interstate 81 lead north about 70 miles, through the prosperous agricultural region around the east end of Lake Ontario, to

7. **WATERTOWN,** population 32,500. Watertown grew up around early lumber-

and gristmills on the falls of the Black River, which drop about 115 feet over dams within the city. Modern mills, still using the river's power, turn out an assortment of products, chiefly paper. Just south of the city center is the

Flower Memorial Library, 229 Washington St., a strikingly handsome · white marble building of classic design, noted for its collection of Indian relics and historical murals. Open free weekdays September through June, 9 a.m. to 9 p.m; Saturday, 9 a.m. to 5 p.m.; July and August, 9 a.m. to 6 p.m; Friday, 9 a.m. to 9 p.m. Across the street is the

Jefferson County Historical Society, 228 Washington St., exhibiting models of waterwheels and early machine tools. Open Tuesday through Friday, noon to 5 p.m.; Saturday, 10 a.m. to 5 p.m. Watertown has one scenic area worth visiting:

Thompson Park, southeast side of town, entrance from State St., with 355 hilly, wooded .acres. There are a small zoo, a swimming pool, and picnic grounds.

West of Watertown is

Sackets Harbor, population 1,300, a resort village on the shore of Lake Ontario. Sackets Harbor was the site of the first battle of the War of 1812, on July 19, 1812, when a British fleet attacked the town and was repelled by one United States ship and some volunteer farmer-soldiers. The battlefield is on Main St. at the lakeshore.

From Watertown Interstate 81 leads north about 25 miles to the St. Lawrence River and a junction with New York 12, on which, four miles east, is the important resort center of

Alexandria Bay, population 1,600, chief community in the beautiful Thousand Islands district, a 50-mile section of the St. Lawrence River. The river channel, five miles wide in some places, is studded with about 1,800 islands, ranging in size from big rocks to several acres. The best way to see the area is to take one of the several boat trips based in Alexandria Bay. Trips last from one and a half to three hours; fares range from $1.50 to $3.50.

A starting point from which to explore the area is the

Thousand Islands International Bridge, four miles west of Alexandria Bay, crossing the St. Lawrence to meet Canadian highway 401. On Hill Island, midway between two bridge spans, is the remarkable

1000 Islands Skydeck, a 400-foot cylindrical tower with a high-speed elevator that whisks visitors to observation platforms at the top, with a snack bar, cafeteria, and gift shop. The tower is open 8 a.m. to midnight, May to mid-October; closed rest of the year. (Admission: adults $1.25, children 35¢.) The most famous sightseeing novelty in the region is

Boldt Castle, on Heart Island, opposite Alexandria Bay. The castle, which has over 100 rooms, was built at a cost of $2 million by George C. Boldt, who rose from dishwasher to head of the company that ran the Waldorf-Astoria Hotel in New York City. Abandoned in 1902 after it bankrupted the builder, the castle is now a fascinating ruin. A ferry to Heart Island operates daily May through October, 9 a.m. to 7 p.m. (Fare: adults 65¢, children under 12 free.) Most tour boats in the area stop at the castle.

From Alexandria Bay, New York 37 leads northeast about 40 miles to

Ogdensburg, population 15,700, which grew from a French wilderness fort called La Presentation, built in 1739. Ogdensburg is an industrial city. Mills use power from a dam in the Oswegatchie River. It is the head of the International Rapids section of the St. Lawrence Seaway. The city has one important attraction for visitors:

Remington Art Museum, 303 Washington St., housed in a mansion built in 1809. The museum is a memorial to Frederic Remington, famed painter of the Old West, and has the most extensive collection of his work in the world, including paintings, bronzes, drawings. Remington (1861-1909) lived in Ogdensburg for a few years. The museum is open Monday through Saturday, 10 a.m. to 5 p.m. (Admission: adults 50¢, 16 and under free with an adult.)

Three miles east of Ogdensburg the St. Lawrence River is spanned by the

Ogdensburg, N.Y.-Prescott, Ont. International Bridge (Toll $1.50), linking

New York 37 with Canadian highways 2, 16, and 401. The bridge, almost three miles long, opened in 1960 and offers a fine view of the St. Lawrence Valley and the Seaway Project to the east. There are a duty-free shop, travel center, and snack bar at the Bridge Plaza, United States end of the bridge.

From Ogdensburg it is about 35 miles northeast on New York 37, closely flanking the St. Lawrence River, to

Massena, population 15,000, on the Raquette and Grass rivers, a few miles south of the St. Lawrence. Massena grew from a sawmill established by French settlers on the Grass River in 1758. It remained little more than a village until a canal connected the Grass River with the St. Lawrence. The canal dropped the water 90 feet, creating a huge electrical power resource, now greatly augmented by power from the St. Lawrence Seaway Project. As a result Massena has become a booming industrial center. A plant of the Aluminum Company of America, just east of the canal, is the only one in the country making aluminum cable, and is the leading producer of structural aluminum shapes.

Massena is the nearest community to the complex of dams and channels that make up the

St. Lawrence Seaway, various units and installations of which are about two miles east of town on New York 37. The seaway, one of the world's great engineering achievements, and a joint project of the United States and Canada, was dedicated in 1959 by Queen Elizabeth and President Eisenhower. The Moses-Saunders Power Dam, stretching over 3,000 feet across the north channel of the river, generates nearly two million kilowatts of power from 32 turbine generators. Visitor attractions include the *Eisenhower Lock,* on New York 131, where one can watch river traffic from an overlook. *Robert Moses State Park,* on islands linked by dams in the river, east of Ogdensburg, north of New York 37, has an overlook from which the great dam and powerhouse may be seen. The *Barnhart Island Power House* at the main dam has a scale model of the whole project, historical exhibits, and audiovisual presentations. Open free daily. In the park are a marina, fishing and swimming facilities, and picnic- and campgrounds.

About 75 miles southeast of Watertown, linked to it by New York 12, and about 50 miles east of Syracuse on the New York State Thruway, is

8. **UTICA,** population 97,000, on the Mohawk River. Utica grew up around a fron-

From Alexandria Bay, New York, on the St. Lawrence River, ferry boats (which operate daily during the summer) carry visitors to see the fabulous Boldt Castle, on Heart Island.

tier fort established in 1758, near the western end of the Mohawk Trail, but remained little more than a village until the opening of the Erie Canal in 1825. Then Utica began to boom. Now essentially an industrial city, its range of manufacture includes tools, electronic components, cutlery, paper products, and fishing tackle.

Points of Interest.

Munson - Williams - Proctor Institute, 310 Genesee St., in the downtown area, with an extensive collection of American art from the 18th century to the present. Adjacent is a handsome Victorian house called Fountain Elms, with five period rooms. Open free weekdays, 10 a.m. to 5 p.m.; until 10 p.m. on Wednesday; Sunday, 2 p.m. to 6 p.m.

Utica Club Brewery, Court and Varick Sts., offers a 30-minute tour, a ride on an old-fashioned trolley, a visit to a Victorian-style tavern, and free beer. Tours 10 a.m. to 5 p.m. Monday through Saturday during July and August; Monday through Friday rest of the year.

Thirteen miles east of Utica the New York State Thruway intersects New York 28, which leads south 20 miles to a junction with New York 80. Eight miles east on New York 80 is the delightful city of

Cooperstown, population 2,600, at the south end of Lake Otsego, source of the Susquehanna River. The town was founded in 1786 by the father of James Fenimore Cooper, author of romantic Indian stories. He grew up in Cooperstown and used the region as the setting for some of his stories, including *The Last of the Mohicans.* In 1839 Abner Doubleday, while attending a military academy, invented the game of baseball in Cooperstown. The main point of interest is the

National Baseball Hall of Fame and Museum, Main St., a handsome building with a vast collection of relics of baseball and famous players. Open daily in summer, 9 a.m. to 9 p.m.; in winter, 9 a.m. to 5 p.m. (Admission: adults $1.25, children 40¢.)

Two other museums associated with the Hall of Fame, which can be visited on a combination ticket (adults $3, children $1), include

Farmers' Museum, one mile north on New York 80, displaying early American farming equipment and kitchen and craft implements. Part of the museum is the re-creation of a pioneer settlement, with a store, schoolhouse, smithy, print shop, and church. There are demonstrations of wool carding, spinning, and weaving, and other pioneer crafts. The most famous exhibit has nothing to do with farming. It is the Cardiff Giant, a 10-foot-high statue used in a historic hoax in 1869, when it was exhibited as a petrified prehistoric man. The museum is open daily in summer, 9 a.m. to 6 p.m.; in winter to 5 p.m., Sunday from noon. (Individual admission: adults $1.50, children 40¢.) Across the street is

Fenimore House, headquarters of the New York State Historical Association, housed in a handsome mansion (not, as some think, the original Cooper mansion, which has long since disappeared). Displays include manuscripts and possessions of James Fenimore Cooper, an extensive collection of American folk art, landscapes by Cole and Durand, and an unusual collection of life masks of famous Americans. Open daily in summer, 9 a.m. to 9 p.m.; to 6 p.m., spring and fall; 5 p.m. in winter. (Individual admission: adults $1, children 40¢.)

Other museums in or near Cooperstown include the

Indian Museum, 1 Pioneer St., on the lakeshore. Exhibits include dioramas and relics of the Indians of New York from prehistoric times. Open daily, spring and fall, 1 p.m. to 5 p.m.; summer, 10 a.m. to 8 p.m.; closed in winter. (Admission: adults 50¢, children 25¢.) In the downtown area is the

Carriage and Harness Museum, Elk St., with an outstanding collection of vehicles and harness housed in a 1903 coach house and stable. Open daily in summer, 9 a.m. to 5 p.m.; closed weekends rest of the year. (Admission: adults 50¢, children 25¢.) Three miles north of town on New York 80 is

Woodland Museum, with nature and historical exhibits, dioramas re-creating scenes from Cooper stories, and a model railway exhibit. Visitors may ride a narrow-gauge logging railway through the forested grounds. Open daily in summer, 9 a.m. to 6 p.m.; closed during the rest of the year.

(Admission: adults $1.50, children 75¢.)

Cooperstown also has a distinctive luxury resort, the

Otesaga Hotel, on New York 80, just north of the village, with landscaped grounds on the lakeshore, a boat dock, and an excellent 18-hole golf course.

From Utica New York 8 leads northeast into the heart of the huge

9. ADIRONDACK FOREST PRESERVE, a

vast tract of state-owned mountain and forest land, extending over more than 2.4 million acres, much of it primitive wilderness. Mt. Marcy, 5,344 feet, the highest mountain in New York, is here, along with dozens of other mountains nearly as high. There are hundreds of lakes, some quite large, and hundreds of miles of streams and rivers. Tiny Lake Tear of the Clouds is the source of the Hudson River.

The preserve, covering more than half of the whole area of the Adirondack Mountains, extends east and west about 100 miles, north and south about 130. Its northern limit is only about 20 miles south of the border of Canada. In recent years the Adirondacks has become one of the most popular year-round resort districts in the country. Scattered through the preserve are dozens of public campsites. Most communities are small. The largest, Saranac Lake, has only about 6,400 people. Nearly all the more important resort communities are in the northern section of the preserve, where lakes are numerous and mountains are higher. Points of special interest include

Blue Mountain Lake, population 250, a resort village almost in the center of the preserve, at the junction of New York 28 and New York 30. Just north of town on New York 30 is the

The majestic calm of New York state's gently rolling, wooded Adirondack Mountains attracts thousands of hikers, climbers, and campers to enjoy the wilderness.

Almost everyone who has lived in northeastern United States identifies bobsledding with Lake Placid, New York. This is the Mt. Von Hoevenberg Olympic Bobsled Run.

Adirondack Museum, with exhibits in 20 buildings relating to the history and development of the Adirondack region, including paintings, dioramas, vehicles, and tools. There is a huge relief map of the region, an 1890 private railway car, and a famous collection of small boats made and used by Adirondack guides. Open mid-June to mid-October, Monday through Saturday, 10 a.m. to 5 p.m.; Sunday, 1 p.m. to 5 p.m. (Admission: adults $1.50, children 50¢.)

About 30 miles north of Blue Mountain Lake on New York 30 is

Tupper Lake, population 5,200, center of an extensive resort district, at the junction of New York 30 and New York 3, which leads east and west through the whole northern section of the preserve, linking most of the important resort areas. Big Tupper Ski Area is about three miles south off New York 30. Tupper Lake is an outfitting point for canoe trips on the Raquette River leading north through a chain of lakes to the Canadian border. From Tupper Lake it is 20 miles northeast on New York 3 to

Saranac Lake, population 6,400, on Lake Flower, long noted as a health resort. The town's most famous point of interest is

Robert Louis Stevenson Cottage, 11 Stevenson Ln., off New York 3, where Stevenson lived for six months during the winter of 1887-88, while undergoing treatment for tuberculosis. Open 9 a.m. to 6 p.m., mid-June to mid-September. (Admission: adults 50¢, children 25¢.)

Eleven miles southeast of Saranac Lake is the Adirondack's most famous community:

Lake Placid, population 3,000, on Lake Placid, site of the 1932 Winter Olympics. Lake Placid is one of the most popular winter sports centers in the country, with a range of indoor and outdoor facilities unequaled in the East. The village is surrounded by mountains, including Whiteface Mountain and Mt. Marcy. On Mt. Marcy is the

Mt. Von Hoevenberg Olympic Bobsled Run, seven miles southeast on New York

73, fastest and most dangerous bobsled course in the country, one and a half miles long, with 26 curves, some banked so high that their surface is vertical. Visitors are permitted to walk the entire length of the run in summer. Some famous sleds are displayed.

Of interest to many visitors is the

Home of 1,000 Animals, about a mile west on New York 86, a zoo owned by an Alaskan game farm, with animals from all over the world, including performing chimpanzees. Open daily, late May to mid-October, 9:30 a.m. to 7:30 p.m. (Admission: adults $1.60, children 70¢.)

From Lake Placid, New York 86 leads northeast about five miles to

High Falls Gorge, where the Ausable River has cut a spectacular canyon through the southern slope of Whiteface Mountain, exposing colorful rock strata in the walls of the gorge. Bridges and trails lead to a Visitor Center, with an extensive display of Adirondack minerals. The center is open May to October, 8 a.m. to dusk. (Admission: adults $1.50, children 60¢.)

About six miles northeast of the gorge, New York 86 leads to the village of Wilmington, nearest community to

Whiteface Mountain Memorial Highway, beginning about three miles west. A toll road, the highway leads eight miles to the crest of Whiteface Mountain, 4,867 feet. At the top is a castlelike summit house and observation tower, reached by a trail or elevator, offering, on clear days, a stunning view of the St. Lawrence to the north and Lake Champlain to the east. (Toll: $1.25 each passenger, maximum $4.50 per car.) The highway is open May through October, weather permitting. Whiteface Mountain Ski Center is off New York 86, about three miles southwest of Wilmington.

East of Wilmington, New York 9N follows the course of the Ausable River northeast, through a scenic area, about 25 miles to the western shore of

10. LAKE CHAMPLAIN, one of the largest and most historic lakes in the East, stretching south from the Canadian border about 116 miles, varying in width from one-half to about 15 miles. Discovered and explored in 1609 by the French explorer Samuel de Champlain, the lake has been a strategic route of travel between New York, Vermont, and Canada for nearly 300 years. From its western shore rise the wooded slopes of the Adirondacks, and across the lake in Vermont are the famed Green Mountains. Navigable by fairly large vessels, Lake Champlain provides a water route between New York City and Canada, linked by canals to the St. Lawrence and the Hudson.

Points of interest start in the north with

Plattsburgh, population 21,300, at the mouth of the Saranac River, which provides power for papermaking, the city's chief industry. Plattsburgh has been a military base since the War of 1812, when it was occupied by British forces. In 1814 Comdr. Thomas Macdonough, with a small fleet, engaged and defeated a stronger British fleet, ending British control of Lake Champlain. An impressive monument on River St., near the city hall, commemorates the event.

Of interest is the

Kent-Delord House Museum, 17 Cumberland Ave., built about 1795, used as British headquarters during the War of 1812. Furniture, portraits, manuscripts, and other relics are exhibited. Open Monday through Saturday, 10 a.m. to 5 p.m. (Admission: adults 50¢, children 25¢.)

About 12 miles south of Plattsburgh New York 9N crosses the Ausable River, which has cut

Ausable Chasm, one of New York's best known tourist attractions. The gorge is 20 to 50 feet wide, 100 to 200 feet deep, and a mile and a half long. The river surges through it in a series of rapids and falls among oddly shaped rocks. Visitors walk halfway through the gorge along protected trails, then take a sightseeing boat through the rapids. The privately owned chasm is open daily from early May to late October, 8:30 a.m. to 6:30 p.m. (Admission: adults $2.40, children $1, including boat ride.)

A few miles south of Ausable Chasm, New York 22 diverges southeast to follow the shore of Lake Champlain. After about 50 miles it enters Ticonderoga, on the La Chute River, which links the southern end of Lake Champlain with the northern end of Lake George.

Two miles east of the city on New York 73 is historic

Photographers are especially fond of Elephant's Head, which rises above the rushing waters of Ausable Chasm, near Lake Champlain in northeastern New York.

Fort Ticonderoga, strategically located at the crest of a mountain between Lake George and Lake Champlain. The first fort was built by the French in 1755. They leveled the top of the mountain, using the stones for the walls of Fort Carillon. In 1758 French and British troops clashed for control of the fort. The French, under Montcalm, won, but in 1759 the British captured the fort, renamed it Fort Ticonderoga. At the beginning of the Revolutionary War, in 1775, Ethan Allen and his Green Mountain Boys overwhelmed the garrison in a daring night attack, dismantled the fort's cannon, and sent them to Boston. Two years later the fort changed hands again, when the British general Burgoyne placed cannon on a higher hill a mile to the south, forced the Americans out, and burned Fort Ticonderoga.

It has now been carefully restored according to the original French plans. A museum on the grounds has an excellent collection of weapons, uniforms, paintings, and relics of the Colonial period and the French and Indian War. The fort and museum are open daily, 8 a.m. to 6 p.m., spring and fall; to 7 p.m. in July and August; closed rest of the year. (Admission: adults $1.50, children 75¢.)

About a mile to the south of Fort Ticonderoga is

Mt. Defiance, reached by a toll road off New York 22. Here, in 1777, General Burgoyne forced the surrender of Fort Ticonderoga. An observation deck provides a fine view of the region. The toll road ($2 per car) is open from May 30 to October 12, 8 a.m. to 8 p.m.; closed rest of the year.

About 40 miles south of Ticonderoga on New York 9N is the resort village of

Lake George, population 1,000, in the eastern Adirondack foothills, at the southern tip of handsome Lake George, which stretches north about 30 miles. The lake varies in width from less than a mile to about four miles, dotted with more than 150 islands. The shores are lined with summer cottages and resorts. Points of interest include

Fort William Henry, south edge of the village off US 9, the restoration of a frontier fort built by the English about 1755 as a defense against French and Indian attacks. The fort was finally destroyed by the French.

Besides the reconstructed barracks and stockade, there is a museum with relics of the period. Visitors may watch military drills and musket and cannon firing and see bullets made. The fort is open daily, May through October, 9 a.m. to 6 p.m.; until 10 p.m. during July and August. (Admission: adults $1.50, children 50¢.)

Strung along US 9, south of Lake George Village, are several amusement parks. They include **Gaslight Village,** replica of a Gay 90s village, with shows and rides (Admission: adults $2.50, children $1.50); **Magic Forest,** about one mile south, with Santa Claus and his workshop, a herd of deer, replica of an Indian village, circus acts, and animal exhibits (Admission: adults $1.39, children 89¢); **Storytown, USA,** about four miles south on US 9, with a western ghost town, jungle safari, and fantasy rides (Admission: adults $2.95, children $1.95). The amusement parks are open during the summer months, usually from 9:30 a.m. to 6 p.m.

About 25 miles south of Lake George Village on Interstate 87 is

Saratoga Springs, population 17,300, a handsome and historic city noted for mineral springs and horse racing. During the last half of the 19th century it was one of the most fashionable resorts in the country.

Saline mineral springs account for the growth and development of Saratoga Springs. The springs were known and used by the Indians from prehistoric days. The earliest spring known to Europeans, now called High Rock Spring, near the center of the town, was a favorite with the Indians, who called it Medicine Spring of the Great Spirit. Settlement of the area around the springs began about 1775. During the last quarter of the 19th century two huge Victorian hotels, the United States and the Grand Union, drew rich and famous patrons from all over the world. Racing and gambling began to be important.

Today the flamboyant hotels and the gambling casinos have disappeared, but the Saratoga Springs summer race season is still one of the most important in the country. The city has also become a summer cultural mecca. Points of special interest include

Casino and Congress Park, near the center of town. The park is the site of Congress

Spring; it has handsome Italian gardens. The lavish mansion, developed as a gambling casino, now houses two museums with exhibits of regional history. Open May through October, 9 a.m. to 5 p.m. (Admission: adults 50¢, under 12 10¢ or free with adult.)

About a mile east of Congress Park is the

National Museum of Thoroughbred Racing, Union Ave. and Ludlow St., with the finest collection of horse racing relics in the country, including portraits of famous racehorses and trophies won. Open free daily, except closed weekends in February.

Opposite the museum is the

Saratoga Race Course, oldest in the country, and one of the most beautiful, in a 45-acre landscaped park. The track, a one and one-eighth mile oval, has a steeplechase course in the center. Races are held late July through August, Monday through Saturday, post time 2 p.m. (Grandstand seats $2, clubhouse $5.)

About half a mile southeast of the racetrack is

Yaddo, a 500-acre landscaped estate, with a mansion, statues, fountains, an Italian garden, and extensive rose gardens. The mansion, a sanctuary for artists and writers, is not open to the public, but the grounds and gardens are open spring through fall.

About three miles south of the center of town, between US 9 and New York 50, is

Saratoga Spa State Park, a complex of health, recreational, and cultural facilities in a 1,500-acre landscaped tract, including swimming pools, tennis courts, picnic areas, two golf courses, a summer theater, and a hotel. One can "take the waters" in luxurious bathhouses, where rates range from $2.25 to $4.50 for baths, massage, etc. The park's most spectacular facility is the

Saratoga Performing Arts Center, which in 1966 became the summer home of the New York City Ballet and the Philadelphia Orchestra. The roofed amphitheater seats 5,000, with space for another 10,000 in the open air. (General admission $2, reserved seats $3 to $7.50.)

About eight miles southeast of Saratoga Springs, just west of the Hudson, is

The Ensign House on the river road, just north of the Saratoga Battlefield, is as it was at the time of that historic battle.

Saratoga National Historical Park, 2,500 acres of rolling, partially wooded hills, preserving the site of one of the most decisive battles of the Revolutionary War. There, in two separate engagements, on September 19 and October 7, 1777, American forces, assembled in a patchwork army under Gen. Horatio Gates, defeated a larger, professional army under colorful Gen. John ("Gentleman Johnny") Burgoyne. The American victory electrified and united the country and brought France openly over to the American side.

A visitor center on the highest hill in the park offers a view of the battlefield and has maps, dioramas, and films describing the battle. A nine-mile road, open April through November, links important features, one of which is the famous Monument to a Leg, commemorating the wounding of Gen. Benedict Arnold during the battle.

About 30 miles south of Saratoga Springs by US 9 or Interstate 87 is

11. ALBANY, the capital of New York, population 122,000, on the Hudson River. The first European to visit the site of Albany was Henry Hudson, who sailed his tiny *Half* Moon up the Hudson in 1609. Five years later two Dutchmen built Fort Nassau on an island in the river. In 1624 a group of 18 Dutch families arrived and established a settlement and a second fort, Fort Orange. Present-day Albany grew from that settlement, under the patroonship of Kiliaen Van Rensselaer. A steady stream of European settlers established sawmills and gristmills and cleared land for farms. The settlement also became the base for a growing fur trade.

Control of the settlement passed to the English in 1664, who renamed it Albany in honor of the Duke of York and Albany. Albany is the oldest city in the country operating under its original charter, granted in 1686.

In 1785 a stagecoach line linked Albany with New York. In 1807 Robert Fulton's *Clermont*, the first steamship to offer regular service on the Hudson, arrived in Albany. But Albany's biggest boom came in 1825, when the opening of the Erie Canal provided a commercial link to Buffalo. Within a few years the population of the city doubled. Albany's docks were soon serving about 15,000 canalboats a year.

30

Floodlighted, the massive, chateaulike granite New York State Capitol in Albany dominates the after-dark Capitol Park scene.

Today Albany has a mile of deepwater docks which handle more than eight million tons of cargo, much of which is transferred to oceangoing vessels. The city is a big grain-shipping port and has the largest single-unit grain elevator in the world. Factories produce paper of all types, billiard balls, chemicals, and many other products.

Routes To and Through. The New York State Thruway swings west on the southern edge of the city, changing its Interstate designation from 87 to 90. Interstate 87 continues north to the Canadian border; Interstate 90 cuts through the northern edge of the city and goes east to Massachusetts, west to Buffalo. Interstate 787 bypasses the city on the east side. Two main highways, US 20 and New York 5, link with north-south US 9 in the heart of the city.

Most points of interest in Albany are near the city's center, which is undergoing massive redevelopment. The most important is the

State Capitol, on State St., which dominates Capitol Park. An ornate building suggesting an enormous French chateau, it cost $25 million to build in 1898. Interior features worth noting include three ornate stairways and handsome legislative chambers. Open Monday through Friday, 9 a.m. to 4 p.m. Free guided tours available.

Governor Alfred E. Smith State Office Building is directly behind the capitol, on Swan St. An observation terrace on the 31st floor, open free, Monday through Friday 9 a.m. to 4 p.m.; until 5 p.m. in summer, is the best place in Albany for a view of the city. Opposite the capitol is the

State Education Building, on Washington Ave. In the rotunda are interesting exhibits of rare books and paintings. The New York State Museum, on the fifth floor, has wide-ranging exhibits relating to the Indians, animals, birds, and geology of New York. Open free daily, 9 a.m. to 4:30 p.m.

North of the capitol is Albany's most historic church:

First Church in Albany, N. Pearl St. and Clinton Sq., the church of a Dutch Reformed congregation organized in 1642. The present building, erected in 1798, contains the oldest pulpit in America, carved in Holland in 1656. Nearby is the historic

Ten Broeck Mansion, 9 Ten Broeck Pl., built in 1798 by Abraham Ten Broeck, Revolutionary War general and mayor of Albany. The restored house has fine furniture of the Federal period and interesting herb and formal gardens. Open free daily, 3 p.m. to 4 p.m.

South of the capitol is the

Schuyler Mansion, Clinton and Catherine Sts., built by Gen. Philip Schuyler in 1762, a handsome Georgian Colonial house. The British general Burgoyne was a prisoner-guest in the mansion after his defeat at the Battle of Saratoga in 1777. In 1780 Alexander Hamilton married Schuyler's daughter Elizabeth there. The house has been restored and contains much of the Schuyler family furniture. Open free, Monday through Saturday, 9 a.m. to 5 p.m.; Sunday, 1 p.m. to 5 p.m.

A short distance south of the Schuyler mansion is

Historic Cherry Hill, S. Pearl St. between First and McCarty Aves., a handsome frame mansion of the Colonial period. Built in 1768, Cherry Hill was the home of the distinguished Van Rensselaer family until 1963. The house, situated on spacious grounds, contains original family furniture, silver, pictures, documents. Open Tuesday through Saturday, 10 a.m. to 4 p.m.; Sunday, 1 p.m. to 4 p.m. (Admission: adults 75¢, children and students 25¢.)

From Albany the New York State Thruway and New York 5 lead northwest 15 miles to

Schenectady, population 71,000, on the Mohawk River. Schenectady began as a Dutch settlement in 1661 and became an important fur trading base. In 1690 it was virtually wiped out in a massacre by French and Indian raiders. A new settlement, protected by a fort, was established in 1705. Schenectady today is one of the most important industrial communities in the country, due largely to the huge General Electric Co. G.E. has its main offices here, as well as factories and a research center, all of which grew from a small machine works established in 1886 by Thomas Edison. Worth seeing is the

Village Stockade, several old houses along the river, in the downtown Front St. area, built during the 18th century. A walking tour is offered by the YWCA, starting from 44 Washington Ave. (Fee: adults $1, children 25¢.)

In the northwest quarter of the city is

Union College, established in 1795, the oldest planned campus in the country. Of special interest is Jackson's Garden, planted over a century ago, combining formally landscaped areas with wilderness sections.

From Albany the deep, wide channel of the Hudson River extends south to New York Harbor. Paralleling the river on the west are Interstate 87 and US 9W. After about 30 miles both highways lead to Catskill, which takes its name from the rugged region just west, the

12. CATSKILL MOUNTAINS, a rolling, heavily wooded region of low mountains, extensions of the Appalachian system, with an average altitude of around 3,000 feet. The Catskills extend west from the Hudson about 50 miles to the Delaware River, north and south about 30 miles. Much of the region is within limits of the 240,276-acre Catskill Forest Preserve.

The Catskills are famous as the legendary home of the bowling dwarfs who put Rip Van Winkle to sleep for 20 years. It is the most popular resort area in the East, less than 100 miles from New York City. There are dozens of camping and picnic areas and hundreds of miles of trails. Two highways lead through east to west, New York 23A in the north and New York 28 through the center.

Once a region of rugged beauty, the Catskills have long since been stripped by lumbering interests of all but occasional patches of good timber, and they are pocked with unsightly quarry holes. Now, under state protection, the forests are beginning to recover. Waterfalls, ravines, and wooded crests provide scenic variety. Places of special interest are situated along the eastern edge of the mountains, near the Hudson. The northernmost is

Catskill, population 5,800, settled by the Dutch in 1662. The town is now a trading center for the mountain region to the west. Nearby is the

Catskill Game Farm, about 12 miles west off New York 32, with more than 3,000 animals, chiefly deer, llamas, giraffes, and zebras. There are rides for children, and picnic areas. Open daily mid-April to mid-November, 9 a.m. to 6 p.m. (Admission: adults $2.25, children $1.)

About 25 miles south of Catskill on US 9W and the New York State Thruway is

Kingston, population 27,500, largest community in the Catskills, a center for diversified industry, with historic associations. One of the first settlements along the Hudson River, Kingston began as a Dutch trading post around 1615. Later Dutch colonists from Albany established a permanent settlement. Kingston's historic moment came in 1777 when the temporary state government, moving about to avoid the British, established the first state government there, adopted the first state constitution, inaugurated the first governor, and held the first session of the state senate. Soon the advancing British seized and burned the town, and the state government became itinerant again. Worth visiting is the

Senate House, 312 Fair St., near the center of town, a picturesque old stone building built in 1676, where the New York Senate met in 1777. Destroyed by the British, it has been carefully rebuilt and is maintained as a museum. Furniture, paintings, and relics relating to the history of New York are exhibited. Kingston has one historic church:

Old Dutch Church, organized in 1659, though the present building, of no architectural interest, was built in 1852. Some relics are exhibited, including letters from George Washington. More interesting than the church is the adjoining graveyard, where New York's first governor, George Clinton, and other Revolutionary leaders are buried.

A point of high interest is a seldom-visited little village:

Hurley, three miles east of Kingston on US 209. Now almost a ghost town, Hurley has been made a National Historic District, to preserve the relics of its early Dutch heritage. There are ten charming Dutch stone cottages along Hurley St., and others nearby. The village, established in 1662, prospered modestly for many years from fertile farms in the valley of Esopus Creek.

Hurley, too, has a fascinating graveyard with many old Dutch graves.

A town of historic interest about 15 miles south of Kingston, just west of the New York State Thruway, is picturesque

New Paltz, population 4,900, settled by a handful of French Huguenot refugees in 1678. They built a row of quaint stone houses on the main street of the village, several of which are open to visitors. The most notable is the **Jean Hasbrouck House,** built in 1712, a thick-walled stone cottage with a high, step roof, of typical Flemish design. Open Tuesday through Saturday, 9 a.m. to 5 p.m.; Sunday 10 a.m. to 4 p.m. (Admission: adults 50¢, children free.)

East of the Hudson River, two parallel main highways lead south into the Greater New York City area: US 9 and the Taconic State Parkway. US 9 links a chain of towns and historic places. The most important, about 75 miles south of Albany, is

13. POUGHKEEPSIE, population 35,500; like most towns in the Hudson Valley it was founded by Dutch settlers, in 1687. It has developed into a diversified industrial community. IBM and Smith Brothers Cough Drops have big plants here. Poughkeepsie is the home of

Vassar College, entrance on Raymond Ave., one of the best known women's colleges in the country, established in 1861 by Matthew Vassar, a local brewer. On the 1,000-acre campus are impressive trees, broad lawns, and Tudor-style buildings. Taylor Hall Art Gallery houses a notable collection of the works of Rembrandt, Whistler, and examples of the Hudson River School. Open free, Monday through Friday, 9 a.m. to 5 p.m., during the school year.

A few miles north of Poughkeepsie on US 9 is Hyde Park (population 3,000), nearest community to three remarkable mansions. About a mile south, off US 9, is the most famous, part of

Franklin D. Roosevelt National Historic Site, including the sprawling mansion that was Roosevelt's birthplace and family home, and the Franklin D. Roosevelt Library and Museum. Franklin and Eleanor Roosevelt are buried in a rose garden on the extensive grounds. The original house, extended and modified over the years, was

The Franklin D. Roosevelt National Historic Site at Hyde Park includes the sprawling mansion that was F.D.R.'s birthplace and family home.

built about 1826 and acquired by Roosevelt's father in 1867. Most of the living areas are open to visitors and are completely furnished with two generations of Roosevelt family possessions, including notable relics of the lives of Franklin and Eleanor Roosevelt during the presidential years, when the home was often a summer White House.

In the Roosevelt Library and Museum are a vast store of documents, books, and pictures acquired by Roosevelt during his years in the White House. There are special exhibits of ship models, photographs, and unusual gifts the president received. The grounds, library, and house are open daily 9 a.m. to 5 p.m. (Admission to the library: adults 50¢, children free.) Visitors are advised to go as early as possible. There are usually long lines on weekends and on Sunday afternoons.

It would be hard to find two houses more different from one another than the Roosevelt home and the second famous estate:

Vanderbilt Mansion National Historic Site, about one mile north of Hyde Park on US 9. Within more than 200 acres of beautifully landscaped grounds overlooking the Hudson River, the incredibly ornate 54-room palace was built in 1898 at a cost of $660,000 for Frederick W. Vanderbilt, son of Commodore Vanderbilt. Italian Renaissance in style, the mansion is furnished with French and Italian pieces of museum quality. House and grounds are open Wednesday through Sunday, 9 a.m. to 5 p.m. The grounds are open free. (Admission to the house: adults 50¢, children free. Same ticket admits to the Roosevelt house.)

The third historic mansion in the Hyde Park area is within

Ogden Mills Memorial State Park, four miles north of Hyde Park on US 9, just outside of the village of Staatsburg. The former estate of Ogden and Ruth Livingston Mills, the park includes nearly 500 acres of wooded and gardened grounds, picnic areas, and a golf course. The 65-room mansion, originally built in 1832, was later redesigned as a French chateau. It is now a museum. Exhibits include priceless antiques and works of art, furniture, rugs, and tapestries. The grounds are open free. The house is open daily, 9 a.m. to 5 p.m. (Admission: adults 25¢, children 10¢.)

About 25 miles south of Poughkeepsie on US 9W is

West Point, the United States Military Academy, with a superb hilltop setting on the west bank of the Hudson River, on 15,000 acres of grounds. The site has been a strategic point since Revolutionary War days, when a huge chain was stretched over the Hudson River to block British ships. In 1780 Benedict Arnold, in command of West Point, made an unsuccessful attempt to surrender it to the British, in the most famous act of treason of the war.

West Point became an officers' training college in 1802, with ten men in the first class. Enrollment now is about 4,500. An information center just inside the South Gate supplies visitors with literature on points of interest, which include

The Cadet Chapel, the Point's single most notable building, of classic Gothic design, with splendid stained glass windows portraying military leaders of biblical times.

Trophy Point, overlooking the Hudson, is studded with cannon, monuments, and relics, including some links of the great chain which once blocked the Hudson.

The Old Cadet Chapel, in the Post Cemetery, has a black marble shield for every American general in the Revolutionary War. A nameless one stands for Benedict Arnold.

West Point Museum, in Thayer Hall, entrance on Cullum Rd., has one of the finest collections of military relics in the country. Notable exhibits include the surrender document of Tokyo Bay, Goering's baton, Mussolini's hat, Yamashita's sword, and flags and souvenirs from every United States military campaign.

Cadet parades are held several days each week during the academic year. A schedule is available at the information center.

From West Point US 9W and New York 218, the Storm King Highway, lead south about five miles to a narrow, highly scenic gorge in the Hudson River, spanned by Bear Mountain Bridge (Toll 25¢). At the west end of the bridge is Palisades Interstate Parkway, which leads south through

Palisades Interstate Park, a heavily wooded, 62,352-acre tract of low mountains, extending southwest in several sections. The two largest sections adjoin each other just west of the Hudson at Bear Mountain Bridge. They include

Bear Mountain State Park, 5,057 acres. Bear Mountain, rising to 1,314 feet, has a toll road leading to the crest. One of the most popular recreation areas in New York, the park offers skiing in winter and swimming, fishing, and boating in summer. There are many miles of nature trails, and trailside museums maintained by New York City's Museum of Natural History. Adjoining Bear Mountain State Park is

A regimental review is the highlight of a visit to the United States Military Academy at West Point. Reviews are held several days each week.

From Bear Mountain, a New York state park, there is a panorama of the Hudson River, Bear Mountain Bridge, and the Hudson Highlands beyond.

Harriman State Park, 45,960 acres, with much wilder and more rugged terrain, all heavily forested. Over a dozen lakes offer swimming, boating, and fishing. Silver Mine Ski Area is near the northern end.

On New York 17, near the southwest edge of the park, is the village of Tuxedo Park, long a sanctuary for the rich, the nearest community to

Sterling Forest Gardens, four miles north of Tuxedo Park on New York 17, then three miles west on New York 210. In 125 forested acres are unusual formal and natural gardens, industrial parks, and housing developments. For children there are Farmyard Theater, animal feeding, and pond fishing. Open daily May through October, 10 a.m. to dusk. (Admission: adults $1.95, children 50¢.)

From the southern end of Harriman State Park the New York State Thruway (Interstate 287) swings east, reaches the Hudson River at the historic city of Nyack, then spans the river at its widest point on the four-mile-long Tappan Zee Bridge (Toll 50¢). East of the Tappan Zee Bridge is

14. TARRYTOWN, population 11,300, chief community of the historic Sleepy Hollow region made famous by Washington Irving. The area has high interest for visitors because of three notable restorations. All are on or just off US 9, which closely flanks the east bank of the Hudson River. West of US 9, at the southern edge of Tarrytown, is

Sunnyside, on W. Sunnyside Lane, the home of Washington Irving from 1835 to 1859. A small, oddly gabled stone mansion of great charm, with 20 acres of beautifully landscaped grounds sloping down to the Hudson, Sunnyside is filled with Irving's furniture and possessions, letters and manuscripts. Open daily, 10 a.m. to 5 p.m. (Admission: adults $1.50, children 75¢.)

The second restoration is

Philipsburg Manor, in North Tarrytown, west of US 9, part of a big estate developed by Frederick Philipse in the late 17th century. The restored area includes a stone manor house, an operating gristmill, a millpond created by a dam across the Pocantico River, wharves, and a warehouse. Open

"Full of angles and corners as an old cocked hat" was the way Washington Irving described his home, "Sunnyside," at Tarrytown.

daily, 10 a.m. to 5 p.m. (Admission: adults $1.50, children 75¢.)

The third restoration is

Van Cortlandt Manor, a few miles north of Tarrytown, just south of Croton-on-Hudson. The Van Cortlandt family owned the house until 1940. The manor, restored to its 18th-century appearance, contains much of the original furniture. On the grounds are extensive gardens, a ferry house, and kitchen with tap room, associated with a family operated ferry over the Croton River. Open daily, 10 a.m. to 5 p.m. (Admission: adults $1.50, children 75¢.)

From Tarrytown, Interstate 287 leads east across central Westchester County about 12 miles to link with the New England Thruway (Interstate 95). Intersecting the Westchester Expressway are several highways which lead south into the Greater New York City area: the Saw Mill River Parkway, the New York State Thruway, the Bronx River Parkway, and the Hutchinson River Parkway. About midway to the link with the New England Thruway the Westchester Expressway passes through

White Plains, population 52,000, county seat of Westchester County and one of the most important suburbs in Greater New York. Many New York City stores maintain branches in White Plains, and many big companies are moving their corporate headquarters here. The town is the site of two historic incidents. The last battle fought in New York between Washington's retreating army and British troops under General Howe took place in White Plains on October 28, 1776. The old farmhouse where Washington made his headquarters, on Virginia Rd., north of the city, has been restored and is open free, Tuesday through Saturday, 10 a.m. to 4 p.m.; Sunday, 1 p.m. to 4 p.m. Closed in winter.

In July 1776, the Declaration of Independence was adopted in White Plains and the State of New York was formally organized. A monument near the center of the city, at S. Broadway and Mitchell Pl., commemorates the occasion.

The following text is a separate section devoted to the extraordinary urban complex of five boroughs that make up New York City.

The Solomon R. Guggenheim Museum, designed by the architectural genius Frank Lloyd Wright, is the home of some of the finest examples of 20th-century art forms.

New York City.

NEW YORK CITY, a unique association of land and channels, is the largest city in this country and one of the largest in the world. It is made up of two separate islands, the eastern third of a nearby larger island, and the southern end of a triangular mainland tip, all separated by saltwater channels, only one of which is a true river. New York's superb harbor has determined much of her history. All the land elements of New York are linked by bridges and tunnels.

Almost 450 years ago a Florentine navigator named Giovanni da Verrazano sailed a tiny ship into New York Harbor, the first European to do so. New York honors him today with a splendid bridge spanning the mouth of the harbor he discovered. In 1609

Henry Hudson, in the pay of the Dutch East India Company, sailed up the Hudson River to Albany. His report to his employers triggered a stream of immigration that has never stopped.

New York City grew far beyond the wildest dreams of men like Verrazano and Hudson. Its development has paralleled the growth of the nation, and today it reigns as the country's financial and cultural capital.

Points of interest are described in the following text. For those who want more detail, a separate guide devoted entirely to New York City is available in this series.

The map on the opposite page shows Manhattan Island and bridge and tunnel links to Brooklyn, Queens, the Bronx.

Millions of people visit the city each year. For most of them, the sights to see and things to do are concentrated on Manhattan Island, starting in the north with

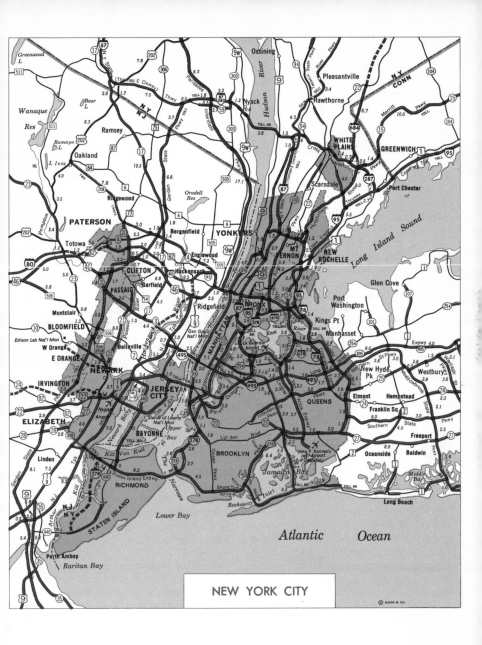

NEW YORK CITY

© RMⓃN & CO.

The Cloisters, a remarkable re-creation of a medieval monastery, housing one of the world's finest collections of medieval art. It can be reached by the IND subway, which stops at 190th St., or by a No. 4 bus. The Cloisters takes its name from several colonnaded walks, each enclosing a garden and containing elements of a different monastery. Outside are more gardens, rampart walks, terraces with commanding views, and a cobblestone drive. The whole building is a dramatic setting for a vast collection of treasures: statues, paintings, tapestries, and even a whole chapel. The Cloisters is open free, Tuesday through Saturday, 10 a.m. to 5 p.m.; Sunday, 1 p.m. to 5 p.m.

About 12 blocks south of The Cloisters on the Henry Hudson Parkway is the George Washington Bridge, the fourth longest suspension bridge in the world.

About 50 blocks south of the bridge Manhattan Island broadens to about a mile

39

in width to include Harlem, sharply divided into two sections. On the east is Black Harlem, a dreary, almost level plain extending from 110th St. to beyond 145th St., the most famous of New York's Negro districts. Vast areas of slums are slowly being replaced by new housing. On the west, thrusting sharply above the Harlem plain, is a rugged ridge called Morningside Heights, or the

COLUMBIA UNIVERSITY—ST. JOHN THE DIVINE DISTRICT, extending from 125th St. on the north to 110th St. on the south. At the northern edge of the district is

Grant's Tomb, Riverside Dr. at 122nd St., a massive, ornate monument to a great soldier and the 18th president. The bodies of Grant and his wife lie in massive sarcophagi at the bottom of a circular crypt. A gallery exhibits Civil War maps, flags, and relics. The monument is open free daily, 9 a.m. to 5 p.m. Just south of 122nd St. is

Riverside Church, one of the largest churches in New York, classic Gothic in design, with a tower rising 392 feet. Bordering the great nave are stained glass windows that rank with the finest in the world. Two chapels, one with the famous Hofmann painting, *Christ in Gethsemane,* open from the nave. The church is open free daily, 9 a.m. to 5 p.m.

By far the most important educational institution in the area is

Columbia University, enrollment about 25,000, with a crowded campus filling the area between 121st and 114th streets and Broadway and Amsterdam Ave. Worth seeing is the central plaza on 116th St., dominated by Low Library.

Columbia began as Kings College in 1754. It is famed for its special schools and departments, most at graduate level. Affiliated institutions include Barnard College for Women, Teachers College, and Union Theological Seminary.

Southwest of the Columbia campus is the

Cathedral of St. John the Divine, between 113th and 110th streets, and Amsterdam Ave. and Morningside Dr., with its entrance at 112th St. Begun in 1892, the cathedral is the largest Gothic building in the world and, seen from the inside, one of the most beautiful. The vast nave soars 124

feet high, and is nearly 600 feet from entrance to altar. The rose window above the entrance is splendid. St. John's is the cathedral of the Protestant Episcopal Diocese of New York. Scattered over the extensive grounds are schools, diocesan offices, and residences. The cathedral is open free daily, 7 a.m. to 8 p.m. in summer; to 6 p.m. rest of the year. Guided tours weekdays, 11 a.m. to 2 p.m.

Though the center of Manhattan, extending south from 110th St. to 59th St., from Fifth Ave. on the east to Central Park West or Eighth Ave. on the west is

CENTRAL PARK—EAST AND WEST. Each district has places of high interest for visitors, as does

Central Park, one of the great parks of the world, with an astonishing range of facilities in 840 acres. The park is landscaped to preserve its natural features, including some wilderness areas; it contains three lakes, two ponds, a loch, and a pool. There are about six miles of bridle paths, 28 miles of walks and trails, and nine miles of roadways. Other features include a fine small zoo, a skating rink, two restaurants, a boathouse, a merry-go-round, a miniature boat basin, a chess and checker house, and bowling-on-the-green courts. The park is open 24 hours a day, year-round.

Central Park West, once a pleasant middle-class district, is undergoing renovation. There are two important places of interest. One is the

American Museum of Natural History, facing Central Park at 79th St., one of the finest museums of its type in the world, with about 60 exhibit halls. Among the most popular are habitat exhibits of North American mammals and African mammals. The dinosaur exhibits are notable. Open free, Monday through Saturday, 10 a.m. to 5 p.m.; Sunday and holidays, 1 p.m. to 5 p.m.

Southwest of the Natural History Museum is

Lincoln Center for the Performing Arts, on a 14-acre site between 62nd and 66th streets, west of Broadway, a superbly integrated association of landscaped plazas, theaters, concert halls, and educational buildings. Completed in 1969 with the opening of the new quarters of the Juilliard School of Music, the Center cost almost $200 million. Buildings include the Metropolitan Opera House, Philharmonic Hall, home of the New York Philharmonic Orchestra, the New York State Theater, and the Vivian Beaumont Theater, home of the Repertory Theater of New York.

Central Park East, extending east from Fifth Ave. to the East River, is completely different in character and history from Central Park West. During the last half of the 19th century it was the most exclusive residential district in New York, and is often referred to as the Gold Coast. Over a period of several decades the east side of Fifth Ave. acquired an almost unbroken row of millionaires' mansions. Many are still there, although now converted to museums, consulates, and schools. Side streets are lined with handsome town houses, many still privately owned. Places of interest include

Museum of the City of New York, Fifth Ave. between 103rd and 104th streets, a handsome Georgian building devoted to the history of New York. There are dioramas, period rooms, and a costume gallery. The theatrical and musical exhibits are among the best anywhere. Open free, 10 a.m. to 5 p.m., Monday through Saturday; after 1 p.m. on Sunday. About 15 blocks south is the extraordinary

Solomon R. Guggenheim Museum, 1071 Fifth Ave., between 88th and 89th streets, designed by the architectural genius Frank Lloyd Wright. The building is circular in design, resembling a truncated cone standing on its small end. Exhibits, chiefly 20th-century art, are placed on a quarter-mile-long display ramp that winds from top to bottom. Open Wednesday through Saturday, 10 a.m. to 6 p.m.; Tuesday to 9 p.m.; Sunday, noon to 6 p.m. (Admission: 50¢, children under 6 free.)

Facing Fifth Ave. from the west, within Central Park, between 80th and 84th streets, is New York's famous

Metropolitan Museum of Art, main entrance at 82nd St., one of the great museums of the world, with more than 360,000 works of art, covering every period from prehistoric to modern. Notable exhibits include an Egyptian temple, superb collections of

arms and armor and American musical instruments, a Costume Institute, and a Junior Museum. The Metropolitan is open free except for occasional special exhibits, Monday through Saturday, 10 a.m. to 5 p.m.; Tuesday to 10 p.m.; Sunday, 1 p.m. to 5 p.m.

Within easy walking distance are two other museums:

The Frick Collection, Fifth Ave. at 70th St., housed in the elegant mansion of Henry Clay Frick, steel tycoon. The collection consists mainly of 18th-century British and French paintings. Open free, September through May, Tuesday through Saturday, 10 a.m. to 6 p.m.; Sunday, 1 p.m. to 6 p.m. No children under ten. A few blocks northeast of the Frick is the

Whitney Museum of American Art, 945 Madison Ave. at 75th St., housed in a new building of remarkable design. The museum, devoted entirely to American painting and sculpture, is open Monday through Saturday, 11 a.m. to 6 p.m.; Tuesday to 10 p.m.; Sunday, noon to 6 p.m. (Admission: adults $1, children under 12 free.)

The southern limit of Central Park is 59th St. It is also the northern limit of New York's

MIDTOWN AREA, which extends roughly from 59th St. to 23rd St., and from the East River to the Hudson. Within this area are most of the city's better hotels, restaurants, shops, department stores, and theaters. Places of special interest include

Museum of Modern Art, 11 W. 53rd St., just off Fifth Ave., with an outstanding collection of modern art and a big sculpture garden behind the main museum. Classic films are shown Sunday through Friday at 2 p.m. and 5:30 p.m. The museum is open Monday through Saturday, 11 a.m. to 6 p.m.; Thurrday to 9 p.m.; Sunday, noon to 6 p.m. (Admission: adults $1.50, children 75¢.)

Facing Fifth Ave. from the east, between 52nd and 51st streets, is

St. Patrick's Cathedral, cathedral of the Roman Catholic Archdiocese of New York. One of the first great Gothic churches in America, it is reminiscent of the Cologne Cathedral, and was completed in 1888.

Opposite the cathedral, extending south

along Fifth Ave. for four blocks and west almost to Seventh Ave., is

Rockefeller Center, largest privately owned business and entertainment center in the world, a closely integrated complex of 18 buildings, with two more under construction, all linked by underground arcades lined with shops.

The RCA Building, 850 feet high, has an observation deck on top, and two notable restaurants on the 65th floor. The delightful Channel Gardens and Lower Plaza link the RCA Building with Fifth Ave. The Lower Plaza, dominated by a fountain and the golden statue of Prometheus, has restaurants on either side and becomes a skating rink in winter and an outdoor dining terrace in summer. Radio City Music Hall, the world's largest indoor theater, is at Ave. of the Americas (Sixth Ave.) and 50th St. Conducted tours of the Center, lasting about an hour, leave at frequent intervals from a lounge in the RCA Building arcade, include visits to broadcasting studios and the Observation Roof. Tours begin at 9:30 a.m. and continue until 5:30 p.m. daily. (Fee: adults $1.90, children $1.20.)

The central east-west street of the midtown area is historic 42nd St. At its eastern end is the

United Nations Headquarters, a complex of remarkable buildings in beautifully landscaped grounds extending from 42nd St. to 48th St., on the east side of First Ave. At the southern end is the Secretariat Building, 39 stories, with side walls of glass and end walls of white marble. Here are the offices of the working staff of the United Nations and of the Secretary General. The Conference Building has three large council chambers and several big committee rooms, all of striking design and decor. The north end of the Conference Building is linked with the General Assembly Building and Auditorium, a building of extraordinary design, where the General Assembly meets. Visitors enter the UN from First Ave. at 45th St. through a plaza leading to the General Assembly Building. Open daily, 9 a.m. to 6 p.m. Guided tours, which leave the lobby of the General Assembly Building at frequent intervals between 9 a.m. and 4:45 p.m. (Fee: adults $1.25, children 50¢.)

From the UN 42nd St. leads west five blocks to

Grand Central Terminal, facing and blocking Park Ave. to the south, with traffic flowing around it on elevated ramps. Massive and ornate, the huge terminal is one of two in New York serving the Penn-Central System. The terminal, completed in 1913, is worth seeing, particularly the vast concourse and its arched blue ceiling set with golden stars.

The terminal is linked by escalators to the

Pan American Building, octagonal in shape, 59 stories, the world's largest privately owned office building, named for its principal tenant, Pan American World Airways. Two blocks west of Grand Central, 42nd St. crosses Fifth Ave. On the southwest corner is the

New York Public Library, headquarters for the world's largest city library system. The monumental building, guarded by two famous stone lions, was completed in 1911. Worth seeing is the great hall on the main floor and the huge third-floor reference and reading rooms.

Two blocks west of Fifth Ave., 42nd St. intersects Broadway and Seventh Ave. The intersection is the southern edge of Times Square and the

Theater District, extending north between Broadway and Seventh Ave. for about ten blocks, and on side streets in both directions. The district is now being renovated, and dozens of shabby old buildings are being replaced by new office towers. Within the area are about 25 legitimate theaters, many big motion picture theaters, TV studios, hotels and restaurants, the offices and plant for the *New York Times,* bars, clip joints, and penny arcades. The area is spectacular at night, thanks to enormous electric signs, some animated.

From 42nd St., Fifth Ave. extends south to 34th St., an important intersection. On the southwest corner is the

Empire State Building, 350 Fifth Ave., world's tallest and New York's most famous building, 1,472 feet high. Each year over 1.5 million people ride to observation decks on the 86th and 102nd floors to get a bird's-eye view of the city. Open daily, 9:30 a.m. to midnight. (Tickets: adults $1.50, children 75¢.)

One block south of 34th St., filling a two-block area between 33rd and 31st streets, Seventh and Eighth avenues, is New York's newest and most spectacular sports and entertainment facility:

Madison Square Garden Center, a huge complex of arena, amphitheater, restaurants, museum, bowling alleys, and convention space. The main arena seats 20,000. Guided tours daily, 9 a.m. to 5:30 p.m. (Tickets: adults, $2.00, children $1.)

South of midtown, points of interest are widely scattered. A worthwhile one, buried in a shabby wholesale district, is

Theodore Roosevelt Birthplace National Historic Site, 28 E. 20th St., a beautifully restored Victorian mansion where Roosevelt was born in 1858. He was the only president born in New York City. The brownstone house is furnished with many family possessions. The museum next door displays a remarkable collection of relics. House and museum are open daily, 9 a.m. to 4:30 p.m. (Admission: adults 50¢, children free.)

From 34th St., Fifth Ave., no longer an important shopping street, continues south to

GREENWICH VILLAGE, a celebrated district which has lost much of the distinctive character that made it famous 50 years ago, when it was the haunt of artists, writers, and Bohemians. Most places of interest are around and near

Washington Square, once a pleasant park with big trees, lined with fine houses. The central feature is Washington Arch, completed in 1895, which was built to celebrate the centennial of Washington's inauguration. Two statues of Washington face up Fifth Ave.

Eighth St., chief east-west street, Greenwich Ave., and the narrow streets west of Sixth Ave. are fun to explore, with their craft and curio shops, restaurants, coffee shops, and psychedelic stores.

East of Washington Square, Broadway leads south about a mile to become the chief north-south street of

LOWER MANHATTAN, the triangular southern end of Manhattan Island where New York began. Places of interest:

Chinatown, on the northern edge, a congested patch of irregular streets. Chatham Square is the gateway to Chinatown, the home of about 6,000 Chinese and the trading center for a worldwide commerce in Oriental merchandise. Chinatown's excellent shops and restaurants attract hordes of visitors. Southwest of Chinatown, Park Row leads to City Hall Park, dominated by

City Hall, one of New York's most charming buildings. A museum on the second floor, displaying historic relics and portraits, is worth seeing. East of City Hall Park is the

Brooklyn Bridge, spanning the East River to downtown Brooklyn, the city's oldest and, to many, its most beautiful bridge.

Facing Broadway, just south of City Hall Park, is

St. Paul's Chapel, between Fulton and Vesey streets, oldest church on Manhattan Island, completed in 1766. George Washington's pew and 14 Waterford crystal chandeliers are outstanding interior features. From St. Paul's churchyard, looking west toward the Hudson River, one can see the rising towers of the

World Trade Center, filling an area bounded by Vesey St. on the north, Church St. on the east, the Hudson River on the west, and Liberty St. on the south. Two identical 110-story towers will rise above a cluster of lower buildings and a five-acre plaza. The whole Center will cover 16 acres.

South of St. Paul's Chapel, Broadway becomes a canyon between towering office buildings. Six blocks south, an even narrower canyon, lined with some of the city's tallest buildings, leads east to the East River. It is

Wall Street, the historic center of the world's biggest financial district. It was named for the wall that was the northern limit of New Amsterdam. Along and near Wall St. are several places of interest:

Trinity Church, facing down Wall St. from the west side of Broadway, founded in 1697, and a few years later endowed by Queen Anne with a large grant of Manhattan Island land. Trinity still owns much of this land. The present Gothic church, blackened with city grime, is the third on the site and was completed in 1846. In the churchyard are the graves of Robert Fulton and Alexander Hamilton.

From Trinity Church it is only a short walk east on Wall St. to Broad St. On the north side of Wall St. stands

Federal Hall National Memorial, a Greek Revival building built in 1842 on the site of Federal Hall, the country's first capitol. There Congress met, and there George Washington in 1789 took the oath of office as president of the United States, at about the spot where the familiar statue of Washington now stands. The handsome old building is now a historical museum. Open free, Monday through Friday, 10 a.m. to 4 p.m.

Federal Hall faces south down Broad St. On the west side of Broad St. is the ornate facade of the

New York Stock Exchange, with entrances at 18 and 20 Broad St., world's largest market for the sale of securities. The Stock Exchange began here under a buttonwood tree in 1792, when a group of New Yorkers met to organize a system for buying and selling securities. The visitors'

The New York Stock Exchange, world's largest market for the sale of securities, is an exciting place to see and feel the financial pulse of the nation.

gallery is open free weekdays except Wednesday, 10 a.m. to 3:30 p.m.

Three blocks south of Trinity Church and Wall St., Broadway ends at historic

BATTERY PARK, which forms the southern tip of Manhattan Island, bounded by Battery Pl. on the northwest, State St. on the northeast, and a curving promenade on the southwest with a superb view of New York Harbor. The park is laced with wide, tree-lined walks, and is filled with memorials and statues. The most important is.

Castle Clinton National Monument, on the southwest edge of the park, a circular brownstone fort completed in 1812, recently restored. In 1824 the fort became an amusement center called Castle Garden. Jenny Lind sang here in 1850. A few years later it became the principal port of entry for immigrants. More than seven million people streamed through it from 1855 to 1890. Soon after 1890 it was converted to an aquarium and remained one until 1941.

A statue of Giovanni da Verrazano, who discovered New York Harbor, is just east of Castle Clinton. Farther east, at the edge of the harbor promenade, is the unique East Coast War Memorial, two rows of huge granite slabs carved with the names and states of men and women lost in Atlantic waters during World War II.

The outstanding point of interest in this area is the

Statue of Liberty, visited by more than a million people a year. A gift of the people of France to the people of the United States, the statue was dedicated in 1886. The hollow bronze figure is fitted with 225 tons of copper sheets rising 151 feet from the base to the tip of the raised torch. The statue stands on a 142-foot pedestal built over the ramparts of a former fort. A narrow spiral stairway (168 steps) leads from the base to the head, where you can see the harbor through narrow windows. The American Museum of Immigration is scheduled to open, in the base of the statue, in 1970. Ferries leave the Battery Park terminal every hour on the hour, 9 a.m. to 5 p.m., daily, with more frequent trips in summer. (Round-trip fare: adults 90¢, children 40¢.)

At the southwest corner of Battery Park, head of State St., is the Staten Island Ferry Terminal. Ferries operate at frequent inter-

vals, and the fare is an incredible 5¢. The trip, which takes about 20 minutes, links Manhattan with

STATEN ISLAND, officially the Borough of Richmond, twice the size of Manhattan Island, 14 miles long and seven miles wide, but with a population of only 290,000. The island, one of the earliest settled places in the area, is a patchwork of scattered towns and villages. One community of interest is

Richmond, near the center of the island, where a number of historic sites and houses, some going back to the 17th century, are being restored. They include the Voorlezer House, 63 Arthur Kill Rd., built about 1696, oldest known elementary school building in the country. Near it is St. Andrew's Church, first constructed in 1713, and rebuilt twice since that time.

East of the southern end of Manhattan Island, linked to it by several bridges and tunnels, is

BROOKLYN, the most heavily populated of New York's five boroughs, with about 2.6 million people; an area of 71 square miles. Brooklyn began as a Dutch village in 1636. Essentially industrial, with port facilities that handle about half of all the tonnage of the New York area, Brooklyn also has residential sections ranging from ghettos to pleasant middle-class districts. Places of interest:

Brooklyn Museum, on Eastern Pkwy. at Washington Ave. The museum is famous for exhibits relating to Egypt, Africa, and the Pacific Islands. It also has Colonial period rooms and an unusual sculpture garden, preserving ornamental stonework from demolished New York buildings. Open free, Monday through Saturday, 10 a.m. to 5 p.m.; Sunday, 1 p.m. to 5 p.m. Directly behind the museum is the

Brooklyn Botanic Garden, famed for a Japanese garden and groves of flowering shrubs and fruit trees. Other features include the Garden of Fragrance for the blind, and herb and wild flower gardens. Conservatories display exotic and tropical plants. The outdoor garden areas are open Monday through Saturday, 8 a.m. to sundown; Sunday after 1 p.m.

The most famous spot in Brooklyn is probably

Coney Island, filling the ocean side of a flat peninsula along Brooklyn's extreme southern edge, reached by Ocean Pkwy. or Shore Pkwy. The name Coney is a corruption of the Dutch word for rabbit, *konijn;* when discovered the land was a sand dune entirely populated with rabbits, who had no use at all for the four miles of superb beach on the ocean side. New Yorkers flocked there in increasing numbers. For some years it was a fashionable resort, but when the subway linked it to Manhattan it became everybody's beach. The newest exhibit is the

New York Aquarium, Boardwalk and W. Eighth St. The aquarium specializes in big marine mammals like whales, walrus, and seals. There are also penguins, and fish of various regions, exhibited in settings as colorful and exotic as the fish themselves. Open May 30 to Labor Day, 10 a.m. to 7 p.m.; rest of the year to 5 p.m. (Admission: adults 90¢, children 45¢.)

QUEENS, the youngest of the five New York City boroughs, is linked to Manhattan by two bridges, the Queensboro (59th St.) and the Triborough, and the Queens-Midtown Tunnel. Queens is the largest borough in area, with 113 square miles. It is the fastest growing in population, and ranks next to Brooklyn, with about two million people. Places of interest:

La Guardia Airport, Grand Central Pkwy., nearest airport to Manhattan and the city's oldest. Recently renovated, it serves domestic flights of most major airlines. About three miles south of La Guardia, west of Grand Central Pkwy., is the

West Side Tennis Club, within the residential district of Forest Hills, at Burns St. and Tennis Pl., the most famous center for professional and amateur tennis in the country. Each summer the club, which has about 60 beautifully maintained grass and clay courts, and a stadium seating 15,000, is the setting for national and international tennis matches.

It is about ten miles from La Guardia on Grand Central Pkwy. and the Van Wyck Expressway to New York's huge and famous

John F. Kennedy International Airport, which occupies almost 5,000 acres of the southern edge of Queens, overlooking Jamaica Bay. JFK is one of the few big city airports using a dispersal system. Most major airlines have their own terminals. It is New York's only airport serving foreign flights, and handles about 20 million air passengers a year.

On the south side of Queens is

Aqueduct Race Track, about 14 miles from Manhattan, just west of Kennedy Airport, between Rockaway Blvd. and Southern State Pkwy. Newest and largest of the city's tracks, it was opened in 1959, seats 60,000, and has a one and one-half mile oval dirt track, a one-mile turf course, and a seven-furlong steeplechase course inside the main oval. Meets are held daily during several periods of the year.

About seven miles northeast of Aqueduct is New York's historic racetrack:

Belmont Park, just east of the New York City line, in Nassau County, off the Cross Island Pkwy. and the Hempstead Tpke. One of the most beautiful racetracks in the country, Belmont Park was reopened in 1968 after several years of renovation. Site of the first racetrack in the American colonies, Belmont opened in 1905, and was for many years one of the leading tracks in the country. It features steeplechase and hurdle racing on a grass course, and flat racing on a mile-and-a-half oval dirt track. Belmont races alternate with those at Aqueduct.

The southern edge of Queens, beyond the wide expanse of Jamaica Bay, is a pencil-thin peninsula, with a chain of

Ocean beaches, extending more than ten miles, from Breezy Point on the west to Rockaway Inlet on the east. There are dozens of separate beach areas, some private, some public, all linked by Cross Bay Blvd.

Of the five boroughs of New York City, the only one not an island or part of an island is

THE BRONX, north of Manhattan, 42 miles of rugged, often wooded, land. On the west is the Hudson River, on the south and southwest the Harlem River, on the southeast the East River, and on the east Long Island Sound.

The Bronx is surprisingly varied in character. Its 1.5 million residents live in a mosaic of communities ranging from some of New York's worst slums to relatively luxurious suburbs. Points of interest:

Yankee Stadium, 161st St. and River Ave., just east of the Harlem River, the home field of the New York Yankees baseball team and the New York Giants football team.

About two miles north of Yankee Stadium, at the crest of a bluff overlooking the Harlem River, is the

Hall of Fame for Great Americans, University Ave. and 181st St., part of the uptown campus of New York University. The Hall of Fame is in an open-air, covered colonnade displaying about 90 bronze busts of Americans who have made significant contributions to the nation. Open free daily, 9 a.m. to 5 p.m. About two miles east of the Hall of Fame is

Fordham University, Third Ave. and Fordham Rd., run by the Jesuits, one of the oldest Catholic universities in the country, with about 11,000 students. The university is famed for its Seismographic (earthquake) Research Center.

East of the Fordham campus is the

Bronx Zoo (New York Zoological Park), Fordham Rd. and Pelham Pkwy., one of the largest zoos in the world. The World of Darkness, opened in 1969, lets one see nocturnal creatures as they appear at night, thanks to special lighting. Other features include a children's zoo, aquatic and exotic bird displays, a reptile house, and a penguin house. Open weekdays, 10 a.m. to 5 p.m.; to 5:30 p.m. on Sunday and holidays. (Admission: Tuesday through Thursday 25¢; free rest of the week.)

Adjoining the Bronx Zoo on the north is the

New York Botanical Garden, entrances from Pelham Pkwy. and Southern Blvd., one of the finest gardens in the world, with 12,000 different plant species in 230 acres. Open free daily, 10 a.m. until half an hour after sunset. There is a $1 parking fee on Saturday, Sunday, and holidays.

New York's southern limit is

LONG ISLAND, nuzzling into the flank of Manhattan Island like a tethered whale, 125 miles long from its stubby western nose to the two slender tails in the east. The only convenient access, except by air, is through New York City, by tunnel or bridge. Two of New York's five boroughs, Brooklyn and Queens, make up the western third of the island, with a combined population of over four million. The rest of the island consists of Nassau County, which adjoins Queens, and the more sparsely settled Suffolk County.

The topography of the island ranges from fairly rugged, wooded hills cupped with deep bays along the north shore, overlooking Long Island Sound, to flat salt marshes along the southern shore, behind thin barrier beaches.

Points of Interest.

U.S. Merchant Marine Academy, Kings Point, reached by Steamboat Rd. from the town of Great Neck. The Academy, the Merchant Marine counterpart of West Point and Annapolis, trains about 700 cadets each year as officers for United States merchant ships and the Naval Reserve. The handsome grounds are open to visitors Saturday, Sunday, and holidays from noon to 5 p.m. Worth seeing are the Administration Building, the former Chrysler mansion, and an interfaith memorial chapel of striking design. Regimental reviews are held each Saturday at 10:30 a.m. between May and November (except during July, when the Academy is closed).

About 15 miles east of the Merchant Marine Academy is

Sagamore Hill National Historic Site, three miles northeast of the village of Oyster Bay, on Cove Neck Rd. Built in 1884, the rambling, 22-room Victorian house, on hilltop grounds of more than 80 acres, was the home of Theodore Roosevelt and his family until his death in 1919. From 1901 to 1909, the eight years Roosevelt was president, Sagamore Hill was the official summer White House. The house is crowded with relics of Teddy Roosevelt's strenuous life: trophies from big game hunts, souvenirs of presidential days, books, pictures, and hundreds of intimate family possessions. Of special interest is Roosevelt's gun room on the third floor. Open daily, 10 a.m. to 5 p.m. (Admission: adults 50¢, children free.)

Fire Island National Seashore, just 65 miles from New York City, opened its first full season of operation in 1966 and gives the visitor a touch of truly primitive beach.

A bird sanctuary and museum, about one mile east of Oyster Bay, on Cove Rd., is maintained as a memorial to Roosevelt, with about 100 varieties of trees and shrubs on a 12-acre tract, linked by a self-guiding trail. The museum exhibits plant and animal life native to Long Island. Theodore Roosevelt's grave is in a small cemetery adjoining the sanctuary.

About 18 miles south of Oyster Bay on the Meadowbrook Pkwy. is

Jones Beach State Park, with five miles of superb beach, a boardwalk, an aqua stadium, and playgrounds. All sections of Jones Beach are linked by Ocean Pkwy., which joins the Robert Moses Causeway, leading across Fire Island Inlet to

Fire Island, 30 miles long and never more than a few hundred yards wide, a barrier beach which has become one of the most unusual resort areas in the country. Much of the island has recently been designated the Fire Island National Seashore. Until completion of the Robert Moses Causeway at its west end, the island could be reached only by ferry. There are virtually no roads on the island, and no private automobiles are allowed. The chain of villages strung along the island are linked only by foot trails and the beach. An unusual feature is a sunken forest of holly trees among the sand dunes.

Main east-west highways of Long Island converge on

Riverhead, population 6,500, county seat of Suffolk County, shipping and buying center for crops like potatoes and cauliflower. East of Riverhead, Long Island divides into two slender, irregular peninsulas (locally referred to as flukes because of their resemblance to the divided tail of a whale), with Great Peconic Bay between. From Riverhead New York 25 leads northeast through the north fluke about 22 miles to the village of

Greenport, population 2,900, processing and shipping center for oysters raked from offshore waters, and a shopping center for summer visitors. From Greenport a system of ferries and highways leads south over a chain of islands to the south fluke, and New York 25 leads east to Orient Point, from which a ferry to New London, Connecticut, operates during the summer.

From Riverhead New York 24 leads eight miles southeast to a junction with New York 27, the Montauk Highway, which links

The Hamptons, a chain of towns on a 35-mile stretch of Long Island's south shore, beginning in the west with Westhampton, ending in the east with Amagansett. In between are Hampton Bays, Southampton, Bridgehampton, and East Hampton. Two towns are notable:

Southampton, a shopping and service center and a world-famous resort. Founded in 1640, Southampton is one of the oldest towns on Long Island. The Halsey Homestead, on S. Main St., built in 1648, is open to visitors. About a mile south of town the shore road runs along behind an incredible row of beach mansions, and past charming St. Andrew's Dunes Church on Dune Rd. Southampton's most important exhibit is

Long Island Automotive Museum, northwest edge of town, on New York 27, with one of the best collections of old and historic automobiles in the country. Open daily, 9 a.m. to 5 p.m., June through September; weekends only in spring and fall; closed in winter. (Admission: adults $1.25, children 60¢.)

From Southampton New York 27 leads east about 15 miles to historic

East Hampton, population 2,200, widely regarded as one of the most beautiful villages in the country. The village green, with a pond in the center, is surrounded by fine old homes. Facing the green is

Home Sweet Home, built around 1660, a shingled cottage of great charm where John Howard Payne, who wrote the song "Home, Sweet Home," was born and lived. Open daily except Tuesday, 10 a.m. to 5 p.m., during July and August; rest of the year until 4 p.m. (Admission: adults 50¢, children free.) East Hampton has several historic windmills. One, near the village green, is the only one on Long Island that still works.

Like Southampton, East Hampton is an

important shore resort, with handsome summer houses strung along the beach to the south.

From East Hampton it is about seven miles northwest on New York 114 to

Sag Harbor, population 2,700, one of the most fascinating villages in New York. Once it rivaled New Bedford, Massachusetts, as a great whaling center. Sag Harbor sea captains who made fortunes from whaling and shipping built fine mansions. Most of them are still here. One of the finest, built around 1845, is now the

Whaling Museum, Garden and Main Sts., once the mansion of ship owner Benjamin Huntting, one of the finest examples of Greek Revival style in the country. A notable collection of whaling gear and relics is displayed. Open from late May to early October, Monday through Saturday, 10 a.m. to 5 p.m.; Sunday, 2 p.m. to 5 p.m. (Admission: adults 50¢; 6-16, 25¢; children under 6 free.)

From East Hampton New York 27 leads east past Amagansett through the center of a narrow finger of rugged land, with high, windswept, almost treeless moors and steep bluffs breaking sharply to the sea, a region unlike any other on Long Island. This is the Montauk area, with big ponds, salt marshes, and dunes, ending in high bluffs at the tip of the peninsula. The only community is the village of

Montauk, population 600, the most easterly town on Long Island, and the eastern terminus for the Long Island Railroad. Montauk began as part of a promoter's dream. Carl Fisher, who developed Miami Beach, tried to make Montauk a great resort and base for ocean shipping, and built a giant hotel as a starter. The plan didn't work. Fisher lost his fortune and for years Montauk was little more than a ghost town. Recently it has become the most important sports fishing center on Long Island.

Five miles east of Montauk, Long Island comes to a dramatic end with

Montauk Point State Park, about 130 acres, on a high, rugged promontory above the sea. The park has picnic areas, a lighthouse built in 1795, and a fine beach which, although unsafe for swimming, is a favorite among surf fishermen.

The famous old Liberty Bell is on permanent exhibition in Independence Hall, Philadelphia. Visitors hear the story of the bell through a tape recording.

PENNSYLVANIA.

PENNSYLVANIA RANKS 33rd in size in the country, with 45,333 square miles. It ranks third in population, nearly 12 million, after New York and California. In shape it is roughly rectangular, slightly more than 300 miles east to west, and about 160 miles north to south. It is bordered on the north by Lake Erie and New York, on the east by New Jersey and New York. In the south the Mason-Dixon line, a straight-line border, is shared with Maryland and West Virginia. Delaware is also a neighbor to the south. Another straight-line border on the west separates Pennsylvania from West Virginia and Ohio.

Pennsylvania is a mountainous state.

Parallel folded ranges sweep through the eastern and central sections in a belt ranging from 40 to 50 miles wide, with some crests rising 2,000 feet above narrow valleys. Different types of mountains flank the neat parallel ranges. In the northeast are the low, tumbled hills of the Poconos. Filling most of the northwest section is the vast Allegheny Plateau, much of it wilderness.

Flanking the mountains are two richly productive agricultural areas. In the northwest the region along the shore of Lake Erie is famed for vineyards, and in the southeast is the enormously fertile Pennsylvania Dutch country.

Pennsylvania claims three important rivers. The Delaware, emerging from sources in New York's Catskill Mountains, forms the eastern boundary of the state. It flows south more than 300 miles to become a wide tidal river below Philadelphia, making that city one of the chief ports of the country. The Susquehanna flows south in a double S-curve through central eastern Pennsylvania, here and there cutting through the mountains to form picturesque water gaps. Pennsylvania's most important river is the lordly Ohio, created from two big rivers, the Monongahela and the Allegheny, which rise in the western mountains and join at Pittsburgh to form the Ohio. In pioneer days the Ohio provided the best route for western migration, and today it makes Pittsburgh an important inland port, connecting that city with the Mississippi Valley and the Gulf of Mexico.

William Penn was not the first European to visit Pennsylvania. Henry Hudson is known to have anchored his *Half Moon* in Delaware Bay in 1609, and six years later the inquisitive Frenchman Étienne Brulé explored the Susquehanna River into the heart of what is now Pennsylvania. The first attempt at settlement came in 1643, when Johan Printz established a settlement on Tinicum Island in the Delaware, near the southern edge of what is now Philadelphia, as the capital of a cluster of Swedish settlements in the Delaware Valley. It had about 300 people when the Dutch from New York took over all the Swedish colonies in 1655, only to lose them to the English in 1664. The real beginning of Pennsylvania came in 1681, when William Penn received a grant from Charles II. Penn himself came to the New World the next year and laid out two square miles on the banks of the Delaware with wide streets

and parks, a "greene countrie towne," to be called Philadelphia, meaning in Greek the "city of brotherly love." In the years that followed Philadelphia became the chief city of the American colonies, larger and richer than any other, a center of culture and industry.

The Pennsylvania wilderness to the west played a part in the French and Indian War of the late 18th century. The French defeated the British in 1755. Later the British built Fort Pitt, which grew into the important city of Pittsburgh.

Before and during the Revolutionary War Philadelphia became a center of political activity. The first and second Continental Congresses were held there, the Declaration of Independence was signed there, the Constitution was adopted there, and Philadelphia was the nation's capital for ten years from 1790 to 1800.

In 1859 the nation's first successful oil well was drilled near Titusville, in Pennsylvania's western mountains.

During the Civil War Pennsylvania sent more than 300,000 men to the Union army, and 34,000 Pennsylvanians took part in the battle at Gettysburg, the only major engagement of the war fought on Pennsylvania soil.

The development of Pennsylvania's huge industrial and commercial interests came rapidly after the Civil War, partly because of the growth of the area around Pittsburgh as the center of the nation's steel and iron industry. Pennsylvania now ranks first in the country in the production of iron and steel, accounting for one-quarter of the total national output. Pennsylvania mines account for nearly all the anthracite coal mined in the country, about 15 million tons a year. It ranks second in bituminous coal. Its 68,000 oil wells produce more oil than any other eastern state.

In volume and variety of manufactured products Pennsylvania is exceeded only by New York. It leads in shoe production, ranks near the top in textiles, petroleum products, chemicals, scientific instruments, railway cars, electrical equipment. Pennsylvania leads all states in processing chocolate, pretzels, and sausage produces, and ranks second in ice cream.

About half of Pennsylvania's 15 million acres of farmland is in crops. There are some 80,000 farms. Pennsylvania leads the nation in growing mushrooms and cigar leaf

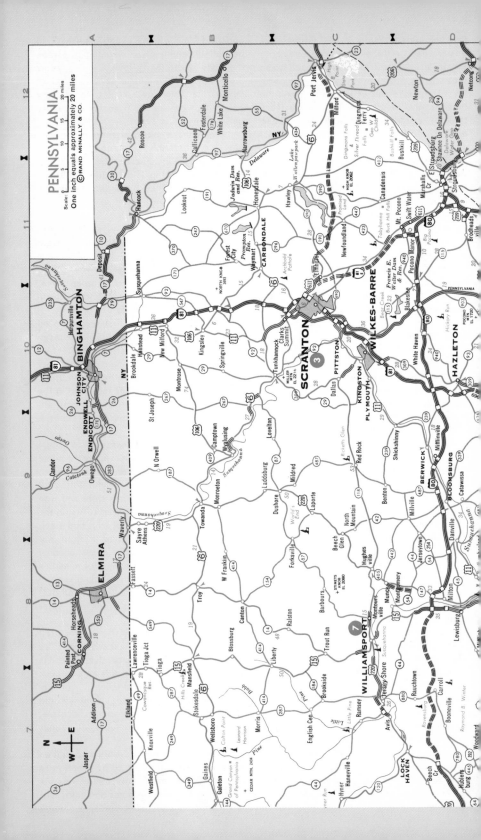

PENNSYLVANIA

Scale:
One inch equals approximately 20 miles
© RAND MCNALLY & CO.

0   5   10   15   20 miles

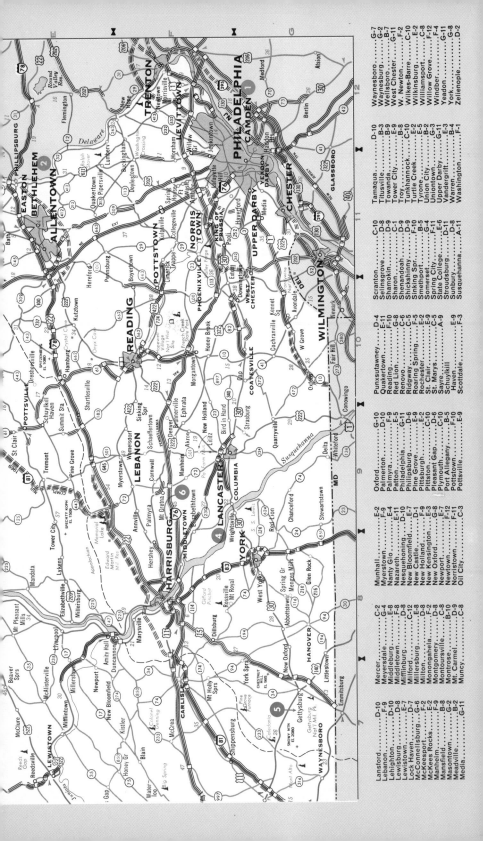

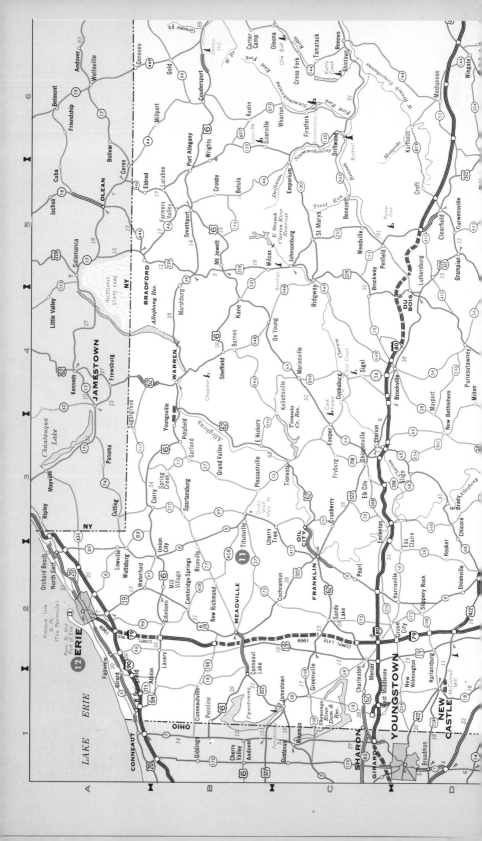

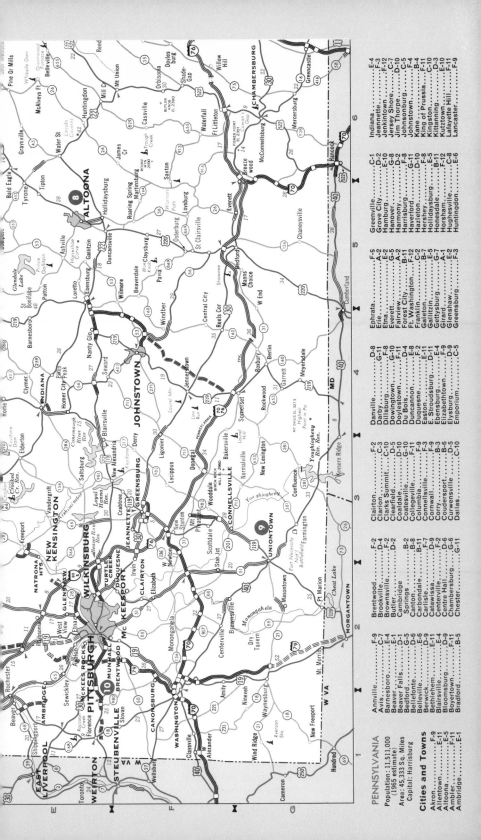

PENNSYLVANIA FACTS

Name. From *Penn* (for William Penn) and Latin word *silva*, meaning wood, or Penn's Woods.

Nickname. Keystone State, because of its central position among the 13 colonies.

Area. 45,333 square miles, 33rd in the United States.

Population. 11,675,000, 1969 estimate, third in the United States.

Admitted as a state. 1787, second among the 13 colonies.

Capital. Harrisburg.

Largest city. Philadelphia 2,000,-000.

State tree. Eastern hemlock.

State flower. Mountain laurel.

State bird. Ruffed grouse.

Industry. Steel, leads the country; also important in electrical machinery, chemicals, coal mining, pretzels, ice cream, chocolate.

Agriculture. Dairy products, Christmas trees, fruits, tobacco, mushrooms.

Odds and Ends. Declaration of Independence written and proclaimed here; U.S. Constitution framed here; the site of George Washington's Valley Forge headquarters, the first national bank, the first capital of the United States, the first major toll highway (the Pennsylvania Turnpike), and the Civil War's most important battle (Gettysburg).

tobacco. Only three states produce more grapes and only four produce more milk, apples, and maple syrup.

The population pattern of Pennsylvania is uneven, with the largest share of the state's nearly 12 million people concentrated in the southeast and east, most of them within a 100-mile radius of Philadelphia. In the northern section of the state west of Scranton there are no large cities except Erie, Pennsylvania's Lake Erie port, in the northwest panhandle. There are no large cities in the central mountain region. Pittsburgh, with about 540,000 people in the city proper and over two million in the metropolitan district, dominates southwest Pennsylvania.

Pennsylvania's highway pattern is controlled by the location of larger cities and gaps through the mountains. Both Philadelphia in the east and Pittsburgh in the west are hubs of intersecting express routes, including toll highways. Two main Interstate routes cross the state east to west. Of these the most famous, now numbered Interstate 76, is the Pennsylvania Turnpike, a pioneer toll road, which began during the early 30s with the conversion of an abandoned railroad right-of-way. It links with the New Jersey Turnpike in the east and the Ohio Turnpike in the west. An extension leads north, connecting Philadelphia with Scranton, and then continues as Interstate 81. Other Interstate routes that link with the turnpike include Interstate 83, 81, and 70. A recently developed northern east-west Interstate route is Interstate 80, entering the state through the Delaware Water Gap in the east and crossing the sparsely settled mountain and forest region to link with the Ohio Turnpike. Along the western side of the state Interstate 79 extends from Erie in the north down to the border of West Virginia, skirting Pittsburgh and linking with all east-west routes. US 15 links Gettysburg with Harrisburg, and then follows the Susquehanna River north through the mountains.

Important points of interest in Pennsylvania are indicated by number in the text and on the two maps on pages 52-53 and 54-55. Points of interest in the eastern half of the state (pages 52-53) start with Pennsylvania's largest and most historic city:

Red-bricked Independence Hall gives today's American a chance to stand in the rooms where the Declaration of Independence was drafted, debated, and signed.

1. PHILADELPHIA, population 2,015,000, fourth largest city in the country, a great seaport, and a center of diversified manufacturing and industry. It began in 1682 as a two-square-mile community on the west bank of the Delaware River, and was carefully planned by William Penn to be a "greene countrie towne."

Within a few years Penn's city was a big success, had more than 6,000 people, and soon became the largest and richest city in the Colonies and a center of culture, industry, and political ferment. Philadelphians were leaders in many fields. Some became rich and built handsome houses. Philadelphia claims many American firsts, like the first bank, the first Bible printed in English, first circulating library, first circus, first daily newspaper, first hospital.

Philadelphia was the center of political control of the Colonies during the Revolutionary period. Two sessions of the Continental Congress met here, in 1774 and again in 1775. The Declaration of Independence was written in Philadelphia, and the Liberty Bell, now its most cherished relic, rang out to proclaim the fact. Philadelphia remained the power center of the Revolution until General Howe and the British army took over the city in 1777. It was the new nation's capital for ten years after the war ended.

After the government moved to the newly established District of Columbia in 1800, Philadelphia's political prestige declined, but its population and industrial development steadily increased. It became important as an educational center, with 19 colleges and universities. Though 50 miles from the mouth of the Delaware River and 60 miles from the ocean, it is the fourth biggest port in the nation, handling nearly 50 million tons of cargo annually, most of it in foreign trade. Philadelphia is the largest petroleum refining center on the East Coast. The city's more than 4,000 factories produce over $5 billion worth of goods a year. Philadelphia leads in manufacturing textiles, ships, surgical instruments, radios, railway cars and locomotives. It is also famous for making hats, ice cream, and cream cheese.

Philadelphia today extends about 25 miles along the Delaware River, and west from the river more than ten miles. Hundreds of residential and industrial suburbs surround the city. In recent years a huge and dramatic urban renewal program has trans-formed the run-down inner city. Much of the Colonial charm of the old city has been restored.

Routes To and Through. The Pennsylvania Turnpike (here numbered Interstate 276) skirts the northern limits of the city. From it two Interstate routes diverge into the center of the city: the Delaware Expressway (Interstate 95) along the Delaware River in the east, the Schuylkill Expressway (Interstate 76) along the Schuylkill River in the west. They merge south of the central business district as Interstate 676, which leads over the Delaware River to link with the New Jersey Turnpike.

Points of Interest.

These fall into three adjoining districts in downtown Philadelphia. The first and most important includes most of the original colonial city, just west of the Delaware River. At its center is

Independence National Historic Park, a four-block area between Second and Sixth, Walnut and Chestnut streets. In the area, best seen on foot, are many historic buildings. At the west end is

Independence Hall, a beautiful Georgian Colonial building, faithfully restored to look as it did when the Declaration of Independence was adopted there in 1776. Here the Second Continental Congress met, the Declaration of Independence was signed, and George Washington accepted command of the American armies. The Constitution was written here. The Liberty Bell and the inkstand used by the signers of the Declaration of Independence are the outstanding exhibits. Open free daily, 8:15 a.m. to 8 p.m. in summer; rest of the year, 9 a.m. to 5 p.m.

West of Independence Hall is

Congress Hall, built in 1787, where Congress met from 1790 to 1800. On the east is old City Hall, built about 1790, the first home of the United States Supreme Court. Independence Park south from Independence Hall to Walnut St. is worth strolling through. It is lighted by 56 gas lamps, one for each signer of the Declaration of Independence. One of the most charming buildings in the park is

Carpenters' Hall, in Independence National Historical Park, is where the stormy First Continental Congress met in 1774 to debate the question of revolution.

Carpenters' Hall, a block east of Independence Square, at 320 Chestnut St. Built in 1770 as a headquarters for master craftsmen, it was loaned by the Carpenters' Guild, which still owns and uses it, for the First Continental Congress in 1774. A small building of classic Georgian design, it has been carefully restored and exhibits relics of the Revolutionary period. Open free daily, 10 a.m. to 4 p.m. One block east is the

First Bank of the United States, 116 S. Third St., oldest bank building in the country, organized by Alexander Hamilton while he was Secretary of the Treasury. It houses the visitor center which serves the park.

About three blocks northeast of the bank is

Christ Church (Episcopal), on the west side of Second St., just north of Market St. The congregation was organized in 1695. The present building, a handsome example of Georgian church design, completed in 1754, was the place of worship for many leaders of the Revolutionary period, including George Washington and Benjamin Franklin. Several signers of the Declaration of Independence are buried in the churchyard. Interior features worth noting include a 1697 baptismal font, a 1744 chandelier, and a distinctive "wineglass" pulpit. The church is open free daily, 9 a.m. to 5 p.m. There are daily services at 12:30 p.m., and several Sunday services.

About a block north of Christ Church is the

Betsy Ross House, 239 Arch St., a tiny, charming Colonial cottage, the home of the seamstress who is said to have stitched together the first American flag, under the guidance of George Washington. The story has never been proved, but the legend persists. The house has been restored and contains relics of the Revolutionary period. Open free daily, 9:30 a.m. to 5:15 p.m. Just east and a little north of the Betsy Ross House is

Elfreth's Alley, one block long, between Second and Front streets. Narrow, paved with cobblestones, the little street is lined with houses over 200 years old, some built as early as 1690. No. 126, maintained as a museum, is restored and furnished in late 18th-century style. It is open free daily, 12:30 p.m. to 4 p.m., April to November; rest of the year weekends only. Information about all the houses on the street is available at the museum.

On the north side of Independence Square, between Fifth and Sixth streets, extending north four blocks, is the handsomely landscaped Independence Mall, replacing the shabby commercial buildings that once blighted the area. On the east side of the mall is

Christ Church Burial Ground, corner of Fifth and Arch streets, where the most famous graves are those of Benjamin Frank-

lin and his wife, Deborah. Just north, filling the whole block between Arch and Race streets, is the

United States Mint, a big new building designed to harmonize with the Colonial character of the area. The entrance is on Independence Mall. Until the completion of the new building the mint was some distance north, at 16th and Spring Garden streets. The oldest and largest of three United States mints (the others are in Denver and San Francisco), it sponsors 30-minute tours every hour on the half hour, 8:30 a.m. to 3:30 p.m., Monday through Friday. Closed mid-June to July 4. Children must be over eight years old, and no cameras are allowed.

Eight blocks east of Independence Mall, on Market St., chief east-west street of the downtown area, is Philadelphia's massive

City Hall, filling Penn Square at the junction of Broad and Market streets. A huge building of unusual design that might be called Victorian Rococo, built around 1895,

Elfreth's Alley is the oldest still-occupied residential street in the United States. Annually its residents parade in 18th-century dress.

it has only one notable feature, a tower rising 548 feet, topped by a statue of William Penn above a four-faced clock. Visitors are admitted to the tower free daily, 9 a.m. to 4:30 p.m.

Points of Interest—northwest of City Hall.

The second area of high interest for visitors begins at City Hall, extends west and northwest, with most places along or near Philadelphia's handsomest street, Benjamin Franklin Parkway. Immediately west of City Hall is

Penn Center, a 12-block area along John F. Kennedy Blvd., the most impressive evidence of Philadelphia's huge redevelopment program, a complex of gleaming new office towers, hotels, shops, and restaurants, which have replaced an industrial slum and the elevated railway tracks that once cut through the heart of the city. The Center, built on several levels, has a landscaped concourse, a skating rink, and some of the city's finest shops. Benjamin Franklin Parkway leads northwest from Penn Center five blocks to Logan Circle. Just south of the Circle is the

Academy of Natural Sciences, at 19th St., the oldest museum of its kind in the country and a noted research center, with wide-ranging nature exhibits and live animal shows. The Academy is open Monday through Saturday, 10 a.m. to 5 p.m.; Sunday, 1 p.m. to 5 p.m. (Admission: adults 50¢, children 25¢.)

Facing Logan Circle from the west is Philadelphia's famous science museum, the

Franklin Institute, at 20th St. The Institute's most celebrated feature is a gigantic seated statue of Benjamin Franklin by James Earle Fraser. One can see action exhibits relating to science, astronomy, chemistry, and physics. Open Tuesday through Saturday, 10 a.m. to 5 p.m.; Sunday, noon to 5 p.m. (Admission: adults $1.25, children 95¢.)

Two blocks northwest of the Franklin Institute is the

Rodin Museum, at 22nd St., a small museum on landscaped grounds, with the finest collection outside of Paris of the work of the French sculptor Auguste Rodin, housed in a copy of the French Musée Meudon. Open daily, 9 a.m. to 5 p.m. (Admission: adults 25¢, children free.)

Four blocks northwest of the Rodin Museum, just beyond the end of Benjamin Franklin Parkway, is the

Philadelphia Museum of Art, at 26th St., one of the country's greatest museums, housed in a huge, handsome building. In addition to wide-ranging general collections covering every period of art, the museum is noted for its Japanese Tea House, Chinese Palace, Medieval Cloister, outdoor Fountain Court, and period rooms. Open daily, 9 a.m. to 5 p.m. (Admission: adults 50¢, children 25¢. Free on Monday.)

Stretching northwest from the Museum of Art is

Fairmount Park, extending about ten miles along the Schuylkill River and Wissahickon Creek, to the northwest limits of Philadelphia. The Schuylkill Expressway leads through the park on the west bank of the river and connects with a network of park drives.

In more than 4,000 rolling, handsomely landscaped acres, the park offers much to see and do: a fine zoo near the southern end, the first zoo in the country; an outdoor amphitheater; a theater; the log cabin used by General Grant as his headquarters during the siege of Petersburg; a Japanese house given to the city by the people of Japan; and Boat House Row; a series of boat houses used by rowing clubs. Six mansions overlooking the river, built by colonial Philadelphians, have been restored. Most of them are open 10 a.m. to 5 p.m., for a nominal admission charge. They include **Lemon Hill,** regarded as a masterpiece of domestic architecture; **Woodford,** built in 1756, housing a famous collection of period furniture; **Mount Pleasant,** built in 1761, with a notable collection of Chippendale furniture. Perhaps the most famous of all is **Strawberry Mansion,** built in 1798, named for the fact that strawberries, imported from South America, were first grown in this country in the estate gardens.

Points of Interest, west of the central business district.

Drexel Institute of Technology, 32nd and Chestnut streets. Randall Hall exhibits a notable collection of German and French art and antique furniture. Open free, weekdays, 9 a.m. to 5 p.m., Saturday until 1 p.m.

Just south of Drexel Institute is the big campus of the

University of Pennsylvania, with more than 100 buildings scattered over a 150-acre campus, its center at about 34th and Walnut streets. Founded by Benjamin Franklin in 1740, the university now has about 19,000 students and a full range of schools and departments, several celebrated for excellence. Places worth visiting include ivy-covered College Hall, where the Continental Congress met in 1778; Franklin Field, on the east side of the campus, a huge sports arena, traditional setting for the Army-Navy football game; and the University Museum, with an outstanding collection relating to the ancient peoples of America, Egypt, and Mesopotamia. Open free, 10 a.m. to 5 p.m.; Sunday after 1 p.m. At the southwest corner of the campus, off University Ave., is one of the finest botanical gardens in the East. Just south of the university is Philadelphia's big new

Civic Center, 34th St. and Civic Center Blvd. The cluster of buildings includes a huge convention hall, an exhibition hall, a commercial museum with exhibits of international arts and crafts, and a panorama of Philadelphia's past, present, and future. Open free, Monday through Saturday, 9 a.m. to 5 p.m.; Tuesday to 10 p.m.; Sunday, 1 p.m. to 5 p.m.

On the west bank of the Schuylkill River, about two miles southwest of the University of Pennsylvania, is

Bartram's Gardens, 54th St. and Elmwood Ave. just off Lindbergh Blvd., the first botanical garden in the country, developed by John Bartram, who is called the father of botany in the United States. A stone house on the site, built by Swedish settlers, was his home for many years. House and gardens are open daily, 8 a.m. to 4 p.m. There is a 25¢ fee to see the house.

About three miles east of the gardens, on the west bank of the Delaware River, is

Gloria Dei National Historic Site (Old Swedes Church), 916 Swanson St., just east of Front St., oldest church in Philadelphia.

The original log church was built in 1677 by Swedish settlers, who began building the present church about 1698. It has the original font, some rare Bibles, and a very early organ. Nonreligious relics include models of Swedish ships that brought the settlers to America. The models hang from the ceiling.

Points of Interest—outside Philadelphia, but easily reached from the city.

Pennsbury Manor, about 18 miles northeast of downtown Philadelphia off US 13, reached by the Bordertown Ferry Road, the country estate William Penn established in 1683. The original manor house was destroyed years ago, but much of the estate has been restored. Visitors may now see the reconstructed bake and brew houses, smokehouse, stable, and handsome gardens. The grounds are open 9 a.m. to 5 p.m. (Admission: adults 50¢, children free.)

Fifteen miles northwest of Philadelphia, just north of the intersection of Interstate 76 with the Pennsylvania Turnpike, is an outstanding shrine and memorial:

Valley Forge State Park, preserving the site where Washington and his 11,000-man army camped during the bitter winter of 1777-78. Three thousand men died of cold and sickness. The 2,300-acre park is on the south bank of the Schuylkill River. Pennsylvania 23 links most points of interest: a new Visitor Center; copies of typical soldier huts; the Potts house, a farmhouse that was Washington's headquarters; National Memorial Arch, commemorating the suffering of the army; Washington Memorial Chapel, with a carillon, stained glass memorial windows, and a museum of Revolutionary War relics. The chapel and museum are open daily, 9 a.m. to 5 p.m. (Admission: adults 25¢, children free.)

Southwest of Philadelphia, about 30 miles from the city center, is one of the most celebrated gardens in the country:

Longwood Gardens, just outside the village of Kennett Square, junction of US 1 and Pennsylvania 52, part of the 1,000-acre estate of the late Pierre Samuel du Pont. Features include both formal and natural gardens, woodland, conservatories and greenhouses, two lakes, and several fountains. The conservatories are open free

Valley Forge State Park preserves the farmhouse that was General Washington's head-quarters during the bitter winter of 1777-78.

daily, 11 a.m. to 5 p.m.; the outdoor gardens, 8 a.m. to sunset.

North of Philadelphia, filling the eastern corner of the state, is picturesque and rugged Bucks County. The county seat is

Doylestown, population, 6,900, center of a rich agricultural district among rolling, partially wooded hills. Doylestown is the shopping center for a large colony of writers and artists who live nearby. The town is famous for the

Mercer Museum, Pine and Ashland streets, housed in a building resembling a castle. The museum maintains a library and contains a remarkable collection of hand tools and implements used on farms and in

crafts and trades going back to pioneer days, before the development of mechanical power. Open Tuesday through Saturday, 10 a.m. to 5 p.m., Sunday, 1 p.m. to 5 p.m. Closed January and February. (Admission: adults 75¢, children 25¢.)

About ten miles east of Doylestown is

New Hope, population 950, a picturesque village, the home of many artists, writers, and musicians. The main street is lined with souvenir and antique shops. New Hope grew from a settlement around a water-powered mill. From April through October mule-drawn barges carry passengers along a historic 1831 canal. The one-hour trip starts from a dock at the south end of town. (Fare: adults $1.10, children 55¢.)

A 14-mile round trip on the New Hope & Ivyland Railroad operates from a terminal on US 202 at Bridge St. The steam locomotive, built in 1911, pulls colorful Victorian coaches. (Fare: adults $1.50, children 75¢.)

Eight miles south of New Hope, on Pennsylvania 32, which closely skirts the west bank of the Delaware River, is

Washington Crossing State Park, a tract of about 500 acres, linked by a bridge to a similar park in New Jersey. The park preserves the area from which George Washington and his army of 2,400 men, during a blinding snow storm on Christmas night, 1776, embarked in small boats to cross the Delaware River, reassemble in New Jersey, and march south to defeat a Hessian army in Trenton. In the Memorial Building, near the embarkation point, is a copy of the famous painting by Emanuel Leutze, *Washington Crossing the Delaware.* (The original hangs in the Metropolitan Museum of Art in New York City.) The embarkation point is marked by a shaft topped by a statue of George Washington, among 13 cedar trees. The old ferry house has been restored as a small museum.

About 45 miles northwest of downtown Philadelphia, via the Northeast Extension of the Pennsylvania Turnpike, is

2. ALLENTOWN, population 109,000, a center for industry and shopping on the west bank of the Lehigh River. Founded in 1762, Allentown was little more than a village when an event occurred which gives it its chief claim to fame. When it became evident in 1777 that Washington could not prevent the British from occupying Philadelphia, the Liberty Bell and the bells of Christ Church in Philadelphia were secretly brought to Allentown and hidden under the floor of the Zion Reformed Church. They were later returned to Philadelphia, but the hiding place became the

Liberty Bell Shrine, in the basement of the Zion Reformed Church, Hamilton and Church streets, where the Liberty Bell was hidden. A copy of the bell is exhibited, along with a large mural of Revolutionary scenes.

About nine miles from Allentown, two miles west on US 22 and seven miles north on Pennsylvania 309, is the

Trexler-Lehigh County Game Preserve, a 1,000-acre tract where herds of buffalo, elk, and deer roam. The preserve is open Sunday and holidays only, from early April to late November. Visitors may drive through in their own cars. (Admission: adults 25¢, children free.)

Immediately east of Allentown, on the east side of the Lehigh River, is

Bethlehem, population 70,000, an industrial city, with the emphasis on steel. The mills and general offices of the huge Bethlehem Steel Corp. are here. In 1741 Moravian immigrants from Bohemia and Saxony built a log community house and church as the center of a new wilderness settlement. The building was completed on Christmas Eve. On the same day Count von Zinzendorf, bishop of the Moravian Church, brought a second group of Moravian immigrants to the settlement. The singing of a Christmas hymn suggested Bethlehem as the name for the settlement.

The Moravian community of Bethlehem today is the largest and oldest in the country, and their church is the national seat of the Moravian religion. One of the oldest Protestant sects, the Moravians have a special interest in music and song; they sponsor a Bach festival each May, featuring their own nationally known choir, a guest orchestra, and soloists.

Points of special interest include

Bethlehem Steel Corp., south side of town, where visitors are welcome at the plant's Charles M. Schwab Memorial Library in the General Office Building, which has exhibits relating to the story of steel. Tours of the plant's research laboratories are available, between 8 a.m. and 5 p.m. weekdays, on advance notice.

Brethren's House, Main and Church streets, built in 1748 as a residence and workshop for single men. The old house, now a part of the Annie S. Kemerer Museum, exhibits fine 18th-century furniture and a notable collection of Bohemian glass. An odd exhibit is the oldest fire engine in the country. Adjoining the Brethren's House is the Main Hall, built in 1854, with notable restored Victorian rooms. The whole museum complex is open free, Monday through Friday, 1 p.m. to 4 p.m. The most notable Moravian building is the

Central Moravian Church, Main and W. Church streets, built in 1806, a fine example of Federal style church design. The church is famous for a trombone choir, which has been playing for special occasions for over 200 years. Near the church is the

Moravian Museum, 66 W. Church St. A five-story log building completed in 1742, oldest building in the city, it is open to visitors Tuesday through Friday, 1 p.m. to 4 p.m. (Admission: adults 50¢, children 25¢.)

Moravian College has two campuses, one for men and the other for women. One of the oldest colleges in Pennsylvania, dating from 1742, it has about 1,200 students. From a visitor standpoint a more interesting college is

Lehigh University, Brodhead and Packer avenues. Founded in 1865, Lehigh, a nationally famous technical school, has about 3,000 men students. The extensive campus, one of the most beautiful in the East, is worth seeing. Buildings of special interest include the Packer Memorial Chapel, named for industrialist Asa Packer, who founded the university. Lehigh is the setting for the Bach Festival each May.

About 55 miles north of Allentown on the Northeast Extension of the Pennsylvania Turnpike is

3. SCRANTON, population 103,000, fifth largest city in Pennsylvania. Though founded in 1771, Scranton was for many years little more than a wilderness settlement. In 1840 George Scranton established blast furnaces, using anthracite coal to make iron by a revolutionary new process. For many years Scranton was the center for the mining and use of anthracite coal. Mines and mills were scattered throughout the nearby mountains. But about 1902 the iron mills moved away, and the anthracite mines began to play out. By the end of World War II Scranton had entered a period of deep depression. It has now revived, largely because of a community fund-raising drive which brought in 24 new industries, with products as diverse as lace, salt, textbooks, plastics, electronic components, electric organs, luggage, and jet fighter planes. Scranton is also the home of the International Correspondence School, largest mail-order school in the country. A pleasant oasis is

Nay Aug Park, east side of town, end of Mulberry St. The park has a waterfall, big formal gardens, a better than average zoo, a lake that offers summer swimming and winter skating, and a natural history museum with excellent displays of stuffed birds and animals. The park's most unusual exhibit is the Brooks model anthracite coal mine, only one of its kind in the world, open free daily, 10 a.m. to 6 p.m., mid-June through August.

East and southeast of Scranton, extending to the Delaware River, is an irregularly shaped region dominated by the Pocono Mountains, which nearly everyone calls the Poconos. The mountains, actually an extension of the Allegheny Plateau, are tumbled and irregular, with no well-defined ranges. There are dozens of lakes and narrow valleys. Small streams flowing through gorges form picturesque waterfalls. The northern limit of the region is Lake Wallenpaupack, largest lake in the Poconos. The Northeast Extension of the Pennsylvania Turnpike skirts the section's western edge. Wind Gap, about 20 miles southwest of the Delaware Water Gap, is the approximate southern limit.

The Poconos, easily accessible from both New York and Philadelphia, comprise Pennsylvania's largest, oldest, and most popular resort area. It began to develop about the middle of the 19th century and now attracts visitors year-round, with a full range of winter sports facilities. There are very few towns in the region—no large ones. Points of interest include

Delaware Water Gap, at the southeast corner of the Pocono area, a spectacularly scenic gorge cut through the mountains by the Delaware River. Main highways pass through the gap, as does the Appalachian Trail. Just west of the gap is Stroudsburg, largest community in the area, on Interstate 80. About ten miles northeast of the gap, on the Delaware River and US 209, is Bushkill, nearest village to two scenic waterfalls. One is

Bushkill Falls, two miles northwest of US 209 on a local road, a series of falls, the largest more than 100 feet high, that carry the Bushkill River through a gorge. Picnic facilities, privately owned, are open mid-April through October, 8 a.m. to dusk. (Admission: adults $1.50, children 50¢.)

At the southeast corner of the Poconos is this spectacularly scenic gorge, Delaware Water Gap, cut through the mountains by the Delaware River.

Winona Five Falls, two miles southwest off US 209, is named for an Indian princess who is supposed to have drowned herself in the falls because her father killed her lover. The area, with hiking trails and picnic facilities, is privately owned, open mid-April through November, 9 a.m. to 6 p.m. (Admission: adults $1, children 35¢.)

From Delaware Water Gap, Pennsylvania 447 leads north about 15 miles to

Buck Hill Falls, population 160, a mountain village adjacent to the Poconos' finest resort, The Inn at Buck Hill Falls, with 6,000 acres of mountain and forest land, including a scenic gorge with spectacular waterfalls. There is a large central lodge with 350 rooms, and a full range of facilities including the best golf course in the Poconos, skiing, trout fishing, and horseback riding over many miles of trails.

About 70 miles west of Philadelphia on US 30 is

4. LANCASTER, population 58,000, chief city and most important trading center for the historic and picturesque Pennsylvania Dutch country.

Settled in 1721, Lancaster was for many years a frontier outfitting point for travel into the western wilderness. Industry developed slowly. Early craftsmen produced the famed Kentucky rifle that became the standby of frontiersmen. For one day, September 27, 1777, Lancaster was the capital of the United States, when Congress, fleeing the approach of British troops to Philadelphia, paused briefly in Lancaster.

Lancaster grew steadily after the beginning of the 19th century, when many members of the Amish, Mennonite, and Brethren sects immigrated from Germany.

Lancaster today is a city of diversified industry. Several plants welcome visitors—Schick Electric, Armstrong Cork, and Hamilton Watch. The city's stockyards are the largest east of Chicago. In 1879 the first successful store in the vast F. W. Woolworth chain was established in Lancaster.

Two information centers provide details on the Pennsylvania Dutch country. They are the Mennonite Information Center, about four miles east on US 30, at 2215 Mill Stream Rd.; and the Pennsylvania Dutch Tourist Information Center, Chamber of Commerce Building, 34 W. Orange St.

Points of high interest within the city are the

Farmers Markets. Market days are Tuesday, Friday, and Saturday. They include: West End Market, 501 W. Lemon St.; Central Market, Center Square; Arcade Market, 113 N. Prince St.; Southern Market, 106 S. Queen St. They feature fresh produce and an astonishing number of Pennsylvania Dutch delicacies made by farm families from the surrounding area.

Places of interest a short distance from Lancaster include the

Pennsylvania Farm Museum, three miles north off US 222, at 2451 Kissel Hill Rd. Tools, farm equipment, and home crafts are displayed, ranging from early firearms and Conestoga wagons to spinning wheels and looms. There are also several period rooms. Open mid-May to mid-October, Monday through Saturday, 8:30 a.m. to 5 p.m.; Sunday, noon to 5 p.m.; shorter hours rest of the year. (Admission: adults 75¢, children free.)

About two miles west of Lancaster on Pennsylvania 23 is

Wheatland, 1120 Marietta Ave., once the home of James Buchanan, 15th president of the United States. Built in 1828, the 17-room house was Buchanan's home until his death in 1868. Carefully restored and furnished with many of Buchanan's possessions, the house has recently been made a National Historic Landmark. Guided tours are available daily, mid-March through November, 9 a.m. to 5 p.m. (Admission: adults 75¢, children free.)

In the village of Lititz, nine miles north of Lancaster on Pennsylvania 501, is the

Pretzel House, the first commercial bakery in the country to make pretzels, a distinctive Dutch product. The bakery began operations in 1861, and is now a museum exhibiting pretzel-making equipment. Open weekdays, June through Labor Day, 10:30 a.m. to 4:30 p.m.; shorter hours rest of the year. (Admission: adults 25¢, children free.)

In Ephrata, about 12 miles northeast of Lancaster on US 222, is

Ephrata Cloister, W. Main St., junction of US 222 and US 322, a group of austere buildings, the home of a semimonastic order, established in 1732 by a German hermit named Conrad Beissel, a member of the Seventh-Day Baptist sect. The order had a Brotherhood, a Sisterhood, and some married couples. The buildings, erected by members of the sect over a period of 20 years, were simple and primitive. At the height of the order's success about 300 people lived here. Many members died of typhus while nursing soldiers during the Revolutionary War. Celibacy contributed to the decline of the order, but it was not finally disbanded until 1929. Ephrata is open between mid-May and mid-October, Monday through Saturday, 8:30 a.m. to 5 p.m.; shorter hours rest of the year. (Admission: adults 50¢, children free.)

About 30 miles northeast of Lancaster on US 222, at the eastern edge of the Pennsylvania Dutch country, is

Reading, population 92,000. Settled in 1748 by two sons of William Penn, on land Penn had bought from the Indians, Reading was one of the earliest iron-making centers in Pennsylvania. Its foundries turned out cannon for both the Revolutionary and the French and Indian wars. Today several hundred Reading factories make automobile parts, machinery, optical goods, and hosiery. Reading's pretzels are exported all over the world. A sightseeing novelty is

The Pagoda, at the crest of a mountain on the eastern edge of the city, a seven-story Japanese pagoda originally built as a hotel, later converted to an observation tower, open free daily.

About eight miles southeast of Reading, off US 422, just north of the village of Baumstown, is the

Daniel Boone Homestead. Boone was born in a log cabin at the site in 1734, and lived there for 16 years. The stone farmhouse which replaced the cabin has been restored and refurnished; it is maintained as a museum of early Pennsylvania days. There are 17 other buildings on the 600 acres of grounds, picnic areas, and campgrounds. House and grounds are open between mid-May and mid-October, Monday through Saturday, 8:30 a.m. to 4:30 p.m.; Sunday after 1 p.m.; shorter hours rest of

PENNSYLVANIA DUTCH

ONE OF THE MOST colorful regions in the East is the Pennsylvania Dutch country of south-eastern Pennsylvania, a land of big, rolling, partially wooded hills rising above wide and fertile valleys. The region, having no precise limits, includes six counties east of the Susque-hanna River and south of Harrisburg. The Pennsylvania Turnpike (Interstate 76) and US 30 cut through it east and west. Lancaster is the most important community. Reading and Lebanon are along the northern limits.

The name Pennsylvania Dutch has nothing to do with Holland but derives from the German word "Deutsch," which means both German and people. German people settled and developed the Pennsylvania Dutch country, made it one of the richest agricultural districts in the world, and gave it a distinctive architecture, decor, dress, and culture.

Because William Penn offered settlers complete religious freedom in Pennsylvania, a steady stream of Germanic people began migrating there after the middle of the 17th century. Most were members of religious sects: Dunkards, Moravians, Amish, Mennonites. They came in such numbers that by the beginning of the Revolutionary War Benjamin Franklin estimated that one-third of the population of Pennsylvania was Germanic in origin.

Most were farmers. In the peace and isolation of farm living they could practice their strict, often strange religious beliefs. Although some of the sects avoided the use of any machinery, and still do, the Pennsylvania Dutch were pioneers in crop rotation and the use of fertilization. They built huge stone and wooden barns, often decorated with colorful re-ligious symbols, to store the bounty of their fields and to house their sleek dairy cattle.

After more than a century, many descendants of the original settlers have hardly changed their way of life. Some groups, particularly the Amish, wear plain, unadorned clothing. Most Amish men wear beards, and the women wear long dresses. Amish people usually travel by horse and buggy or wagon.

Pennsylvania Dutch housewives are likely to be prodigious cooks. Favorite dishes are shoofly pie, sauerbraten, homemade sausage, and heavily seasoned soup. Many of the men are fine craftsmen, turning out sturdy furniture and colorful pottery. Women do weaving and quilting.

The Pennsylvania Dutch Tourist Information Center at 34 W. Orange St., Lancaster, supplies maps of the Pennsylvania Dutch country and addresses of craft shops, markets, and exhibits.

the year. (Admission: adults 50¢, children free.)

The most important relic of iron-making in the area, 15 miles southeast of Reading on US 422, then ten miles south on the Birdsboro-Warwick Road, is

Hopewell Village National Historic Site, at the center of 6,000-acre French Creek State Park. Hopewell was an early iron-making village that turned out pig iron and iron products from 1770 until 1883, using ore mined nearby and charcoal from the surrounding forests. During the Revolu-tionary War, ironworkers made cannon and cannonballs for Washington's army. In one building alone, where 16 molders worked,

more than 5,000 stoves a year were once produced.

Much of the original village has been restored, and the rest will be restored soon. Original products of the Hopewell Furnace are exhibited in the visitor center, which also offers an orientation film. A self-guiding tour leads to the charcoal house, ruins of an anthracite furnace, tenant houses, iron-master's mansion, the cast house, and other buildings.

The restored area, more than 800 acres, is open free daily, July through Labor Day, 8 a.m. to dark; shorter hours rest of the year.

About ten miles southeast of Lancaster on Pennsylvania 741 is the

Pennsylvania Dutch country of southeastern Pennsylvania is characterized by wooded hills rising above fertile valleys dotted with pleasant farms such as this.

Strasburg Railroad, in operation since 1832, which offers a nine-mile trip to nearby Paradise and back, on old-fashioned cars pulled by a steam locomotive. The railroad makes eight trips a day between late June and early September; reduced schedule rest of the year. (Fare: adults $1.25, children 50¢.)

Gun fanciers will enjoy a visit to the Eagle Americana Shop & Gun Museum, two miles west of Strasburg on Pennsylvania 741. A collection of Pennsylvania-Kentucky rifles, other weapons, and early American crafts are displayed in an old stone mill, open weekdays mid-April through October,

10 a.m. to 5 p.m.; to 7 p.m. on weekends. (Admission: adults $1, children free.)

From Lancaster US 30 leads west across the Susquehanna River about 25 miles to

York, population 51,000, second largest (after Lancaster) city in the Pennsylvania Dutch country. Settled in 1741, it was the first frontier outpost west of the Susquehanna. For several months during the Revolutionary War, York was the nation's capital. Between September 30, 1777, and June 27, 1778, while the British occupied Philadelphia, Congress met in York where they adopted the Articles of Confederation and issued the first Thanksgiving Day proclamation.

York today is the center of a rich agricultural district. Its mills and factories turn out refrigerating and air-conditioning equipment, false teeth, pretzels, wallpaper, and turbines. US 30 leads through the center of town as Market St., intersecting a business section of north-south Interstate 83, the main route of which bypasses the city on the east.

York, like Lancaster, has several busy farmers' markets, each open at least three days a week, selling homemade specialties from Amish and Dunkard farms. The markets are City Market, 606 S. George St.; Central Market, Beaver and Philadelphia streets; Farmers' Market, in business since 1866, Market and Penn streets.

Other points of interest include

Museum of York County, 250 E. Market St., maintained by the local historical society. Exhibits concentrate on local history before 1830, and include a diorama of the town's Continental Square and a scale model of an earlier village square. There is also an excellent genealogical library. The historical society is also responsible for the restoration of two of the city's historic buildings. They are the

Golden Plough Tavern, 157 W. Market St., built in 1741, a half-timbered brick country inn of medieval German design, believed to be the only one of its type in the country. The stone house next door, called the General Gates House, built in 1751, was the setting for an incident during the American Revolution when General Lafayette, by toasting General Washington, ended an anti-Washington officers' rebellion. The tavern and the Gates House are open Monday through Saturday, 10 a.m. to 5 p.m.; Sunday, 1 p.m. to 5 p.m. (Admission for both: adults 75¢; 12-18 35¢; children under 12 free.)

About 30 miles southwest of York, US 30 leads to

5. GETTYSBURG, population 8,000, the site of the most important battle of the Civil War, which occurred on the first three days of July, 1863. Before the battle Gettysburg was a quiet country town, settled in the last years of the 18th century. It had two small colleges and was a shopping center for a rich agricultural district noted for its apple orchards.

Today Gettysburg draws several million visitors a year. Most of the highways entering Gettysburg from the south and southeast pass through the battlefield, which covers about 25 square miles, most of it now within

Gettysburg National Military Park, with more than 1,400 monuments and statues and 30 miles of paved highways lined with hundreds of markers and relics of the battle. Within the battlefield area is the 20-acre Gettysburg National Cemetery, with the graves of 3,706 soldiers who died in the battle, about 1,000 of them unknown. When the cemetery was dedicated on November 19, 1863, Abraham Lincoln delivered a 296-word speech that has become one of the most famous speeches in the English language, the Gettysburg Address.

The Battle of Gettysburg began almost by accident, when patrols of Gen. Robert E. Lee's army of 75,000 men, heading north after the victory at Chancellorsville, encountered Gen. George Meade's Union army of 97,000.

Lee's immediate objective was Harrisburg, 35 miles to the northeast. His psychological objective was to break the fighting spirit of the Union army with a decisive victory. The encounter led to the total involvement of both armies. Throughout the three days of bitter fighting the Union forces generally occupied interior lines, repulsing converging Confederate attacks from the outside. Much of the action occurred along and between two ridges extending south from the town, Seminary Ridge on the west and Cemetery Ridge on the east. Two main highways, US 15 and Pennsylvania 134, roughly parallel the two ridges. The battle resulted in a Union victory, but at a cost of 23,000 men. Confederate losses were 28,000.

The story of the Battle of Gettysburg is made clear at the fine new Visitor Center, on US 15 and Pennsylvania 134, which has exhibits and dioramas, free maps and literature. Don't miss the famous 356-foot cyclorama of Pickett's charge, a high point of the battle, when 15,000 Confederate troops advanced against deadly Union fire on the third day of fighting. (Admission: adults 50¢, children free.) One can get a good view of some sections of the battlefield from the center's rooftop observation deck. Places of high interest near the center include

Gettysburg National Cemetery,
a short distance north. The place where Lincoln delivered his address is at the west entrance to the cemetery, marked by the Soldiers' National Monument.

The area around the Visitor Center and the National Cemetery can best be explored on foot. Farther afield, a car will be needed. One can drive his own, or take a two-hour tour of the battlefield with a licensed guide for $7 per car. Points of interest:

High Water Mark,
also called the Angle, on Cemetery Ridge, south of the Visitor Center, where Union forces, firing from behind a stone wall, stopped Pickett's charge on the last day of the battle. Afterward General Lee began the retreat that ended almost two years later when he surrendered at Appomattox. West of High Water Mark is the

Virginia Memorial,
at the crest of Seminary Ridge, near the point where Pickett's charge began. The memorial is a statue of Lee astride his horse Traveler.

General Meade Statue
is east of High Water Mark, near his farmhouse headquarters, now restored.

Near the southern end of the battlefield is

Devil's Den,
a cluster of boulders that sheltered Confederate sharpshooters. Northwest of Devil's Den are the Wheatfield and the Peach Orchard, two areas of fierce fighting.

Other places of interest include

Eternal Light Memorial,
on Oak Ridge, north side of the town of Gettysburg, scene of the first day of battle. A 40-foot shaft topped by a huge bronze urn with an ever-burning flame, it was dedicated by President Roosevelt in 1938, on the 75th anniversary of the Battle of Gettysburg. Gettysburg Battle Theater, south on US 15, 975 Steinwehr, has a miniature battlefield with 25,000 animated figures. A diorama and film re-create the battle. (Admission: adults 75¢, children 40¢.)

Gettysburg National Museum,
opposite the National Military Cemetery, on US 15, has a huge electric map illustrating the story of the battle. The associated museum has what may be the world's largest collection of Civil War relics. (Admission: adults 75¢, children 40¢.)

Lincoln Room Museum,
Wills House, on the town square of Gettysburg, preserves the room where Lincoln stayed and where he is believed to have completed the Gettysburg Address. (Admission: adults 60¢, children 40¢.) Both of these establishments are open daily, mid-March through November; closed rest of the year.

From Gettysburg US 15 leads northeast 27 miles to a junction with the Pennsylvania Turnpike, and eight miles beyond, after crossing the Susquehanna River, enters

6. HARRISBURG,
population 73,000, capital of Pennsylvania, on the east bank of the Susquehanna. In 1710 John Harris, for whom the city is named, established a trading post on the site. Harris and his descendants developed the wilderness settlement and operated a ferry over the river. Harrisburg was selected as the capital in 1810.

Since that time, though the city has important industry, particularly steel mills, Harrisburg has been chiefly concerned with state business.

Routes To and Through. Harrisburg is easily bypassed on several Interstate routes. The Pennsylvania Turnpike (Interstate 76) skirts the southern edge of the city, links just west of the river with north-south Interstate 83, which cuts through the main business section, and links with partially finished Interstate 81 at the northeast edge of the city. Main US highways are US 22 and US 15, the Gettysburg Pike.

Harrisburg is dominated by

The Capitol,
in handsomely landscaped, 13-acre Capitol Park. Huge and splendid, designed in classic Renaissance style, it has a towering dome rising 272 feet, modeled after St. Peter's in Rome. The ornate building spreads over more than two acres, and has hundreds of rooms. Details worth noting include bronze doors, some fine stained glass windows, and a magnificent marble staircase like the one in the Paris Opera

House. Open daily, free, between 8:30 a.m. and 5 p.m. Nearby is the relatively new

William Penn Memorial Museum, on the northwest corner of Capitol Park, a round six-story building next to a 20-story tower. Exhibits include a country store, typical craft shops, old automobiles and vehicles of all kinds, and period rooms. The most famous exhibit is an enormous painting, *The Battle of Gettysburg,* one of the largest framed paintings in the world. Open free, Monday through Saturday, 9 a.m. to 5 p.m.; Sunday from 1 p.m.

A pleasant feature of Harrisburg is the

River Parkway, or Front St., extending for five miles along the east bank of the Susquehanna River. The parkway links with five bridges spanning the river. Memorials, sunken gardens, and a pleasant river promenade make the parkway popular with walkers as well as drivers.

Near the southern end of the parkway, corner of Washington St., is the city's oldest building:

John Harris Mansion, 219 S. Front St., built in 1766, for many years the home of the city's founder, now the headquarters of the Dauphin County Historical Society. Dolls, Indian relics, and 18th-century furniture are displayed. Open free, Monday through Saturday, 1 p.m. to 4 p.m.

Two communities of high interest are east and west of Harrisburg. The most famous is

Hershey, population 9,000, about 12 miles east of Harrisburg on US 322. Hershey is the home of the world's largest chocolate factory, founded in 1903 by Milton S. Hershey, who grew up on a Pennsylvania Dutch farm nearby. The chief streets are Chocolate and Cocoa avenues.

Hershey is a planned community, with several points of high interest. The most important is the huge

Hershey Chocolate Factory, 19 E. Chocolate Ave., producing chocolate and cocoa in many forms, including incredible quantities of the world-renowned Hershey Bar. Free 40-minute tours are offered Monday through Friday, from 8:15 a.m. to 3:30 p.m.

Not far from the chocolate factory, near the center of town, just off Park Blvd., is

Hershey Park, given to the town by Mr. Hershey, with a zoo, golf course, lake, sports arena, fountain, and facilities for boating and swimming. The park is a setting for events throughout the year, ranging from professional hockey and ice shows to Pennsylvania Dutch exhibits. On the north edge of the park, Derry Rd., is the

Hershey Museum, exhibiting an atticlike collection of antiques and oddities, chiefly of Pennsylvania Dutch, American Indian, and German origin. There is a notable collection of Stiegel glass. The most famous single exhibit is the remarkable Apostolic Clock, on which animated figures tell the story of Christ. The museum is open daily, 10 a.m. to 5 p.m. (Admission: adults $1; 12-15 30¢; 6-11 20¢.)

Overlooking Hershey from the north, at the crest of a high hill, is the

Hershey Hotel, built by Mr. Hershey during the Depression to provide work for local laborers and craftsmen. The hotel, in several thousand acres of landscaped grounds, has a huge circular dining room unobstructed by pillars. The hotel is famous for 23 acres of gardens. The roses and tulips are outstanding.

About 20 miles west of Harrisburg, between the Pennsylvania Turnpike and Interstate 81, is the historic city of

Carlisle, population 16,600, settled in 1720, a strategic frontier outpost in the western wilderness, an outfitting base for campaigns against the French during the French and Indian War. Three signers of the Declaration of Independence lived here, as did Molly Pitcher, Revolutionary War heroine. Her grave is in a Carlisle cemetery. Points of interest include

Carlisle Barracks, US 11, north side of town, a frontier barracks established by the British during the French and Indian War. During the Revolutionary War the Hessian Guardhouse was built by Hessian prisoners. For 39 years, 1879 to 1918, the buildings were the home of the Carlisle Indian Industrial School, recently named a National Historic Landmark. The school at one time had about 1,000 students (including famed athletes like Jim Thorpe); it was the only Indian school in the country not on a reservation. The Barracks is now the home of the senior unit of the Army War College. The grounds are open to the public, and the museum is open free, Sunday, 1 p.m. to 5 p.m. On the west side of town is

Dickinson College, established in 1773, tenth college chartered in the United States, second oldest in Pennsylvania. President James Buchanan was a member of the class of 1809. Worth seeing on campus is "Old West," the oldest building, recently made a National Historic Landmark. Built in 1804 by Benjamin H. Latrobe, architect of the Capitol in Washington, it is a distinguished example of post-Revolutionary design. Of interest is the

Hamilton Library, 21 N. Pitt St., near the center of town, with relics of early Carlisle history. On display is the first American-made printing press, built in 1787.

From Harrisburg, US 11-15 leads north through a sparsely populated region of forested mountains, closely flanking the west bank of the Susquehanna River, one of the most scenic drives in the state. About 75 miles north of Harrisburg the route reaches

7. WILLIAMSPORT, population 40,000, on the north bank of the Susquehanna, largest city in north central Pennsylvania. Established as a wilderness trading post in 1795, it was not until the middle of the 19th century that Williamsport became a booming lumber town. Logs cut from surrounding forests were floated down the river on huge rafts. After the lumber boom ended, Williamsport became the center for a rich farming district. Plants manufacture flashlight bulbs, computer and radio components, aircraft engines, and steel wire. About a half mile south of town on US 15 is the

Little League Baseball International Headquarters, where Little League Baseball originated, and where the Little League World Series is played each August on Lamade Field.

About 25 miles southwest of Williamsport, on US 220 and the Susquehanna River, is

Lock Haven, population 11,900, which began as a lumber camp about the middle of the 19th century. In Lock Haven is the

The Hershey Museum, on the north edge of Hershey Park, has an excellent re-creation of an early Pennsylvania Dutch kitchen, complete with all of their strange utensils.

Piper Aircraft Corp., 820 E. Bald Eagle St., one of the world's largest makers of private aircraft. Tours weekdays at 10 a.m., 11 a.m., 2:15 p.m., and 4 p.m.

Lock Haven is a gateway to the dramatically scenic forest and mountain area of northern Pennsylvania. Access to it is gained by a very scenic stretch of Pennsylvania 120 extending for 75 miles along the Susquehanna River, and north from the village of Driftwood to the town of Emporium. The whole route has been designated

Bucktail State Park, commemorating a Civil War regiment of frontiersmen whose regimental insignia was a bucktail. There are camping and picnic facilities along the route, but in general the area is remote and isolated, with small towns and villages, and few service facilities.

From Williamsport US 15 leads north through the forest about 40 miles to a junction with east-west US 6. On that highway, 13 miles west, is

Wellsboro, population 4,400, in the heart of a scenic area of mountain and forest. Wellsboro has one notable industry, a plant of the Corning Glass Co., which makes more light bulbs, Christmas tree ornaments, and radio tubes than any other factory in the world. The Chamber of Commerce, 40 Main St., offers bus tours of the canyon country to the west. Tours last three and a half hours. (Fare, including lunch: adults $6.50, children $3.25.) Exploring the rugged canyon in one's own car is not recommended, since much of the route is over old logging roads. Of particular interest is the

Grand Canyon of Pennsylvania, or Pine Creek Gorge, 1,000 feet deep and about 50 miles long. The most scenic part of the gorge is within two state parks, Leonard Harrison State Park, ten miles southwest of Wellsboro on Pennsylvania 660, and the adjoining Colton Point State Park.

About 35 miles apart in the heart of the Allegheny Mountains of south central Pennsylvania are two industrial cities, Altoona and Johnstown. The biggest is

8. ALTOONA, population 66,000, which began in 1849 as a construction base for the Pennsylvania Railroad (now the Penn-Central), inching west over the rugged slopes of the mountains. US 220 leads

through the city north to south, intersects east-west US 22 five miles south of town. Altoona today has diversified industry, but repair shops of the Penn-Central still provide many jobs. Before Altoona was a railway construction base it was an important iron-making center. The main point of interest in the town is the

Baker Mansion, Baker Blvd. and 35th St., built in 1840, a handsome Greek Revival house that was the home of the local ironmaster, now maintained as a museum by the county historical society. Unusual hand-carved Belgian furniture and relics of the early railway days are displayed. Open free, June through September, Saturday only, 1 p.m. to 4:30 p.m.

In the heart of the mountains, five miles west of Altoona, is

Horseshoe Curve, perhaps the most famous curve of railway track in the world, which makes it possible for main-line trains of the Penn-Central to negotiate a steep mountain slope. When it was built about 1850 it was regarded as an engineering triumph. The curve makes a huge 2,375-foot sweep, almost a complete circle, permitting trains to climb or descend at a vertical rate of 91 feet per mile. A highway overlook about midway on the curve provides a fine view. A huge locomotive and caboose are displayed.

From Altoona US 220, US 22, and US 219 lead through the mountains 35 miles southeast to

Johnstown, population 43,000, one of the earliest western Pennsylvania steelmaking centers, built in a narrow mountain valley near the junction of three rivers. The city has had three disastrous floods since 1862, as the result of the collapse of dams built in the Conemaugh River, about 15 miles east. The worst was in May 1889, when the lake behind the dam was full to overflowing with the runoff of spring rains. A wall of water surged into the valley, engulfing the town, killing nearly 3,000 people and causing damage estimated at $25 million. A third flood in 1936 resulted in heavy property damage but no loss of life.

Johnstown's most unusual feature is the

Inclined Plane Railway, with huge cars that carry 50 passengers and one automobile 502 feet from the heart of Johnstown to a residential suburb at the top of the mountain. The 71 percent grade is said to be the steepest in the country. The Johnstown terminus is at Vine and Union streets. Cars operate Monday through Saturday, 7 a.m. to 11 p.m.; Sunday and holidays, 9 a.m. to 10 p.m. (Fare: adults 45¢, children 15¢.)

On US 119, in the southwest corner of Pennsylvania, is

9. UNIONTOWN, population 17,200, in the heart of Pennsylvania's bituminous coal district, a city almost entirely devoted to coal and its by-products, steel, and glass. The city is a junction of main highways, including historic US 40, the first National Road. On that highway, 11 miles southeast, is the

Fort Necessity National Battlefield, over 300 acres, the site of the first battle of the French and Indian War. Here Lt. Col. George Washington, commanding a small company of Virginia militia, built a primitive stockaded fort. On July 3, 1754, Washington and his men fought off a larger force of French and Indians. A surrender was negotiated, but the fort was burned down by the French after Washington and his troops left. Not until 1953 did archaeological research reveal the location and character of the fort. It has been reconstructed on the original site. A visitor center, with maps, pictures, and slides, tells the story of the fort and the wilderness campaigns. The fort and visitor center are open free daily.

On US 40, overlooking the fort, is

Mount Washington Tavern, a stagecoach stop on the National Road for about 40 years after 1820. Now a museum, furnished with pioneer relics typical of the period of its use, it is open free daily. A mile west of Fort Necessity on US 40 is

Braddock Park. Gen. Edward Braddock and his men were ambushed by French and Indians near the French outpost of Fort Duquesne (present-day Pittsburgh) on July 9, 1755. Lt. Col. George Washington, the general's aide, helped the remnants of Braddock's army carry the wounded general back to this spot. Braddock died four days later, and his body was placed in a secret, unmarked grave. In 1804 it was removed

A thrilling panorama of Johnstown nestled in the crevices of the Allegheny Mountains is offered to the riders of the Inclined Plane Railway.

to the park, where it is marked by a granite monument.

About 40 miles north of Uniontown, by either Pennsylvania 51 or US 119 and the Pennsylvania Turnpike, is Pennsylvania's great western metropolis:

10. PITTSBURGH, population 530,000, the urban core of a district where more than 2.4 million people live and work. A great industrial city, center of the nation's chief coal mining and steelmaking district, and headquarters for some of the country's largest companies, Pittsburgh owes its growth and character to two factors. One is its location, at the junction of two big rivers: the Allegheny, flowing in from the northeast, and the Monongahela, from the southeast. They form the Ohio River, one of the great rivers of the world, flowing west through the vast, rich Ohio Valley.

The second factor is Pittsburgh's proximity to vast resources of coal, iron, and limestone in the mountains to the east.

Around 1715, trappers and hunters roaming the forests of the region described the meeting of the two rivers, a place so obviously strategic that it was chosen by the French in 1754 as the site for a frontier fort called Fort Duquesne. The French, who claimed the whole region, first had to drive out a small force of Virginia troops. This triggered the French and Indian War, which continued for almost 20 years. In 1758 the British defeated the French. They subsequently burned Fort Duquesne and built Fort Pitt, which is how Pittsburgh got its start and its name.

When the Revolutionary War ended, the British withdrew. With the opening of the Northwest Territory Pittsburgh began to grow. Pittsburgh was a gateway to the settlement of the Ohio Valley. Immigrants bound for the new lands beyond the mountains found that the best way to reach them was to float down the Ohio River from the frontier settlement of Pittsburgh. Pittsburgh began to supply settlers with nails, shovels, and axes. As early as 1816, when it was incorporated as a city, Pittsburgh was a busy manufacturing center, with dozens of factories belching out soft coal smoke. It took 130 years, billions of dollars, and a remarkable civic redevelopment program to get rid of the smoke.

Now the wide channel of the Ohio, which carried the rafts and keelboats of settlers west, helps make Pittsburgh the most important inland river port in the country, handling more than 54 million tons of freight a year.

The little factories that made nails, shovels, and axes for the pioneers have grown into huge mills. The Pittsburgh area produces one-quarter of all the steel used in the country. Pittsburgh is the home of the world's largest producers of aluminum, air brakes, and plate and window glass; it also has the largest cork factory in the world. From the area come 40 million tons of bituminous coal each year.

Routes To and Through. The topography of the Pittsburgh area, a cluster of steep hills cut by the curving channels of three rivers that converge in a huge Y-shaped valley near the center of the city, dictate the route of most highways.

Motorists approaching the city from the east on the Pennsylvania Turnpike (Interstate 76 and 80S) have the option of bypassing the city center by either of two routes. Interstate 70 diverges west from the Turnpike at New Stanton, and leads into West Virginia and the Ohio Valley. Just east of Pittsburgh the Turnpike becomes Interstate 80S, sweeps northwest around the city to Ohio and a junction with the Ohio Turnpike. At the east side of Pittsburgh Interstate 76 extends into the center of the city as the Penn Lincoln Parkway (US 22-30), links in the downtown area with Interstate 79, which leads to the Greater Pittsburgh Airport. A main north-south highway is US 19.

To reduce congestion, Pittsburgh has established the Belt Route Plan. Each of the five routes involved is color-coded Red, Orange, Yellow, Green, or Blue, and directional arrows are used at main intersections. Most of the Belt Routes follow secondary roads that are relatively traffic-free.

Most points of interest in Pittsburgh are grouped in two areas: the downtown section, a triangular district just east of the junction of the Allegheny and Monongahela rivers, and a more extensive area three miles further east.

Points of Interest —downtown. Start with the place where Pittsburgh began:

Point State Park, also known as the Golden Triangle, a triangular tract of 36

76

handsomely landscaped acres where the Monongahela and Allegheny rivers meet to form the Ohio, site of three pioneer forts. The last was Fort Pitt, built by British troops in 1764. A blockhouse of that fort is still there, the only pre-Revolutionary building left in Pittsburgh. The park has a museum with exhibits relating to the pioneer period. Three bastions of Fort Pitt have recently been reconstructed, and outlines of the fort are traced on the grounds. A handsome fountain symbolizes the meeting of the waters.

The whole area to the east of the park, once a shabby commercial district, is now being redeveloped in one of the most spectacular civic improvement programs in the country. The most conspicuous feature is

Gateway Center, a cluster of gleaming new office towers and a hotel rising above 23 landscaped acres, among pools, foun-

tains, flower gardens, and wooded walks, all built over a huge underground garage. East and south of Gateway Center more than 40 new buildings have been completed or are going up. Notable among them are the new headquarters for the United States Steel Corp., rising 64 stories, the tallest building in Pittsburgh; the Gulf Oil Building, 44 stories, second highest in the city, with a sightseeing deck that provides a striking view of the district; and the 30-story, aluminum-sheathed Alcoa Building, headquarters for the Aluminum Company of America.

Just east of the heart of the Golden Triangle area is the new

Civic Arena, Washington Place, Centre and Bedford avenues, a remarkable all-weather amphitheater with a retractable dome three times the size of St. Peter's in Rome. The arena accommodates about 13,000, and is in almost constant use for

Pittsburgh owes a good part of its growth and character to its location at the junction of the Allegheny and Monongahela rivers.

events ranging from summer opera to trade shows and hockey games.

Dramatic views of the Golden Triangle and downtown Pittsburgh are gained from the crest of Mount Washington, which rises steeply from the south bank of the Monongahela River. Though the crest can be reached by city streets, a more enjoyable route is by two

Inclined planes, the last of several that once climbed Pittsburgh's steep hills. The Monongahela Incline has a lower terminal on W. Carson St., opposite the Pittsburgh and Lake Erie Railway Station. At the top, Grandview Ave., there is an observation deck. The Incline operates Monday through Saturday, 5:30 a.m. to 1 a.m.; Sunday and holidays, 8:45 a.m. to midnight. Fare is 15¢ each way. The second incline, the Duquesne, is a little farther west on Carson St., opposite Point State Park, just west of the Fort Pitt Bridge.

From the Golden Triangle area the parallel routes of the Penn Lincoln Parkway (Interstate 76) and the Boulevard of the Allies lead east along the north bank of the Monongahela. About three miles east of Point State Park, Forbes Ave. diverges northeast as the chief street of a district with several notable places of interest. They include the

Cathedral of Learning, Fifth Ave. at Bigelow Blvd., just north of Forbes Ave., part of the University of Pittsburgh, which spreads over 120 acres north of Forbes Ave. The strikingly designed Gothic building is the tallest academic building in the world, rising 42 stories. There is an observation deck at the 36th floor. Worth seeing inside are 18 international classrooms, each furnished and decorated in a different national style. Guided tours of the building are available Monday through Friday, 9 a.m. to 5 p.m.; Saturday, 1 p.m. to 4 p.m.

Just east of the Cathedral of Learning is the

Heinz Chapel, a gift to the university from the H. J. Heinz family, world's biggest makers of pickles, whose huge plant is in Pittsburgh. A small building of great charm, designed in French Gothic style, the chapel is famed for superb stained glass windows.

Across the street from the Cathedral of Learning, on the south side of Forbes Ave., is the renowned

Carnegie Institute, 4400 Forbes Ave., a splendid building containing two museums. The Museum of Art is famed for special exhibitions of contemporary painting and sculpture held every three years. The Museum of Natural History has what is generally regarded as the world's best collection of fossil dinosaurs. Both the art museum and the natural history museum are open free, Monday through Saturday, 10 a.m. to 5 p.m.; Sunday after 1 p.m.

Extending over nearly 500 acres south of the Carnegie Institute is

Schenley Park. The Penn Lincoln Parkway (Interstate 76) leads along its southern edge. The Boulevard of the Allies, Schenley Dr., and Panther Hollow Rd. lead through it. The park has all sorts of recreational facilities, including a golf course, tennis courts, and a swimming pool. Its most famous feature is the

Phipps Conservatory, in the northwest section of the park, just off Schenley Dr. Extending over about three acres, the conservatory maintains 12 greenhouses with constantly changing floral displays. Its orchid collection is one of the best in the country. The conservatory is open daily, 9 a.m. to 5 p.m., and 7 p.m. to 10 p.m. It is free except during special shows, when the fee is: adults 50¢, children 10¢.

About five miles northeast of the downtown area, in a rolling, wooded district overlooking the Allegheny River, is the notable

Pittsburgh Zoo, spreading over 65 acres in Highland Park, reached from the downtown area by Fifth Ave. and Washington Blvd., with an entrance from Butler St. The big zoo, with more than 1,500 animals, has some special features: a 300-foot tunnel with exhibits of rare nocturnal animals, a children's zoo with baby animals, wild and domestic, and the Aqua Zoo, consisting of an Amazon River section with creatures like the stingray and electric eel, and a North American section, with a penguin colony, and pike, crab, and trout pools. Open daily, 10 a.m. to 5 p.m. (Admission: adults $1, children 25¢.)

About 18 miles northwest of downtown Pittsburgh, on the west bank of the Ohio River, reached by Pennsylvania 65, is one of the state's most interesting communities:

Ambridge, population 12,900, named for the American Bridge Co., its chief industry, established here in 1902. But long before, beginning in 1825, the town was called Economy, the third of three communities dedicated to communal living established by a German immigrant named George Rapp.

The first of the Rapp communities was established at Harmony, Pennsylvania, in 1804. In 1814 it moved to New Harmony, Indiana, where a very successful community was established. In 1825 Rapp brought his followers back to Pennsylvania and established Economy. It became prosperous from farming and the skilled craftsmanship of its people, who operated several factories and financed railroads and other enterprises in western Pennsylvania. Following the death of George Rapp in 1847 the community began to decline, in part due to the practice of celibacy. Economy went out of business completely in 1905, and in 1916 the community buildings were taken over by the State of Pennsylvania as

Old Economy Village, a two-block area with 17 original buildings, restored and

furnished with relics of the communal period. Buildings that can be visited include the 35-room Great House—home of George Rapp—gardens, the Feast Hall, a church, wine cellars, craft shops, community kitchen, and granary. Cobblestone streets link the buildings. The village is open Monday through Saturday, 8:30 a.m. to 5 p.m.; Sunday, 1 p.m. to 5 p.m., in summer; shorter hours rest of the year. (Admission: adults 50¢, children free.)

From a few miles north of Pittsburgh, Interstate 79, leading north to Lake Erie, intersects east-west Interstate 80 after about 60 miles. Ten miles east of the intersection Pennsylvania 8 diverges northeast from Interstate 80, leading after about 35 miles to

11. TITUSVILLE, population 8,400, center of a rich agricultural district, famous for the drilling of the world's first successful oil well, on August 27, 1859, by Col. Edwin L. Drake. This event led to an immediate oil boom in Pennsylvania.

Drake Well Memorial Park is about one mile southeast off Pennsylvania 8. It has an operating copy of the first Drake derrick

In Drake Well Memorial Park, near Titusville, stands a reconstruction of the world's first successful oil well, completed on August 27, 1859.

and engine house, a museum with exhibits relating to the history of the oil industry, tools, maps, a library, and a notable collection of photographs of oil industry pioneering. The park and museum are open daily during the summer, 8:30 a.m. to 5 p.m.; rest of year, 9 a.m. to 4:30 p.m.; Sunday all year, 1 p.m. to 5 p.m. (Admission: adults 50¢, children free.)

About 15 miles south of Titusville on Pennsylvania 8, at the junction of US 62, is a city that became famous as the center of Pennsylvania's oil industry, appropriately named

Oil City, population 17,000, on the banks of *Oil Creek and the Allegheny River. Oil City became a boomtown almost overnight when oil was discovered at Titusville. Derricks lined the banks of Oil Creek as far north as Titusville. Within five months Oil City grew from a population of one family to 10,000. Between 1860 and 1870 about 18 million barrels of oil were shipped out of Oil City to Pittsburgh. Oil and gas are still the chief business of the city.

From Oil City the Allegheny River, closely flanked by US 62, extends northeast 45 miles through a hilly, heavily forested region to

Warren, population 14,200. Warren grew from a lumber shipping point. Huge rafts of logs were floated down the Allegheny from Warren to Pittsburgh and points west. On the fringe of Pennsylvania's oil producing district, Warren is now a center for diversified manufacture, but is best known as a gateway to

Allegheny National Forest, spreading over 473,000 acres of rugged hills, threaded by over 250 miles of trout streams. Several main highways and hundreds of miles of minor roads, many of them former logging roads, extend through the forest and link primitive areas and tiny, remote villages with names like Owls Nest, Hearts Content, and Pigeon. In the heart of the forest is a tract of 4,000 acres of virgin hardwood, one of the largest in the country. There is fine fishing and hunting in season for deer, turkey, bear, and grouse. On the northern edge of the forest is the

Kinzua Dam and Allegheny Reservoir, about ten miles east of Warren, reached by

Pennsylvania 59. A flood control project, the dam, 179 feet high and 2,000 feet long, creates a 27-mile-long lake of great beauty extending north into New York, offering a full range of recreational facilities including swimming, boating, fishing, camping, and picnicking. There are boat launching ramps at many points along the shore.

About 30 miles southeast of Warren on US 6, a scenic route through the forest, is

Kane, population 5,400, one of the highest towns in Pennsylvania, with an altitude of more than 2,000 feet, famed as a sanctuary for hay fever sufferers because its cool mountain air is almost free of pollen. Kane is also an eastern gateway for the Allegheny National Forest, and an outfitting base for hunters and fishermen. A nearby point of interest is

Lobo Wolf Park, six miles east on US 6, with the largest pack of wolves in captivity, including several lobos, or timber wolves. Open daily between 10 a.m. and 7 p.m. One can watch the wolves being fed Sunday at 4:15 p.m. (Admission: adults $1, children 50¢.)

About 115 miles north of Pittsburgh, Interstate 79 leads through the shallow northwest panhandle of Pennsylvania to the shore of Lake Erie, and into

12. ERIE, population 134,000, Pennsylvania's only Great Lakes port and her third largest city. The city handles a huge traffic in lake cargo, chiefly oil, ore, grain, and lumber. Erie is also an industrial center, producing boilers, engines, electric motors, and power equipment. It is the home of one of the largest plants of the General Electric Co.

Erie has had a long and unusual history. In 1753 the French erected a wilderness fort on the long curved finger of land extending into Lake Erie, which created an excellent natural harbor. They named it Fort Presque Isle. It became a strategic control point for the western wilderness, and was fought over for many years to come. The English occupied the fort but were driven out by Indians. In 1795 Gen. Anthony Wayne led an expedition to Erie and built a new fort; he died there the next year. In 1813 Comdr. Oliver Hazard Perry came to Erie to build a fleet to fight the British, then in control of the Great Lakes. His nine-vessel fleet was built entirely from timber cut from forests near Erie. With this fleet Perry defeated the British in a battle farther west on Lake Erie, near Sandusky. The battle made Perry famous.

Routes To and Through. Most main highways passing through Erie parallel the lake. They include Pennsylvania 5 and Pennsylvania 5A through the center of town, and US 20 a little south. East-west Interstate 90 skirts the southern edge. Two main highways entering from the south are Interstate 79, terminating at the junction with US 20, and US 19, which becomes State St., the main north-south street.

Points of special interest, most of them in the downtown area, include

USS Niagara, foot of State St., a reconstruction of Perry's flagship. Open in summer, Tuesday through Saturday, free, 8:30 a.m. to 5:30 p.m.; Sunday after 1 p.m.; rest of the year, 9 a.m. to 4:30 p.m. During winter the lower deck is closed. Nearby is another relic:

Prow of the USS Wolverine, built in 1843, first iron-hulled warship built on the Great Lakes. It is open free, 8:30 a.m. to 4:30 p.m. A short walk away is the

Old Customs House, at 407 State St. Built in 1839, modeled on the Pantheon, it is an excellent example of Greek Revival design. Now headquarters for the county historical society, it is open free, Monday through Friday, 1:30 p.m. to 5 p.m.

Also in the downtown area is the

Wayne Blockhouse, Third and Ash streets, on the grounds of the Pennsylvania Home for Soldiers and Sailors, a copy of the blockhouse General Wayne built as part of the fort he established in 1795. The present blockhouse, built over Wayne's original grave, is open free daily, late May to mid-September, 10 a.m. to 4 p.m.; rest of the year by appointment only. Erie's most interesting civic feature is the peninsula extending from it and its harbor at

Presque Isle State Park, filling the slender, seven-mile-long finger extending into Lake Erie, reached by scenic Peninsula Drive. The park has conservation areas, a 110-acre lake, free bathhouses, fishing and boating, a monument to Commodore Perry at the place where he took command of his fleet, and a lighthouse at Land Point, on the site of the first lighthouse built on the Great Lakes, in 1813.

The USS Niagara, flagship of Comdr. Oliver Hazard Perry, was sunk in Misery Bay, north of Erie. A reconstruction of the ship stands at the foot of State Street in Erie.

Atlantic City, besides being the home of the Miss America Pagent, is famous as a beach resort and host for numerous political and commercial conventions.

NEW JERSEY.

NEW JERSEY has a split personality. From its earliest days the northern half of the state has been oriented culturally and economically to the vast urban complex of New York City, sharing with New York the Hudson River and huge New York Bay. But southern New Jersey turns west, toward Philadelphia, with which it shares the wide Delaware River.

New Jersey has the greatest population density of any state in the country, the highest gross farm income per acre, the greatest variety of industrial production, and more miles of highway per square mile than any other state.

New Jersey is a small state—7,836 square miles—46th in the country. It is about 165 miles, as the crow flies, from the mountainous northwest corner to the low, sandy tip of Cape May in the south. In width it ranges from 35 miles near the center to 65 miles in the north. Except for one straight-line land border with New York, all of New Jersey is framed by water. In the west is the winding channel of the Delaware River, separating New Jersey from Pennsylvania. In the south is the Delaware River and Delaware Bay. Most of New Jersey's eastern border is the Atlantic Ocean, beyond a chain of barrier beaches and sand spits. The beaches end with Sandy Hook, at the entrance to New York Bay. Beyond that the eastern limit is the Hudson River, with New York City to the east.

Topographic features of New Jersey vary greatly. In the northwest are low, wooded mountains studded with lakes. They rise to 1,803 feet in the extreme northwest corner and are known as the New Jersey Highlands. East of the mountains lies a 20-mile-wide belt of rolling hills that drops down to a wide, level coastal plain. This is the Piedmont, which includes the Fall Line, where small rivers break into the coastal plain. In the Piedmont, from the Hudson River to the Delaware, are most of New Jersey's major population centers.

Almost abruptly, southeast of the Piedmont, begins a vast, level, sparsely populated plain. This plain extends all the way to the Atlantic and is filled with barrens, forests, and coastal marshes, all laced with little winding rivers. Much of this area is semiwilderness.

Though New Jersey is more densely populated than any other state, more than 70 percent of the land area is in farms and forests, and more than two million acres in forest and woodland. New Jersey farms are among the most productive in the nation. Vegetables, fruits, and dairy products bring in more than $250 million a year. New Jersey is nicknamed "The Garden State."

Around 1620 the Dutch began to establish settlements along the Hudson River, closely linked to the Dutch settlement at New Amsterdam, now New York City. A little later the Swedes settled in the Delaware River valley. In 1664 the English seized New Amsterdam and all the Dutch settlements, both in the north and south. Soon William Penn, who was developing the area of eastern Pennsylvania around Philadelphia, took over the southern section of New Jersey, where Penn's Quaker followers had established a settlement at Salem around 1674. It was not until 1702 that the two divided areas were merged into one province under a royal governor.

During the Revolutionary War New Jersey saw more military action than any of the other colonies. More than 100 major and minor engagements were fought in the state, including the decisive battles of Trenton, Princeton, and Monmouth. Washington twice established his winter headquarters at Morristown. Twice, toward the end of the Revolutionary period, New Jersey housed the new nation's temporary capital—first at Princeton, later at Trenton.

New Jersey's industrial dominance began late in the 18th century with the development of mills along the Fall Line and iron mines in the Highlands. Today New Jersey ranks first in chemical products, third in apparel, and high in instruments, textiles, rubber, plastics, pharmaceutical products, printing, and papermaking. Seven oil refineries have a capacity of more than 500,000 barrels a day, and New Jersey's several ocean ports on New York Bay and the Hudson River trans-ship more petroleum products than any city in the East.

Research and invention have contributed to New Jersey's huge industrial production. Thomas Edison lived and worked in New Jersey for many years and there invented the electric light, motion picture, and radio. Other ingenious New Jersey citizens invented and developed the first American steamship to cross the Atlantic, the first electric sewing machine, the first locomotive, the first linen thread factory, the first silk looms, and the first revolver.

New Jersey has the highest concentration of urban communities in the country, strung along the corridor between New York and Pennsylvania, with the greatest density at each end. In the north, opposite New York City, about two million people live in an unbroken complex of cities and towns, of which Newark, New Jersey's largest city (385,000), is the core.

Opposite Philadelphia is Camden, with 110,000 people in the city proper and several hundred thousand more in industrial and residential suburbs. Trenton, the capital, about midway between New York and Philadelphia, has about 102,000. Outside the industrial-residential corridor, the largest city is the coastal resort of Atlantic City, with about 60,000 people.

New Jersey's most important highways extend north and south. Chief routes are the New Jersey Turnpike, a toll road, generally regarded as the most heavily traveled in the country. Parallel to the Turnpike are US 1, extending from Trenton northeast across the state; US 130; and the developing route of Interstate 295. Running through the entire state from north to south is the Garden State Parkway, paralleling the Turnpike in the north, swinging southeast to link the chain of resorts along the coast. Main east-

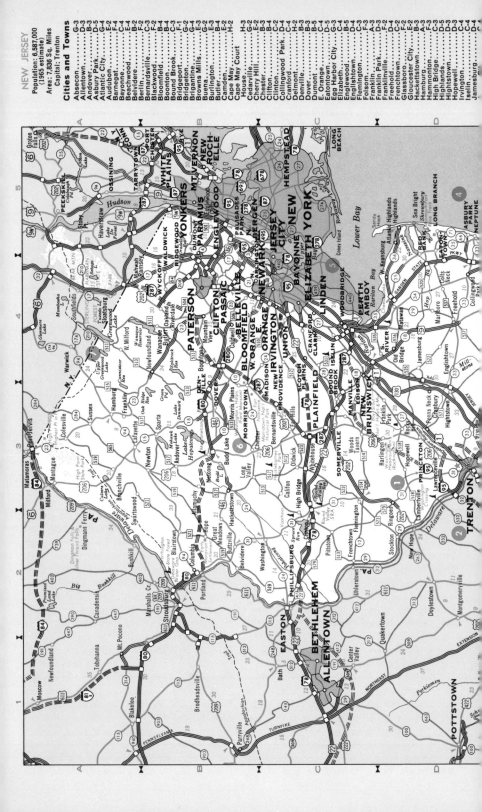

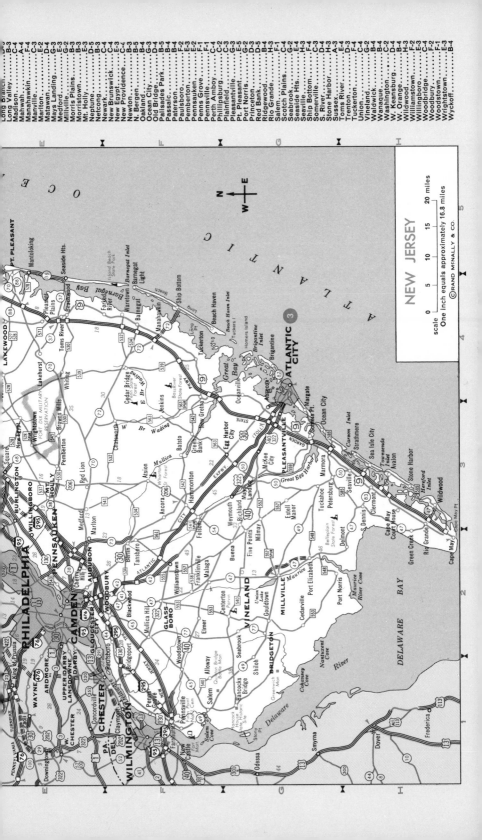

NEW JERSEY

scale

0 5 10 15 20 miles

One inch equals approximately 16.8 miles

©RAND McNALLY & CO.

NEW JERSEY FACTS

Name. From Jersey, an island in the English Channel.

Nickname. Garden State.

Area. 7,836 square miles, 46th in the United States.

Population. 7,106,000, 1969 estimate, eighth in the United States. Most heavily populated state: 869 people per square mile.

Admitted as a state. 1787, third among the 13 colonies.

Capital. Trenton.

Largest city. Newark, 385,000.

State tree. Red oak.

State flower. Purple violet.

State bird. Eastern goldfinch.

Industry. Leads the country in rail and truck shipping; has one of the country's largest ports; is first in chemicals; is important in apparel, plastics, rubber, textiles, drugs, oil refining.

Agriculture. 71 percent of state is farmland, producing vegetables, poultry, fruits, dairy products. Highest farm income in country.

Odds and Ends. Most heavily traveled highways of any state; famous ocean resort (Atlantic City).

west routes include the Atlantic City Expressway, a limited-access toll road between the Camden-Philadelphia area and Atlantic City. Two main Interstate routes crossing the northern end of the state east to west are Interstate 78 and Interstate 80. A developing Interstate highway will eventually swing around the whole huge industrial-residential complex centered in Newark, linking with all main highways leading through the area. The scenic Palisades Interstate Parkway leads north from the George Washington Bridge over the Hudson River, along the crest of the Palisades cliffs, linking with the Garden State Parkway and the New York State Thruway.

Major points of interest in New Jersey are indicated by number on the map on pages 84-85, described in associated text, starting with historic:

1. PRINCETON, population 12,700, one of the most attractive cities in the country and a leading center for education and research. Settled by Quakers in 1685, Princeton prospered when the College of New Jersey, founded by royal charter in 1746, moved to Princeton in 1756. The college became Princeton University in 1896. In

1776 New Jersey's first legislature met in Princeton's Nassau Hall. In 1777 Washington surprised and defeated a larger British force in the Battle of Princeton. From 1902 to 1910 Woodrow Wilson, later governor of New Jersey and president of the United States, was the president of Princeton and the first president of that university who was not a clergyman.

Princeton today is almost wholly devoted to education and research, with several schools and colleges in addition to Princeton University. The most celebrated is the Institute for Advanced Study, where Albert Einstein worked during the last years of his life. But Princeton is also highly regarded as a residential community. Any visit should include a tour of some of the older, tree-lined streets, with fine homes and estates—many going back to colonial days. Several are of historic interest. The center of interest is

Princeton University, with a rolling, beautifully landscaped campus spreading over more than 2,500 acres, in several sections. The older, main section flanks Nassau St., Princeton's main north-south street, just east of the business center at Palmer Square.

The university has about 5,000 students, until recently all men (it became partially coeducational in 1969). A guide service operates from the Visitor Center in Stanhope Hall, southwest of Nassau Hall. Tours start at 9:30 a.m. Monday through Saturday and continue at two-hour intervals. Sunday tours start at 2 p.m. Buildings of special interest include

Nassau Hall, just east of the main gates of the university at Palmer Square, the oldest and most interesting building on the campus, completed in 1756. For half a century it housed the entire college. During the Revolution, Nassau Hall was both a barracks and a hospital for American and British troops. For six months in 1783 it was the nation's capitol, and the Continental Congress met in its library. Though most rooms are now used for administrative purposes, two are open to visitors. They are Memorial Hall, with the names of all Princeton men who have died in the service of their country. Adjoining it is the strikingly handsome Faculty Room, with portraits of Princeton presidents and important alumni. Just north of Nassau Hall is the

Firestone Library, like most of Princeton's buildings designed in English Gothic style, one of the finest university libraries in the country, containing two million books. Some of its special rooms and collections include the John Foster Dulles Library of Diplomatic History, a notable Arabic and Oriental collection, and an outstanding collection of rare books and magazines. The library is open Monday through Saturday, 9 a.m. to 6 p.m., Sunday, 2 p.m. to 5 p.m. Immediately behind the library is the

University Chapel, traditional English Gothic in design. Of interest are stained-glass windows portraying the life, teaching, and influence of Christ. A short distance northeast of the chapel is Princeton's most interesting new building, housing the

Woodrow Wilson School of Public and International Affairs, a striking building facing a reflecting pool and fountain.

From an architectural standpoint Princeton's most interesting group of buildings is the

Graduate School, on a knoll west of the main campus, where the Battle of Princeton was fought. The first residential graduate school in America, its notable features include the great dining hall and the Grover Cleveland Memorial Tower. Associated with the graduate school is a fascinating walled garden.

Morven, located in Princeton, is the official home of the Governor of New Jersey and was built in 1701 by Richard Stockton, a signer of the Declaration of Independence.

A notable extension of Princeton, not on the main campus, is the

James Forrestal Research Center, a memorial to the nation's first secretary of defense, a Princeton graduate. The center has its own 825-acre campus about two miles north of the Penns Neck traffic circle (New Jersey 571). The center is part of the university's advanced training and research program in aeronautical engineering and chemical and nuclear sciences. The huge complex of buildings and facilities of the center is open to visitors by special arrangement. Of interest in the town of Princeton is the

Princeton Battle Monument, south end of Nassau St., which commemorates the battle of January 3, 1777. The monument, a 50-foot shaft of limestone, was designed by Frederick MacMonnies.

Just west of the monument is Princeton's most historic house:

Morven, 55 Stockton St. Since 1957 the old house, built in 1701, has been the official residence of the governor of New Jersey. A handsome Colonial mansion on spacious, landscaped grounds, it was for five generations the home of New Jersey's illustrious Stockton family, one of whom was a signer of the Declaration of Independence. During the Revolutionary War Cornwallis made his headquarters here. The house is open by appointment on Tuesday between 2 p.m. and 4 p.m.

Another historic house worth visiting is

Rockingham, five miles north of Princeton on County 518, in the village of Rocky Hill. Also known as the Berrien Mansion, the house was Washington's headquarters in 1783 when the Continental Congress was meeting in Princeton. Washington wrote and delivered his farewell address to his army here. Open Tuesday through Saturday, 10 a.m. to 5 p.m.; Sunday, 2 p.m. to 5 p.m. (Admission: adults 25¢, children free.)

About ten miles southwest of Princeton, linked to it by US 206, is New Jersey's capital:

2. TRENTON, population 103,000. Settled in 1679 and the capital since 1790, Trenton is essentially an industrial city. More than 400 Trenton mills and factories, some established in colonial times, turn out a wide range of products, particularly pottery (for which the city is famous), wire rope, and rubber products.

Trenton's moment in history occurred the night of December 26, 1776, when George Washington, having crossed the ice-clogged Delaware River, won a decisive victory over the British troops garrisoned in Trenton. The Battle of Trenton is commemorated by the

Trenton Battle Monument, N. Broad St. and Pennington Ave., the highest point in

Trenton, the capital of New Jersey, has numerous historical markers, such as this one at Cadwalader Park, commemorating Washington's crossing of the Delaware.

The McKonkey Ferry House, in Washington Crossing State Park, is where General Washington rested after crossing the Delaware and before marching to Trenton.

the city. It marks the place where Washington's artillery began to bombard Trenton. The monument, a 155-foot granite shaft, with an observation platform and a statue of Washington on top, was built in 1893. There is a 25¢ charge for the elevator ride to the observation deck (children free). The monument is open weekdays except Monday, noon to 5 p.m., Sunday, 2 to 5 p.m.

Places of interest near the river include the

State Capitol, 121 W. State St., built in 1792. There is little left of the original building, which has been greatly modified over the years with rebuilding and extensions. Worth seeing inside is a collection of battle flags. Just west is a new

Cultural Center, a three-building complex. The state museum has exhibits relating to New Jersey's archeology, geology, history, flora, and fauna. Open free Monday through Saturday, 9 a.m. to 5 p.m.; Sunday, 2 p.m. to 5 p.m. The planetarium features

up-to-date exhibits of space vehicles.

From the visitor standpoint the most interesting buildings in Trenton are the

Old Barracks, S. Willow St., opposite W. Front St. Built in 1758, they are the finest examples of Colonial barracks in the country and were used throughout the Revolutionary War. Here British and Hessian troops were roused from sleep by Washington's artillery on December 26, 1776. Now restored and maintained as a museum, with exhibits of Colonial and Revolutionary relics, the barracks are open weekdays in summer, 10 a.m. to 5 p.m., shorter hours rest of the year. (Admission: adults 75¢, students 50¢, children 25¢.) Farther east, north of the river, is the

Trent House, 539 S. Warren St., just west of US 1A. The oldest house in Trenton, it was built in 1719 by William Trent, who became chief justice of New Jersey, and for whom Trenton is named. The house is now a museum. Notable features include copies of

The Old Barracks, located in the city of Trenton, was built in 1758 and is considered to be one of the finest examples of Colonial barracks in the country.

original draperies, fireplaces, woodwork, and an unusual stairway. It is open in summer Monday through Saturday, 10 a.m. to 5 p.m.; Sunday after 1 p.m.; shorter hours rest of the year. (Admission: adults 25¢, children 10¢.)

A place of interest closely associated with Trenton is

Washington Crossing State Park, eight miles northwest on New Jersey 29, a tract of 783 wooded acres on the Delaware River that marks the point where Washington's army crossed from Pennsylvania, in the dead of night, to begin the march to Trenton. Of special interest is the McKonkey Ferry House, now a museum, where Washington and his officers rested while his soldiers ferried over the river. Now restored, the ferry house is open weekdays, 10 a.m. to 5 p.m.; Sunday, 2 p.m. to 5 p.m. (Admission: adults 25¢, children free.)

Interstate 295 leads southeast from Trenton parallel with the Delaware River. It links with US 130 five miles southeast of Trenton. Thirty-five miles southwest of the junction of Interstate 295 and US 130 is

Camden, population 109,000, center of a vast sprawl of industrial districts and residential communities, all satellite to Philadelphia, opposite downtown Camden. Camden is almost completely industrial. The main plants of RCA-Victor and Campbell Soup are here. Three toll bridges link the Camden area with Philadelphia to the west. From north to south they are Palmyra Bridge, leading into northeast Philadelphia, carrying New Jersey 73; in the center Benjamin Franklin Bridge, linking downtown Camden with the heart of Philadelphia, carrying US 30 and Interstate 76; and the Walt Whitman Bridge, linking south Camden with South Philadelphia, carrying Interstate 676.

Among points of interest for visitors is

Walt Whitman's Home, 330 Mickle St., in the heart of the downtown area. Whitman lived in the modest frame house, built in 1848, from 1873 until his death in 1892. Many of his papers and possessions are displayed. Open 10 a.m. to 5 p.m., Tuesday through Saturday; Sunday after 2 p.m. (Admission: adults 25¢, children free.)

One might also want to visit Whitman's

tomb, in Hareleigh Cemetery, Haddon Ave. and Vesper Blvd., on Camden's west side. The tomb is a gray stone vault which the poet designed himself.

Three parallel main highways lead southeast from the Camden area across the level plain of southeast New Jersey. They are US 30; the Atlantic City Expressway, a limited-access toll road; and US 322, which starts at the ferry leading to Chester, Pennsylvania. All converge after about 55 miles on

3. ATLANTIC CITY, population 58,000, largest of New Jersey's many shore resorts on the chain of fine ocean beaches that stretches for more than 100 miles along the Atlantic from Cape May to Sandy Hook.

Built on and dominating offshore Absecon Island, Atlantic City is linked to the mainland by the three highways leading from Camden. They all intersect north-south Garden State Parkway eight miles west of the city.

Atlantic City was a remote fishing village that began to develop after the coming of the railroads, around 1850. The two natural factors which have made Atlantic City so popular as a seaside resort are a mild climate, thanks to its proximity to the Gulf Stream, and a superb ocean beach. In 1870 the first boardwalk was built, extending more than five miles along the beach. An amusement pier was built out into the ocean. There are now five big piers, with an incredible range of facilities to beguile visitors. Atlantic City was successfully promoted as a fine place for meetings and conventions, and it has the world's largest convention hall. The city sponsors an endless series of events, from art shows to tuna tournaments. The most celebrated event is the annual Miss America contest. Dozens of hotels, resorts, and rooming houses—large and small, luxurious and modest—have been built to accommodate the more than 16 million visitors that flock to the city every year. Besides inventing the seaside boardwalk, the rolling chairs that trundle along it, and amusement piers, Atlantic City claims one other significant first: the introduction into this country of the picture postcard. Facilities and points of interest include

The Boardwalk, 60 feet wide and eight miles long, on the beach, flanked by an unbroken row of hotel and associated facilities. Only Miami Beach has more hotels. The most celebrated features of the boardwalk are the rolling wicker chairs, most of them seating two, which are pushed or pedaled by a bicycle mechanism. First introduced in 1884, they can be rented by the hour, the day, or longer. Extending into the ocean from the boardwalk are the famous

Amusement Piers. They include the Steel Pier, at Virginia Ave., more than 2,000 feet long, with movie houses, a ballroom, and assorted exhibits. Another is Central Pier, at Tennessee Ave., with a 380-foot observation tower at the ocean end, an aquarium, and a miniature golf course. Others are Garden Pier, with an art center; Steeplechase Pier, at Pennsylvania Ave., which is mostly for children; and Million Dollar Pier, with an Italian village and games for young and old.

On the west side of the boardwalk is the city's celebrated

Convention Hall, or Auditorium, the largest in the world, seating 41,000 people, with an enormous stage and one of the world's biggest pipe organs, with 32,000 stops.

The nearest thing Atlantic City has to a historic point of interest is its

Absecon Lighthouse, Rhode Island and Pacific avenues, named for the island where it stands, built in 1857, soon after Atlantic City was settled. It was in use until 1933. Now restored, it offers a stunning view to visitors willing to climb the 167-foot tower. The lighthouse is open May through October, Monday through Saturday, 10 a.m. to 5 p.m.; Sunday, noon to 5 p.m.; closed rest of the year. (Admission: adults 25¢, children free.)

An unusual point of interest, easily reached from US 30, about halfway between Atlantic City and Camden, is

Batsto, on New Jersey 542, about ten miles east of its junction with US 30. The village, now restored, was once the center of a bog iron ore and glassmaking district. During the Revolutionary War the Batsto Iron Works provided the iron essential to the American cause. The furnaces continued in use until 1848. The restored village includes the mansion home of the ironmaster Charles Read, a gristmill, and part of the ironworks. Guided tours are conducted daily from late

May to Labor Day, 10 a.m. to 6 p.m.; rest of the year, 11 a.m. to 5 p.m. Grounds are open free, sunrise to sunset. (Tours: adults $1; 12-18, 25¢; children 10¢.)

The restored village is the chief visitor attraction of a distinctive area—Wharton State Forest, a 150-square-mile tract of pine woods, boglands, and winding streams. Canoe trips through the wilderness are popular. Within the forest, which is accessible from US 206 at the western end, New Jersey 542 in the south, and New Jersey 563 in the east, are picnic areas and camp and trailer grounds.

From Atlantic City, the Garden State Parkway leads southwest, close to the ocean and the chain of barrier islands. Spur roads lead east from the Parkway to the small towns and resorts that face the ocean. About 40 miles from Atlantic City is

Cape May, population 4,500, one of the oldest beach resorts in the country, settled in 1631. Cape May became popular as a resort during the mid-18th century and continued to draw visitors, particularly from Philadelphia and New York, for more than a hundred years. The late period of its popularity resulted in more Victorian houses than can be found anywhere else in the country. Now engaged in a restoration program, Cape May has a fine beach, flanked by a paved promenade. The beach is famous for "Cape May diamonds," actually chunks of quartz which have been rounded by the action of the surf. Cape May is one of the few towns in the country with a horse-drawn trolley. It takes visitors through most of the older part of town. (Round trip: adults 75¢, children 35¢.) Cape May is the terminus for the

Cape May-Lewes (Delaware) Ferry, the only connection between the southern end of the Garden State Parkway and US 13, on the Delmarva Peninsula. The 16-mile trip across Delaware Bay takes 70 minutes. There are frequent daily crossings during the summer, and six daily round trips the rest of the year. Summer service is maintained between 6:30 a.m. and 9:30 p.m.

The Garden State Parkway leads northeast from Atlantic City about 25 miles to a junction with New Jersey 72 (Interchange 63), which leads seven miles east to pencil-thin Long Beach Island, with a chain of tiny beach settlements overlooking the ocean. At the tip of the 18-mile-long island is

The famous Barnegat Lighthouse in Island Beach State Park has seen over 200 ships

Barnegat Lighthouse, one of the most famous lighthouses in the country. More than 200 sailing ships have been wrecked on Barnegat Shoals. The first lighthouse, built in 1834, was destroyed by tides. The present one, rising 172 feet, was built by Gen. George C. Meade between 1856 and 1858 and continued in use until 1927. One can climb the lighthouse's 217-step spiral stairway for a spectacular view. (Admission: adults 25¢, children free.) Barnegat Lighthouse State Park has a fine beach and picnic area, as well as fishing from a stone jetty.

About 30 miles north of Barnegat Lighthouse begins a closely packed area of long-established shore resorts. The best known is

4. **ASBURY PARK,** population 18,500, one of New Jersey's largest and most popular beach resorts. Named for Francis Asbury, first American bishop of the Methodist Episcopal Church, it was established as a sanctuary for vacationing Methodists in 1871, an outgrowth of a Methodist camp meeting at nearby Ocean Grove. The town has long since outgrown any religious flavor and maintains a fine beach, a mile-long boardwalk, and a big convention hall. The beach is open May 30 to September 15.

wrecked on the Barnegat Shoals.

To use the beach and associated facilities such as locker rooms, a beach club, and a saltwater pool, a fee is paid: adults $1.50, children 75¢, weekends and holidays; weekdays, adults $1, children 50¢.

Several points of historic interest are easily reached from Asbury Park. Of these the most interesting is about eight miles southwest, just west of the junction of the Garden State Parkway and New Jersey 34. It is

Allaire Deserted Village, within a 2,000-acre state park. The village, recently restored, was established in 1822 by James Allaire as the site of an ironworks using bog ore. At one time about 500 ironworkers lived here, turning out all sorts of iron pots, pipes, and utensils, from a bog ore furnace and forge. Restored buildings include the enameling furnace, carpenter and blacksmith shops, Allaire's house, workmen's houses, bakery, store, carriage house, and community church. The village can easily be explored on foot, with the help of a self-guiding map from the visitor center. Open May through August, Monday through Saturday, 10 a.m. to 5 p.m.; Sunday from noon. Closed Monday rest of the year. (Admission: adults 25¢, children free.)

One can also see Allaire Village the easy way—on the Pine Creek Railroad, an antique, narrow-gauge railroad with six cars and a locomotive which toots and puffs through the park on weekends, late spring through early fall, noon to 5:30 p.m. (Fare: 25¢.)

From Asbury Park, New Jersey 26 leads north along the shore about 15 miles to New Jersey's most celebrated natural curiosity:

Sandy Hook, a slender, five-mile-long finger of land that thrusts north from the mainland to form the south side of Lower New York Bay. Sandy Hook Lighthouse, 85 feet high, built about 1763, is the oldest standing lighthouse still in use in the country. Its beacon has guided countless ships into New York Harbor. The lower section of the hook is

Sandy Hook State Park, a 470-acre tract that offers fishing, ocean bathing, and nature study in a unique area that includes a heron rookery and the largest holly forest on the Atlantic coast.

From the base of the Sandy Hook peninsula, New Jersey 36 leads northwest along the shore of Sandy Hook Bay to link with the Garden State Parkway. That highway then swings north to a sprawling complex of industrial and residential communities opposite New York City, of which the leading city is

5. **NEWARK,** population 390,000, largest city in New Jersey and chief community in one of the most heavily industrialized districts in the country. Dozens of communities, including a few pleasant residential enclaves, are knit together in a vast urban mosaic by a network of main highways and city streets.

The whole district extends about 20 miles north to south, from Perth Amboy, opposite the southern end of Staten Island, north to beyond Hackensack. Important communities—all industrial—include Perth Amboy (38,500), Elizabeth (118,000), Bayonne (72,500) Jersey City (269,000), Hoboken (45,000), Passaic (53,000), Paterson (144,000), and Hackensack (35,000).

Though most of the area is closely built, there is one curious, completely uninhabited section called the Hackensack Meadows, northeast of Newark. Named for the Hackensack River, which meanders sluggishly through the eastern edge, the meadows are a saltwater swamp about five miles long and one or two miles wide. Repeated efforts to discover a bottom on the bog have failed.

Routes To and Through. Most people who enter this area are passing through, usually as fast as possible, since the air is generally freighted with smog and industrial fumes. Main north-south highways include the New Jersey Turnpike, along the eastern edge, from which spur sections lead east into New York City. The Garden State Parkway links with all main east-west routes and with the New York Thruway. An alternate north-south route through most of the area is US 1-9. An express route leading from the center of the district northwest into New York State is New Jersey 17.

Main east-west highways are, from south to north: Interstate 287, US 22, Interstate 78, Interstate 280, and Interstate 80. Places of interest include the

Catholic Cathedral of the Sacred Heart, 89 Ridge St., at Clifton and Park avenues, northwest section of the city. One

of the largest and most beautiful cathedrals in the country, French Gothic in design, it closely resembles Rheims Cathedral in France. Its twin towers rise 232 feet. Features of note include more than 200 stained glass windows and handsome bronze doors.

Three examples of the work of Gutzon Borglum, sculptor of the Mount Rushmore Memorial, are in Newark. The best known is a seated bronze figure of Abraham Lincoln in front of the County Court House, in the downtown area. Also downtown, in Military Park, is "The Wars of America," with 42 figures of soldiers from most of this country's wars. The third, at Broad and Washington streets, is the Bridge Memorial—a shaft with figures of an Indian and a Puritan at the base, marking the site of a 17th-century marketplace.

Three miles south of Newark, between US 1-9 and the Turnpike, is huge

Newark Airport, one of several airports operated by The Port of New York Authority. One of the oldest airports in the country, and the first to serve New York City, Newark Airport is involved in a massive redevelopment program. Just east of the airport, separated from it by the New Jersey Turnpike, is the

Port of Newark, also operated by The Port of New York Authority. One of the most modern seaports in the country, its facilities extend over approximately 700 shore acres. The port handles nearly five million tons of cargo each year.

About four miles northwest of Newark, linked to it by Interstate 280, in the residential suburb of West Orange, is

Edison National Historic Site, Main St. and Lakeside Ave., a tract of about 18 acres preserving buildings and equipment used by Edison for many of his experiments, and also his library, papers, and models of his inventions. One of the principal units is

The Laboratory, built by Edison in 1887. Here he worked for more than 40 years, receiving more than 500 patents. Among his most famous inventions, for which models are shown, were the phonograph, electric light, motion picture equipment, and electric generator. You can see Edison's movies in the first motion picture theater, called the "Black Maria." Not far away is

The Edison National Historic Site, in West Orange, exhibits some of Thomas Alva Edison's most famous inventions. Shown below in foreground are some early wax cylinder phonographs and the first coin-in-slot "Juke Box," and in the background can be seen a "Long Waisted Mary Ann," an early Edison dynamo.

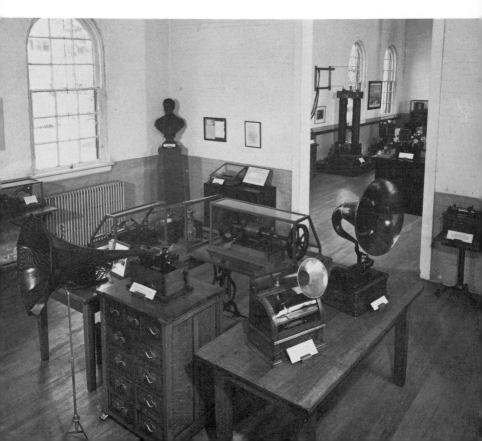

Glenmont, Edison's 23-room house in a 13-acre estate called Llewellyn Park, where Edison lived from 1886 until his death in 1931. The Victorian mansion is furnished as it was when Edison lived here. For most visitors the most interesting room is a second-floor sitting room containing Edison's "thought bench," where he said he thought out many of his inventions. Guided tours of the house can be arranged at the laboratory, start hourly between 10 a.m. and 4 p.m., Monday through Saturday.

The tombs of Edison and his wife are located on the grounds behind the house.

Another historic house, about eight miles northwest of Newark in the town of Caldwell, is the

Grover Cleveland Birthplace, 207 Bloomfield Ave., a state historic site. Grover Cleveland, the 22nd and 24th president of the United States, was born in the house in 1837 and lived there for four years while his father was the Presbyterian minister here. The house was the church manse. The house has been restored and furnished with

Palisades Interstate Park is shared by the states of New York and New Jersey. This view is from the top of the Palisades at Alpine, New Jersey.

possessions of the Cleveland family and relics of the period when he lived. It is open Tuesday through Saturday, 10 a.m. to noon and 1 p.m. to 5 p.m.; Sunday, 2 p.m. to 5 p.m. (Admission: 25¢.)

The only area of scenic interest near Newark begins about 15 miles northeast, near the northern end of the New Jersey Turnpike. It is

Palisades Interstate Park, a strip of parkland extending along the crest of the sandstone cliffs along the west bank of the Hudson River, opposite the northern end of Manhattan Island and the Bronx. The park begins at the western end of the George Washington Bridge, extends north for about 13 miles in New Jersey, and continues in several sections into New York. The New Jersey section contains about 2,500 rugged acres in a strip which is at some points only a few hundred yards wide. The park is served by two highways—Palisades Blvd. (US 9W) along the western edge, and the highly scenic Palisades Interstate Parkway through the center, with frequent overlooks offering fine views of the river and the New York skyline. There are trails leading from the overlooks to picnic areas on the river shore.

About 20 miles west of Newark, on the eastern edge of the New Jersey Highlands, is

6. MORRISTOWN, population 21,000, seat of Morris County. A quiet residential city set among wooded hills, Morristown was settled in 1710. It became important during the Revolutionary period as the center of an iron industry and a powder mill. Morristown today is the most important historic site in New Jersey, and the state's most interesting city, because of

Morristown National Historical Park, in three sections in and near Morristown, relating to houses and facilities used by George Washington and his army during two winter encampments. They include the

Ford Mansion, 230 Morris St., a handsome, spacious Colonial mansion built by Col. Jacob Ford, Jr., the owner of the city's powder mill. In the winter of 1779, Colonel Ford's widow invited General and Mrs. Washington to live in the mansion while the army went into winter quarters nearby. The

house has been beautifully restored and refurnished. It contains many of the original Ford possessions and some relics of Washington's stay. It is open daily, 10 a.m. to 5 p.m. (Admission: adults 50¢, children free.) Just behind the mansion is the visitor center and the

Historical Museum and Library, one of the best specialized museums in the country. There is a Gilbert Stuart portrait of Washington and one of Washington's swords.

The library has more than 60,000 books, documents, records, and prints relating to the Revolutionary War. The library is open free, Monday through Friday, 8:30 a.m. to 4:30 p.m. The museum is open the same hours as the Ford Mansion, on the same admission ticket.

A second area of the historical park is

Fort Nonsense, western side of the city, on top of a high hill, reached by Washington St. The earthen fort was built during the winter of 1777, some say to keep the soldiers busy; hence its name. The third and for many visitors the most interesting unit of the park is

Jockey Hollow, three miles southwest, where 10,000 men were encamped during the bitter cold winter of 1779-80. Within an area now preserved as a wildlife sanctuary are reconstructed huts typical of those the soldiers lived in. Here one can visit the army hospital, so primitive that smoke from fires built in the center of the room found its way out through holes in the roof rather than through a chimney. The Wick House, a typical 18th-century farmhouse, used by Maj. Gen. Arthur St. Clair during the encampment, and now restored and refurnished, is open free, Tuesday through Saturday from 1 p.m. to 5 p.m.; Sunday, 10 a.m. to 5 p.m.

Northwest of Morristown, wooded hills become forested mountains, extending northwest about 30 miles to the border of Pennsylvania and the Delaware River, and northeast to the New York state border. These are the New Jersey Highlands, with dozens of lakes and state parks and few towns of any size. The main highways are east-west Interstate 80 and north-south US 206. About 15 miles northwest of Morristown is

Lake Hopatcong, largest lake in New Jersey, center of a summer resort district. The lake, between heavily forested slopes, is about seven miles long and has a 50-mile shoreline. Near the southern end is a pioneer relic:

Waterloo Village, near the town of Stanhope. Recently restored, it looks about as it did during the middle years of the 18th century. The restoration includes a church, store, mill, several houses, and a blacksmith shop. Buildings are open mid-June to mid-September, Tuesday through Sunday from 10 a.m. to 6 p.m., and April to November, weekends only. (Admission: adults $1.50, children 75¢.)

Two places of interest are along New Jersey's northeast border, among wooded mountains. One is

7. RINGWOOD MANOR, reached by New Jersey 511, off New Jersey 23, to the village of Ringwood, then two miles northeast on an unnumbered road. The 78-room mansion, of no particular architectural distinction, was the center of an important ironmaking district during the 18th century. It was the home of celebrated industrialist Peter Cooper, founder of New York's Cooper Union, and later occupied by his associate Abraham S. Hewitt, one of the leading ironmasters of the 19th century. The mansion, set in a handsome formal garden, is open May 1 to October 31, Monday through Friday, 10 a.m. to 4 p.m.; Saturday and Sunday to 5 p.m. (Admission: adults 25¢, children free. Parking 50¢.)

The park surrounding the mansion, more than 1,000 acres, has a lake and forest trails, and offers picnicking, fishing, and nature study.

About 30 miles northwest of Ringwood Manor, New Jersey's mountains reach their highest point, 1,803 feet, in the heart of

High Point State Park, 12,268 acres, on Kittatinny Ridge. At the crest of High Point Mountain is a war monument and a spectacular view of New Jersey, Pennsylvania, New York, and the rugged valley of the Delaware River to the west.

Southwest of High Point is

Stokes State Forest, 13,000 acres, covering much of the Kittatinny Mountains, with some of the most rugged terrain in the East. The forest offers fishing, hunting, picnicking, and camping. Tillman Ravine, near the southern end, is a picturesque gorge in a primitive area. The Appalachian Trail, which follows mountain ridges from Maine to Georgia, cuts through the southern section.

Ford Mansion, in Morristown (New Jersey) National Historical Park, is where General and Mrs. Washington lived during the winter of 1779.

The Zwaanendael Museum at Lewes was erected to commemorate the first settlement in Delaware by the Dutch, in 1631.

DELAWARE.

DELAWARE is the second smallest state in the country—only Rhode Island is smaller. But it was the first of the 13 original states to adopt the Constitution, its per capita income is one of the highest in the country, some of its industries are the biggest and richest in the world, and its convenient and legally stable business laws have made it the corporate headquarters for almost 60,000 companies.

Delaware is 2,057 square miles in area, 96 miles long, varying in width from 30 miles in the south to nine miles in the north. It shares the Eastern Shore Peninsula, also called the Delmarva Peninsula, with Maryland and Virginia. In the north, a unique semicircular border separates Delaware from Pennsylvania. The Delaware River, Delaware Bay, and the Atlantic Ocean form

the eastern border. Topographically, Delaware is nearly all flat or rolling coastal plain, with extensive areas of marshland along the coast. The only large river is the Delaware, shared with New Jersey and Pennsylvania. The Fall Line, separating the Atlantic Coastal Plain from the Piedmont through half a dozen Mid-Atlantic states, is close to the channel of the Delaware River.

Delaware was first sighted by the explorer Henry Hudson in 1609. On the same voyage he later discovered New York's Hudson River. In 1610 Samuel Argall was driven off course while returning to Jamestown. He then explored Delaware Bay and named it for Lord de la Warr, provincial governor of Virginia.

It was some time before any attempt was made to settle the area of Delaware. The

DELAWARE FACTS

Name. From Lord de la Warr, provincial governor of Virginia.

Nickname. First State, since it was the first colony to ratify the Constitution.

Area. 2,057 square miles, 49th in the United States.

Population. 538,000, 1969 estimate, 46th in the United States.

Admitted as a state. 1787, first of the 13 colonies.

Capital. Dover.

Largest city. Wilmington, 92,500.

State tree. American holly.

State flower. Peach blossom.

State bird. Blue hen chicken.

Industry. Predominantly chemicals, home of Du Pont, world's biggest chemical company; also apparel, textiles.

Agriculture. Poultry, fruits, vegetables.

Odds and Ends. Highest per capita income of any state, official corporate home of more companies than any other state.

first attempt ended in disaster around 1631, when 28 Dutchmen came ashore near the present city of Lewes in southern Delaware and established a community called Zwaanendael, meaning Valley of Swans. The settlement was destroyed and all the inhabitants were massacred by Indians in 1632.

In 1638 Swedish settlers established Fort Christina on the Delaware River in northern Delaware. A monument in Wilmington marks the site of the fort. The Dutch tried again in 1651 by establishing Fort Casimir, later known as New Amstel, which grew into New Castle, Delaware's most interesting Colonial city today. The Dutch soon took over the Swedish settlements, but in 1664 an English fleet took New Amsterdam and New Amstel away from the Dutch. Delaware was under British control until 1776, when the "Three Lower Counties on the Delaware River" became the state of Delaware.

Only one small Revolutionary War skirmish was fought on Delaware soil. The dispute took place at Cooch's Bridge on September 3, 1777, and is remembered as the first time the American flag was flown in battle. About the same time a Delaware citizen, Oliver Evans, invented the automatic milling process. New Castle was already an important milling area because of

the availability of high-quality grain, waterpower, and cheap transportation. The millers' quick adoption of the new process strengthened the already established industry.

Another mill, established in 1802, would later set the stage for Delaware's future. This was a powder mill, established by Éleuthère Irénée du Pont, which would in time grow to become the center of one of the world's greatest industries. In and near Wilmington today are big Du Pont plants, as well as the headquarters of the Hercules, Atlas Chemical, and General Chemical companies.

Agriculture plays a big part in Delaware's economy, with an emphasis on poultry raising and fruit farming. Commercial fishing is also important.

Except for the Wilmington metropolitan area, where two-thirds of the state's population is concentrated, and a rapidly growing urbanized area in central Kent County, the population pattern of Delaware is rural. There are dozens of small towns and villages. Only about ten communities have more than 2,500 people.

The highway pattern of Delaware is relatively simple, except in the north. There are two main north-south highways, US 13 and US 113. In the north, where main highways converge on Wilmington and the Delaware Memorial Bridge, the pattern is more complex. US 40 and the New Jersey Turnpike cross the Delaware River on the bridge and there merge with Interstate 295 and Interstate 95. US 13 and US 301 enter Wilmington from the south.

Points of interest are indicated by number on the map on pages 108-109, described in associated text, starting with

1. LEWES, population 2,700, site of the first Dutch settlement in Delaware, in 1631. Within a year all the settlers were massacred by Indians. But other settlers came, and Lewes prospered. For over 300 years it has been the base for professional pilots who guide ships up and down the Delaware River.

Lewes today is a picturesque seaside town of quiet charm, with weather-beaten old buildings and churches. It is a base for sport and commercial fishing and crabbing, and it has a fine ocean beach. It is the southern terminus for a ferry linking Lewes with Cape May, New Jersey, across Delaware Bay. The ferry operates year-round, with several daily crossings. Crossing time is 70 minutes. (Fare, car and driver: $4.25, .$1 for each additional passenger.)

Lewes's most notable exhibit is a relatively new one:

Zwaanendael Museum, Savannah Rd. and King's Hwy., built in 1931 to celebrate the 300th anniversary of the ill-fated Dutch settlement. The museum is a copy of the town hall at Hoorn, The Netherlands, home of David de Vries, leader of the settlement. The museum has Colonial, Dutch, and Indian exhibits. Open free Tuesday through Saturday, 10 a.m. to 5 p.m.; Sunday from 12:30 p.m. Closed Monday.

Browsers find Lewes a fascinating little town. Several old buildings have been restored and are maintained by the local historical society. One ticket (adults 50¢, children 25¢) admits the tourist to all that are open. A point of interest nearby is

Cape Henlopen State Park, one mile east of Lewes on Delaware 18, a wooded point of land that divides Delaware Bay from the Atlantic Ocean. The park, on the site of former Fort Miles, has some fine beaches and offers swimming, fishing, and camping.

About six miles southeast of Lewes on Delaware 14 is

This aerial view of Cape Henlopen's "jeweled finger" shows the usually calm waters of Delaware Bay (right) and the mighty Atlantic (left).

Rehoboth Beach, population 1,500, Delaware's oldest and most popular ocean resort. Long a favorite with people fleeing the summer heat of Washington, D.C., Rehoboth has a boardwalk, a fine ocean beach, and a variety of accommodations ranging from modest to luxurious. Diversions include fishing, golf, and swimming. A famous fishing spot nearby is

Indian River Inlet, about eight miles south on Delaware 14, connecting the Atlantic with Rehoboth and Indian River bays. Sportsmen, fishing either from the rocks or head boats, regard Indian River as the most rewarding fishing spot in Delaware. The seven-mile strip of land north of the inlet is Delaware Seashore State Park.

About 35 miles northwest of Lewes on US 13 is Delaware's capital:

2. DOVER, population 15,500, on the St. Jones River, near the center of the state. The marketing and shipping center for a rich agricultural district, Dover is one of the oldest settled communities in the state. William Penn directed the laying out of Dover Green in 1683. The Green is still there, surrounded by handsome and historic buildings. Dover became the capital in 1777. Points of special interest include the

Old State House, east side of the Green, a handsome Georgian building built in 1787, the second oldest state house still in use in the country. Maryland has the oldest. Portraits of important Delaware citizens are exhibited inside. Open free Monday through Friday, 8:30 a.m. to 4:30 p.m.

A short walk from the Green, on US 13A, chief north-south street of Dover, is the

Delaware State Museum, 316 S. Governor's Ave., housed in several buildings. The main exhibits are in a Presbyterian church built in 1790. Displays relate to Delaware history, agriculture, resources, and crafts. There are interesting portraits and period rooms. One exhibit is a log cabin typical of those built by early Swedish settlers. Another building houses a big collection of Victor talking machines and records. The museum is open free, Tuesday through Saturday, 11 a.m. to 5 p.m.; Sunday, 2 p.m. to 5 p.m. Closed Monday.

One of Delaware's finest mid-18th century houses is the

John Dickinson Mansion, five miles southeast on US 113, then east on the Kitts-Hummock Rd. Built in 1740, it was the boyhood home of Dickinson, known as the "Penman of the Revolution." Dickinson helped draft the Articles of Confederation. The house, handsomely restored, exhibits furniture and silver typical of the Colonial period and has an interesting formal garden. Open free, Tuesday through Saturday, 10 a.m. to 5 p.m.; Sunday, 1 p.m. to 5 p.m.; closed Monday.

Nature lovers should see the

Bombay Hook National Wildlife Refuge, a wilderness tract of salt marsh extending about 12 miles along the Delaware River. The entrance is ten miles northeast of Dover, just north of the village of Leipsic. The refuge has a large population of migratory birds and waterfowl, and deer and smaller animals. Open daily, dawn to dusk.

A place of historic and religious interest about ten miles south of Dover on US 113, just north of the village of Frederica, is

Barratt's Chapel, built in 1780, known as America's Cradle of Methodism. Francis Asbury and Thomas Coke met here in 1784 to organize the Methodist Church, and here first administered communion. A small museum—open free Tuesday through Saturday, 9:30 a.m. to 5 p.m.; Sunday, 1 p.m. to 5 p.m.—exhibits documents and relics relating to the history of Methodism in the region. About 25 miles north of Dover, US 13 is joined by US 301. At the junction is the historic village of

3. ODESSA, population 468, once a prosperous grain-shipping port, named for the Russian grain port on the Black Sea. There are several fine old houses in Odessa:

The Corbit-Sharp House, south of Main St., is one-half mile east of US 13. Classic Georgian in design, the house was built between 1772 and 1774 by a Quaker named William Corbit. It remained in his family until 1938, when it was acquired by Rodney Sharp. It was beautifully restored and furnished and presented to the Winterthur Museum (Wimington), which maintains it. The mansion is noted for its architecture and for the quality and character of its rooms. The formal garden adjoining it is one of the handsomest in Delaware. Open

Tuesday through Saturday, 10 a.m. to 5 p.m.; Sunday, 2 p.m. to 5 p.m. (Admission: adults $1.50, children 50¢.)

Next to the Corbit-Sharp House is the

David Wilson Mansion, a good example of Georgian architecture of the Colonial period, exhibiting the furniture and possessions of the original owner and others, including William Corbit. Open April through November, Tuesday through Saturday, 10 a.m. to 5 p.m.; Sunday, 2 p.m. to 5 p.m. (Admission: adults 75¢, children 25¢.)

From Odessa US 13 leads north, crossing the Chesapeake and Delaware Canal on a high bridge. Two miles north of the bridge Delaware 72 leads east to

Delaware City, population 1,650, the home of a big oil refinery of the Tidewater Oil Company. It is the nearest mainland point to historic Pea Patch Island, site of

Fort Delaware, a massive, five-sided fort built in 1859. During the Civil War it was the major naval defensive location in the Delaware Valley and later served as a prison for captured Confederate troops. As many as 12,500 men were packed in at one time. Built in swampland, Fort Delaware was

so unhealthy that more than 2,000 Rebel prisoners died in periodic epidemics. The fort continued in use as a military base until 1945. It is now being restored and has a museum displaying Civil War relics. The island and fort are reached by ferry from Delaware City, operating on weekends during the summer every hour on the hour, noon to 7 p.m. (Round-trip fare: adults $1, children 50¢.)

From Delaware City, Delaware 9 leads north about 12 miles, closely following the banks of the Delaware River, to the historic city of

4. NEW CASTLE, population 5,000, tucked away under the soaring approaches to the Delaware Memorial Bridge, just north. New Castle began as Fort Casimir, established by Dutch settlers in 1651. It was seized by Swedes in 1654 and retaken by the Dutch under Peter Stuyvesant a year later. The settlement soon spread beyond the limits of the fort, acquiring the name of New Amstel in 1656. It was captured by the English in 1664, who renamed the town New Castle. William Penn first landed in America at New Castle in 1682, having acquired the town and all the land within a radius of 12 miles in a grant from the Duke of York. New

Pea Patch Island State Park is the site of historic Fort Delaware, which served as a prison for Confederate soldiers during the Civil War.

Castle was the capital of the "Three Lower Counties on the Delaware River" until 1776, and the first capital of the new state of Delaware during the next year.

The old town, with its narrow streets, a few of them cobbled, is a browser's delight —a living museum of the Dutch, Colonial, Federal, and Empire periods of architecture. It is best explored on foot. Many historic houses and gardens are open to visitors for the annual event, "A Day in Old New Castle," third Saturday in May, 10 a.m. to 5 p.m. (Combination ticket: adults $3.50, children free.)

The Green is near the center of town, a landscaped square with handsome old trees, laid out by Peter Stuyvesant in 1655.

Old State House, south side of the Green, was Delaware's colonial capitol and first state house. Its dome was used as a landmark for the survey that established the Mason-Dixon line in 1763. Open daily, 11 a.m. to 4 p.m.; Sunday, noon to 4 p.m. Also on the Green, at the north end, is historic

Immanuel Church, a building of great charm, with a square tower topped by a slender, soaring spire. The parish was organized in 1689, the present building erected in 1703. It is the mother church of the Episcopal Diocese of Delaware. Exhibited inside are a handsome silver communion service donated by Queen Anne in 1710, old tapestries, and historic records. Many prominent Delawareans are buried in the adjoining churchyard. On the east side of the Green, a narrow, cobbled street extends one block south to Delaware St. About midway on the block is an arsenal built in 1812, now a pleasant restaurant. Facing the Green on the west is a row of old houses. The most interesting is the

Old Dutch House, 32 E. Third St., a tiny, picturesque cottage with a steep roof and wide eaves, built before 1704, and prob-

Immanuel Church, in New Castle, was constructed in 1703, although the parish was organized in 1689. It is the mother church of the Episcopal Diocese of Delaware.

ably the oldest house in Delaware. It is filled with early Dutch furniture and household equipment. Open April to December, 11 a.m. to 4 p.m. (Admission: adults 50¢, children free.) At the corner of Delaware and Fourth streets is the famous

Amstel House, built before 1730, home of Nicholas Van Dyke, seventh governor of Delaware. In the house are period furniture and historic portraits. Open daily except Wednesday and Sunday, 11 a.m. to 5 p.m. (Admission: adults 50¢, children free.)

South of the Green is the

Old Presbyterian Church, Second St., built in 1707, open 10 a.m. to 5 p.m.

One block south of the Presbyterian church, on The Strand, a picturesque, cobblestoned street, is the

Read House, built between 1797 and 1801, a fine example of Georgian architecture, with notable boxwood gardens. It has been handsomely restored and furnished and contains a famous Robert E. Lee collection. Open only on "A Day in Old New Castle."

One of the most interesting buildings in New Castle is just west of the river, about two blocks southeast of Read House, the

Original Ticket Office, built in 1832, eastern terminus of the New Castle and Frenchtown Railway. The railway, one of the first in the country, crossed the Delmarva Peninsula to Elk River, Maryland, where passengers could take boats to Baltimore. Other boats carried passengers from New Castle to Philadelphia. A restored section of the original track shows how wooded rails were fastened to stone crossties.

Delaware St. leads west to link with US 40, which merges into Interstate 295 before crossing the Delaware Memorial Bridge. Interstate 95 leads north to

5. WILMINGTON, population 85,000, by far the largest city in Delaware, and more than any other city the "Chemical Capital of the World." Here are the headquarters, research laboratories, and plants of the vast Du Pont Company, and the plants of the Hercules, Atlas, and General Chemical companies among others. The original mill of the Du Pont Company, north of Wilmington, is a fascinating place to visit.

Wilmington extends for several miles along the west bank of the Delaware River, about a mile east of the junction of the Christina River and Brandywine Creek, which join in a marsh east of Wilmington. Wilmington's industrial prominence, starting in the early 18th century, resulted from a combination of the navigability of the deep Christina River with the power of falls on the swift Brandywine. Mills were established on the Brandywine near Wilmington and extending up the valley.

Wilmington began as a Swedish settlement in 1638 when Fort Christina was built at a point now called "The Rocks," on the Christina River. In 1655 the Swedes surrendered control to the Dutch, who sent an expedition from New Amsterdam, led by Peter Stuyvesant, the peg-legged governor of that Dutch settlement. The Dutch lost control to the English in 1664.

Land along the Christina was laid out as a town in about 1730, and in 1734 it was called Willingtown. Quakers became the dominant influence in the new village, officially named Wilmington in 1739. The town grew rapidly and soon outstripped New Castle. Among the businesses established several generations later, in 1802, was the pioneer American powder plant of E. I. du Pont de Nemours, a French immigrant.

Routes To and Through. Interstate 95 provides a fast trip through the heart of the city. Interstate 495 is under construction along the eastern edge. Two main highways from the southwest, US 13 and US 202, lead through the city. They diverge in Wilmington's north end, US 202 leading north into Pennsylvania, US 13 northeast along the Delaware River. A scenic bypass of the downtown area is Delaware 141, which links most points of interest west and north of the city. Places of interest include

Site of Fort Christina, foot of E. Seventh St., in a park near the junction of Brandywine Creek and the Christina River, where the Swedes landed in 1638. A massive memorial topped by the model of a 17th-century sailing vessel, designed by Swedish sculptor Carl Milles, was given to Wilmington by Sweden in 1938. Also in the park is a copy of a typical Swedish log house. Nearby, at Seventh and Church streets, is

Old Swedes Church, built in 1698, and in almost continuous service ever since. Graves in the fascinating old churchyard go back to 1719. The house adjoining the church, built in 1690, is now a museum.

Thirteen blocks northwest of Old Swedes Church, near the business center of Wilmington, is

Old Town Hall, Sixth and Market streets, built in 1798. A Georgian building of great charm, it is now a museum, with a wide-ranging collection of relics, portraits, silver, maps, and documents. Open free weekdays, 10 a.m. to 5 p.m.; closed during August.

At the north edge of the city is the

Delaware Art Center, Kentmere Pkwy. at Woodlawn Ave., Delaware's only art museum, with a notable collection of the works of Howard Pyle, Andrew Wyeth, and John Sloan. Open free Monday through Saturday, 10 a.m. to 5 p.m.; Sunday, 2 p.m. to 6 p.m.

Just north of the northern edge of the city, about a mile and a half east of US 202, is

The Hagley Museum, on Brandywine Creek and Delaware 141, one of the most unusual museums in the country. It is almost entirely devoted to the industrial history of the United States, particularly the Mid-Atlantic states. The museum spreads over 185 acres along the Brandywine. A free, open-air jitney bus carries visitors on a three-mile, 20-minute trip past millraces and distinctively shaped granite powder mills that were in operation as late as 1921. The main exhibit building, an 1814 textile mill, has models and dioramas of water, flour, paper, iron, and textile mills. One exhibit is a talking map of the region. The museum is open free, Tuesday through Saturday, 9:30 a.m. to 4:30 p.m.; Sunday, 1 p.m. to 5 p.m.; closed Monday.

Two miles northwest of the Hagley Museum, on Delaware 52, in a region of rolling, partially wooded hills and handsome estates, is one of the most remarkable museums in the world:

The Henry Francis du Pont Winterthur Museum, developed in a great country house within a private park of great beauty. The house, which is now the Main Museum, has over 100 period rooms, each authen-

tically furnished, and the finest collection of American decorative arts in the country, spanning 200 years, from 1640 to 1840. Included are furniture, textiles, silver, pewter, ceramics, paintings, and prints, which the late Mr. du Pont began collecting in the 1920s.

Because of the manner in which the collections are displayed, only 80 visitors are permitted to tour the Main Museum daily—40 in the morning, 40 in the afternoon, by advance reservation. Tours are conducted in groups of four, accompanied by a trained guide. Visitors must be at least 16 years old. The charge is $2.50 per person for each half-day tour, which lasts about two and a half hours. The morning tour begins at 9:30

An armillary sundial, its metal rings representing the positions of important circles of the celestial sphere, is seen in the Winterthur Gardens.

The graceful Montmorenci Staircase is only one of the many examples of American decorative art that can be found in the Winterthur Museum.

a.m., the afternoon tour at 1:30 p.m. It takes a full day to see all the rooms. For reservations, write to the Reservation Office, Winterthur Museum, Winterthur, Delaware 19735.

No appointment is needed to see ten period rooms in the South Wing, open from 9:30 a.m. to 4 p.m. (Admission: adults $1, children 50¢.)

Winterthur is open daily except Sunday and Monday. The Main Museum is closed for a week before and a week after a special Spring Tour, beginning in late April.

The equally renowned Winterthur Gardens, spreading over 60 acres, exhibit almost every tree, flower, and shrub that will grow in Delaware. All areas are linked by self-guiding trails, and each type of plant and tree is labeled. Some trees are over 300 years old. In the Garden Pavillion near the museum is a large cafeteria, where lunch is served year-round. The gardens are open Tuesday through Sunday, 10 a.m. to 4 p.m., from early April through late May, and during the month of October. (Admission: adults $1, children 50¢.)

Children and railway buffs will enjoy the

Wilmington & Western Railroad, four miles west of Wilmington on Delaware 41, just north of the junction with Delaware 2. One can take a four-and-a-half-mile ride on an old-time steam train, through a scenic valley to the picnic grounds on the top of Mount Cuba, and back. The railway operates from early May to late October. Trips start at 1 p.m., 2:15 p.m., and 3:30 p.m. (Fare: adults $1.25, children 50¢.) Opposite the station is an old water-powered gristmill, still in operation.

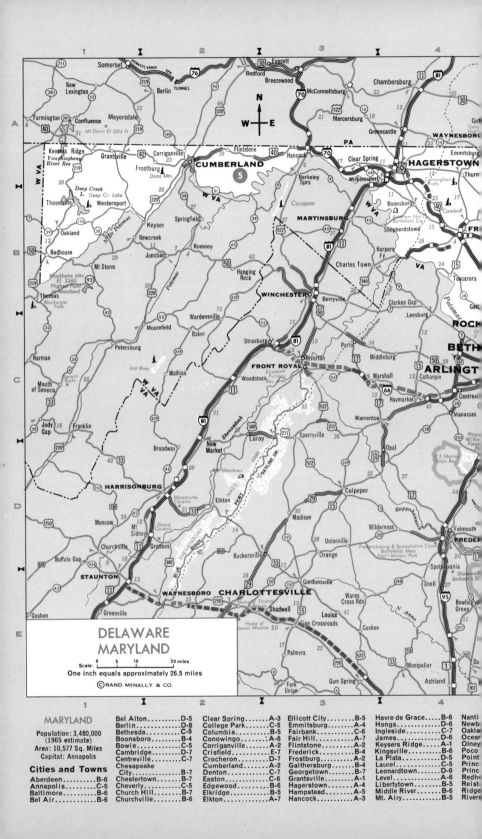

MARYLAND

Population: 3,480,000
(1965 estimate)
Area: 10,577 Sq. Miles
Capital: Annapolis

Cities and Towns

DELAWARE
MARYLAND

Scale: 0   5   10   20 miles

One inch equals approximately 26.5 miles

©RAND McNALLY & CO.

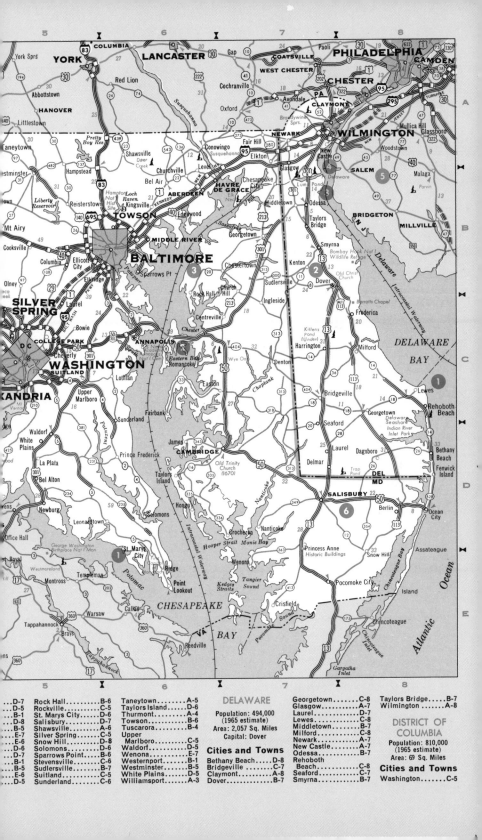

This is a closeup view of a Maryland Brickend Barn, a kind of structure found only along the Maryland-Pennsylvania border.

MARYLAND.

MARYLAND is a varied state. Her shape is remarkable, with a triangular western panhandle almost pinched off by West Virginia and Pennsylvania. The sea has taken a huge bite from her coastal plain to make one of the biggest saltwater bays in the country. Her topography ranges from heavily wooded mountains in the west to isolated ocean beaches to the east. Her products range from tobacco to poultry, oysters to coal and timber, ships to sugar, pipe organs to steel.

Maryland is 10,577 square miles in area, the 42nd state in size. It is 198 miles wide along the northern border, the famous Mason-Dixon line. It is 125 miles long at the longest point, 1.9 miles long at the shortest. Maryland is bordered by Pennsylvania north of the Mason-Dixon line, Delaware and the Atlantic Ocean on the east. Almost all the southern border is the winding channel of the Potomac River, with Virginia and West Virginia to the south and west. The District of Columbia cuts a rectangular notch into the middle of Maryland north of the Potomac. The highest point is

Backbone Mountain, in the western panhandle, rising to 3,360 feet.

Maryland is divided into four distinct topographical regions. The easternmost is the Eastern Shore, a picturesque flatland with the majestic sweep of Chesapeake Bay extending along its irregular western shore. The whole state of Delaware is chopped out of the northeastern section of the Eastern Shore, and Virginia snips off its southern tip. This leaves Maryland with only 30 miles of Atlantic shore. Across the 20-mile width of Chesapeake Bay, the coastal plain continues in the south to the channel of the Potomac River. This is Maryland's Tidewater region, forested, graced with splendid estates. In the north, beyond Washington, D.C., the coastal plain merges into the Piedmont Plateau, dominated by the great city of Baltimore. The rolling hills of the Piedmont break into the mountains of the western panhandle, including ranges of the Blue Ridge and Appalachian mountains.

The modern history of Maryland begins with Verrazano, the Italian explorer, who is thought to have landed on the Eastern Shore in 1524. John Smith charted the Chesapeake Bay area in 1608. In 1634 two boatloads of colonists, under a grant made by King Charles of England to George Calvert (Lord Baltimore), came ashore in southern Maryland and established St. Marys City. Both the city and the colony were named for Henrietta Maria, wife of King Charles. Most of the colonists were Roman Catholics fleeing persecution in England. Though Lord Baltimore was seeking a New World haven for Catholics, he also guaranteed religious freedom to all settlers. In 1649, the colony's general assembly passed the Toleration Act, formalizing the earlier guarantees.

Early settlers planted tobacco and soon prospered from this livelihood. Southern Maryland has been an important tobacco-producing district ever since.

In 1688 Maryland became a royal province, with St. Marys City as the capital. A replica of the capitol building is there today. In 1694 the capital was moved to Annapolis.

Maryland developed steadily through the 18th century. Religious freedom guaranteed by law drew people of all faiths. Tobacco commanded high prices in the world market, and planters built splendid homes in southern Maryland's Tidewater region. Many of them still exist. Shipping tobacco and other products, like timber, required a port and a shipbuilding industry. Baltimore, with its fine harbor, was the natural choice. Today it is one of the world's great ports and a center for shipbuilding.

Maryland's soldiers participated in most Revolutionary War battles. In the War of 1812 the British navy tried to seize Baltimore. Fort McHenry's defenders resisted, unfurling an enormous American flag over the ramparts. When he saw it still flying after a night of bombardment, a Maryland lawyer named Francis Scott Key was inspired to write "The Star-Spangled Banner."

Maryland helped develop the National Road, the first interstate highway, which opened the lands west of the mountains to settlement. In time the National Road became the nation's first transcontinental highway. Maryland shipbuilders designed the famed Baltimore clippers, vessels that carried American products to the far corners of the world. Maryland helped develop the Baltimore and Ohio, the nation's first railroad.

Three major Civil War battles were fought on Maryland soil. The most famous was at Antietam in western Maryland.

The first ice-cream freezer, refrigerator, and typesetting machine were developed in Maryland.

Maryland's present prosperity rests on a healthy balance between agriculture, fishing, and industry. Its seafood and poultry industries are among the nation's biggest. Baltimore claims the world's largest steel mill; Hagerstown, the world's biggest pipe organ factory. The port of Baltimore handles more than 45 million tons of ocean cargo a year.

Except for Baltimore, which has nearly a million of Maryland's total population of 3.6 million, Maryland has no very large cities. Some cities around the 50,000 mark like Bethesda, Silver Spring, and College Park, are actually suburbs of Washington, D.C. Only 20 cities exceed 10,000.

Maryland is served by a fine system of state and national highways, including several Interstate routes, converging on Baltimore. A circular beltway around the city links with all main roads. Interstate 95 angles from the northeast to link Baltimore and Washington, Interstate 70 links Baltimore and Frederick, and Interstate 70S links Frederick with Washington, D.C. Interstate 83 leads into Baltimore from the north. Other main highways include US 50, an ex-

MARYLAND FACTS

Name. For Queen Henrietta Maria, wife of Charles I.

Nickname. Free State, Old Line State.

Area. 10,577 square miles, 42nd in the United States.

Population. 3,789,000, 1969 estimate, 21st in the United States.

Admitted as a state. 1788, seventh among the 13 colonies.

Capital. Annapolis.

Largest city. Baltimore, 905,000.

State tree. White oak.

State flower. Black-eyed Susan.

State bird. Baltimore oriole.

Industry. Food products, particularly seafood and poultry; boatbuilding, steel, wood products, missiles, electronic equipment, electric tools.

Agriculture. Small farms producing corn, wheat, tobacco, poultry, fruits.

Odds and Ends. First clipper ship, steam locomotive, and railway in the United States; home of the United States Naval Academy; scene of the writing of "The Star-Spangled Banner" and the Civil War's bloodiest battlefield (Antietam).

press route to Annapolis, which crosses Chesapeake Bay on a spectacular bridge, continues east and south to Ocean City, and north-south US 301, which bypasses Washington to the east and links Virginia and Tidewater Maryland with Annapolis.

In the material that follows, points of special interest are numbered on the map on pages 108-109, described in associated text. We begin with

1. **ST. MARYS CITY,** population 300, on Maryland 5. In 1634 two ships, the *Ark* and the *Dove*, sailed up St. Marys River with Maryland's first colonists, under the leadership of Leonard Calvert, brother of Cecil, the second Lord Baltimore. St. Marys City was the capital of the colony until 1694, and during that time it grew to be a substantial community. But when the capital was moved to Annapolis in 1694, it became almost a ghost town.

St. Marys City revived briefly in 1934 when it celebrated the 300th anniversary of its settlement. Part of the celebration was the building of a replica of the

Old State House, first built in 1676. The austere brick building is open free daily, 10

a.m. to 5 p.m.; until 4 p.m. during the winter. Nearby is the churchyard of

Trinity Church, built in 1829 with the bricks from the original statehouse. In the churchyard the Leonard Calvert Monument marks the site of a mulberry tree under which Calvert bought land from the Indians and established Maryland's first local government. Nearby, the Freedom of Conscience Monument commemorates the 1649 Toleration Act.

About 12 miles southeast of St. Marys City on Maryland 5 is

Point Lookout, where there is a lighthouse and a 500-acre state park. The ten-mile-wide Potomac is on one side and Chesapeake Bay on the other. The park has fine beaches and offers swimming, fishing, camping, and boating.

About 15 miles northwest of St. Marys City on Maryland 5, just east of the village of Hollywood, is

Sotterly, still a working plantation, with a handsome Colonial mansion built in 1730, open to the public during summer months.

From St. Marys City, Maryland 5 leads

northwest through the Tidewater region. After about 50 miles it intersects US 301. About 90 miles north of St. Marys City, off US 50, is

2. ANNAPOLIS, population 30,000, capital of Maryland since 1694, home of the United States Naval Academy and one of the most interesting Colonial cities in the country. It is also an important sports and commercial fishing center, with a superb location, where the Severn River meets Chesapeake Bay.

One of the oldest cities in America, Annapolis was settled in 1649 and later received a charter from Queen Anne (hence its name). In many ways it has changed little since Revolutionary days. Georgian houses still line the narrow brick streets which radiate from the state capitol. One of the most historic buildings is the

State House, near the center of town, a red brick Georgian building with a towering wooden dome. Built between 1772 and 1779, it is the oldest state capitol still in use. In 1784 the Continental Congress met here and ratified the treaty with Britain which established American independence. In the senate chamber, George Washington resigned his commission as the leader of the American armies. The room, handsomely restored, has a notable portrait collection. An unusual exhibit is the Flag Room, with the only official American flag known to have been carried in a Revolutionary battle. On

The red-bricked, Georgian-style State House in Annapolis is the oldest state capitol in the country still in use.

the grounds is a curious, cross-shaped building built in 1735, the oldest public building in Maryland. It was once the state's treasury and a meeting place for the Provincial Council. Northwest of the State House is

St. Anne's Church, most historic church in Annapolis, built in 1859, the third church built on the site since the first one was erected in 1699. It is worth visiting to see a superb stained glass window. Northeast of the State House is

St. John's College, College Ave. and King George St., established in 1696, third oldest college in the country (after Harvard and William and Mary). Though small, with only 300 students, the college has a reputation for excellence. A long list of distinguished alumni includes Francis Scott Key, who graduated in 1796. Campus buildings worth seeing include the handsomely restored McDowell Hall, a fine Colonial chapel, and the college library, which began operations in 1697. It was the first public library in the country.

Few cities in the country have more fine Colonial mansions than Annapolis. Those that can be visited include

Hammond-Harwood House, Maryland Ave. and King George St., about three blocks northeast of the State House. Generally regarded as one of the finest examples of Georgian Colonial design in the country, it was built in 1774. It has been beautifully restored and refurnished and has unusually fine interior woodwork. Open Monday through Saturday, 10 a.m. to 5 p.m.; Sunday, 2 p.m. to 5 p.m., March through October; rest of the year until 4 p.m. (Admission: adults $1, children 25¢.) Across the street is the

Chase-Lloyd House, 22 Maryland Ave. Completed in 1771, it was built by Samuel Chase, one of the signers of the Declaration of Independence. It was later acquired by Edward Lloyd, governor of Maryland, whose daughter married Francis Scott Key. The first floor is open daily except Sunday, 10 a.m. to noon, 2 p.m. to 4 p.m. (Admission: adults 50¢, children 25¢.) Other historic houses are noted on a map issued by Historic Annapolis Inc., 18 Pickney St.

For many visitors, the most important place in Annapolis is the

United States Naval Academy, on the west bank of the Severn River. One of the world's great military schools, the Academy trains officers for the Navy and the Marine Corps. Enrollment, controlled by Congress, averages about 4,000. On the beautifully landscaped grounds are more than 200 buildings.

Established in 1845, the Academy was almost completely rebuilt in French Renaissance style in 1899. Some buildings, like the Academy Chapel, are architecturally distinguished. Bancroft Hall is the largest dormitory in the world.

Visitors enter the grounds through the main gate, Maryland Ave. at Hanover St. There is a Visitor Information Center at the Field House, Gate No. 1. Grounds are open daily from 9 a.m. to 7 p.m.; buildings close at 5 p.m.

Things to see include the Naval Museum, just inside the entrance gate, and the Academy Chapel, which dominates the grounds just south of the Administration Building. Famed for its superb stained glass windows, the chapel has a crypt with the tomb of John Paul Jones, the great naval hero, resembling the tomb of Napoleon in Paris. Near Bancroft Hall is a bronze copy of the original wooden figurehead of the USS *Delaware*. The figure, called Tecumseh, after an Indian chief, is a kind of patron saint of midshipmen.

The mustering of the brigade of midshipmen in front of Bancroft Hall takes place during the school year weekdays at 12:05 p.m., Saturday at 12:15 p.m., Sunday at 12:30 p.m. More spectacular are dress parades held each Wednesday during the spring and fall at 3:30 p.m., on Worden Field, north of the Academy's main grounds.

From Annapolis, the express route of Maryland 2 leads into the big urban district that dominates all of northern Maryland. At its center is

3. BALTIMORE, population 905,000, the seventh largest city in the United States, one of the nation's greatest ocean ports, a leading manufacturing center, and a community of high historic interest. It is the core of a metropolitan district with more than two million people.

Baltimore was founded in 1729 by act of the colony's Provincial Assembly, who were seeking a port to handle the growing volume of coastal and foreign shipping. It has been Maryland's chief port ever since. During the American Revolution and the War of 1812, swift Baltimore-built privateers harassed British ships with such success that British naval leaders called Baltimore "a nest of pirates." Baltimore shipyards became famous. The *Constellation*, the first warship built for the United States Navy, was launched in Baltimore in 1797.

The most famous episode in Baltimore's history occurred during the War of 1812 when British forces, having seized and burned Washington, sought to do the same thing in Baltimore. But Baltimore's Fort McHenry resisted. Baltimore patriots stitched together an enormous American flag and raised it over the fort, where it flew through 25 hours of bombardment. Francis Scott Key, Maryland-born lawyer and captive on a British ship, saw it flying there and wrote the poem which, set to music, became "The Star-Spangled Banner."

Soon after the end of the war, the clipper, a new type of sailing vessel, which was first built in Baltimore yards, began to establish records in world commerce and helped make Baltimore one of the world's great ports. Baltimore was the eastern terminus of the country's first railway, the Baltimore and Ohio, begun in 1829. Completion of the railway, plus her port and shipbuilding activities, made Baltimore an increasingly important industrial center.

Baltimore dedicated the country's first Roman Catholic cathedral in 1821, started using the first electrically operated streetcar in 1885, and a few years later opened the country's first medical clinic.

Routes To and Through. Main highways converge on Baltimore from all directions, several passing through the center of the city. All of them link with the Baltimore Beltway, Interstate 695, which offers a fast bypass of the congested city center. The highways include Interstate 83, terminating near the city center; US 1; Kennedy Memorial Highway, a toll road which goes southwest to Washington as the Baltimore-Washington Expressway; US 40; Maryland 2, entering from the south as the Annapolis-Baltimore Ritchie Highway; and Interstate 70N, terminating in the western section of the city. Points of interest are widely scattered and are described in several sections, starting with

Points of Interest—central section.

The heart of the city is undergoing a massive program of renovation and redevelopment that fortunately has left many places of historic interest untouched. The main business and shopping streets are here. Starting in the south, points of interest include

U.S. Frigate Constellation, moored at Pier 4, just off Pratt St. Built in Baltimore yards and launched in 1797, the frigate is the oldest ship in the United States Navy and may be the oldest ship in the world still afloat. Open daily, July to Labor Day, 10 a.m. to 5 p.m.; shorter hours rest of the year. (Admission: adults 50¢, children 25¢.) Northeast of the *Constellation* is the

Flag House, 844 E. Pratt St., a museum dedicated to the flag that inspired "The Star-Spangled Banner." In 1814 it was the home of Mary Pickersgill, who made the enormous flag that flew over Fort McHenry. It contained 15 stars and measured 30 by 42 feet. An exact copy is displayed in the house—the original is in the Smithsonian Institution. The house is open Tuesday through Saturday, 10 a.m. to 4 p.m.; Sunday, 2 p.m. to 4:30 p.m. (Admission: adults 50¢, children free.)

In the heart of the business section are several places of interest close enough together so one can walk from one to the other. They include

Peale Museum, 225 N. Holliday St., named for Maryland's great portraitist, Rembrandt Peale, who built the house in 1814. The country's oldest museum building, it contains much of Peale's work and a fine collection of architectural drawings. Open free, Tuesday through Saturday, 10:30 a.m. to 4:30 p.m.; Sunday, 1:30 p.m. to 5:30 p.m. Closed weekends in August, and Sunday in June and July.

A few blocks southeast of the Peale Museum is a city landmark, the

Old Shot Tower, E. Fayette and Front streets, a massive, windowless tower 234 feet high, with a hollow core down which molten lead was dropped into tanks of water to form round shot. Built in 1828, it is the oldest of several similar shot towers still standing in the country. Closed.

Northwest of the Peale Museum, around

The U.S.F. Constellation was the first ship of the U.S. Navy and was launched in Baltimore in 1797.

beautiful Mount Vernon Place, are several places of interest. At the center of Mount Vernon Place is the

Washington Monument, an impressive 178-foot column, with a 16-foot statue of George Washington on the top. The first important monument honoring Washington, it was completed in 1829. There is an observation deck near the top (25¢ fee) and a free historical museum at the base. Open daily, 10 a.m. to 4:30 p.m. Nearby is the

Maryland Historical Society, 201 W. Monument St., a general museum with a fine library. Its most prized exhibit is the original

manuscript of "The Star-Spangled Banner." There are also nine period rooms, portraits of famous Americans, and other exhibits of Americana, with the emphasis on Maryland. The library is open Tuesday through Saturday, 9 a.m. to 5 p.m. The museum is open Tuesday through Saturday, 11 a.m. to 4 p.m.; Sunday, 1 p.m. to 5 p.m. Both free.

A short distance south of Mount Vernon Place is the

Basilica of the Assumption of the Blessed Virgin Mary, Mulberry and Cathedral streets. The cornerstone was laid in 1806. The church, designed by Benjamin Latrobe, architect of the Capitol in Washington, was dedicated in 1821, the first Roman Catholic cathedral in the United States. John Carroll, the country's first archbishop, and Maryland's famed Cardinal Gibbons are buried in the crypt. Near the cathedral is

Walters Art Gallery, 600 N. Charles St., a city-owned museum with an extensive collection of fine art, sculpture, manuscripts, and prints, covering most of the world's art epochs from early Egyptian to modern. Open free September through June: Tuesday through Saturday, 11 a.m. to 5 p.m.; Sunday from 2 p.m. During July and August: Monday through Saturday, 11 a.m. to 4 p.m.; Sunday, 2 p.m. to 5 p.m.

Points of Interest—outlying areas.

Baltimore's most historic point of interest is about three miles southeast of the city center at the tip of a peninsula guarding the inner harbor. It is

Fort McHenry National Monument, reached by Light St. (Maryland 2) south, then southeast on Fort Ave. Built between 1794 and 1805, in the shape of a five-pointed star, the fort protected Baltimore from attack by sea until after the Civil War. On September 13, 1814, the British fleet, sailing up the Patapsco River from Chesapeake Bay, bombarded the fort for 25 hours. In the final hours of the attack, at dawn, Francis Scott Key, detained in a British ship during the bombardment, was able to see an enormous flag flying over the ramparts of the fort. The stirring words of "The Star-Spangled Banner" were the result. Much of the fort has been restored to its appearance as it was during the War of 1812, except for the cannon on the ramparts, which are Civil War models. The flagstaff is in the same position as it was during the bombardment, and a flag flies from it night and day, though not as big as the original. The fort's Visitor Center has historical displays. Open daily mid-June to Labor Day, 8 a.m. to 8:30 p.m.; rest of the year, 9 a.m. to 5:30 p.m.

About a mile west of the central business section is the

Baltimore and Ohio Transportation Museum, at Pratt and Poppleton streets. Enter the museum through Mount Clare Station, built in 1830, the first railway station in the country. The museum is crowded with old locomotives and cars—both originals and copies—and railway gear of all kinds, dating from 1829. Open free, 10 a.m. to 4 p.m., Wednesday through Sunday.

For a pleasant change of pace, visit

Druid Hill Park, in the northwest part of the city, between Interstate 83 and US 140. A rolling, handsomely landscaped tract of 674 acres, the park has several small lakes, many scenic drives, and the Baltimore Zoo, with about 1,000 animals. Also in the park is Maryland House, a natural history museum, with exhibits of Maryland animal and plant life, fossils, and minerals. Open free daily except Monday, 10 a.m. to 4 p.m.

About a mile and a half northeast of Druid Hill Park is Baltimore's renowned

Johns Hopkins University, Charles and 34th streets, founded in 1876. The handsome campus is worth seeing. Homewood House, built in 1800, was the home of Charles Carroll, Jr., and is now the Administration Building. The Medical Center has its own campus at Broadway and Monument St. Since its establishment in 1889 the center has had many medical firsts.

In the northwest corner of Baltimore is Maryland's famous

Pimlico Race Track, Belvedere and Park Heights avenues, just south of Northern Pkwy. The Preakness, one of the oldest thoroughbred races in the country, has been run here annually since 1873. Stables can accommodate more than 1,000 horses. Pimlico stages two meets, spring and fall. Post time is 1:30 p.m. (Admission: grandstand $1.75, clubhouse $4.)

From Baltimore, US 40 follows the route of the historic National Road, begun in 1806. It extends north through the Piedmont hills about 45 miles to

4. FREDERICK, population 23,500, shopping center for one of the richest agricultural districts in the East, with special emphasis on the breeding of fine horses. Frederick has several associations with the Civil War. Toward the end of the war, Jubal Early, Confederate cavalry leader, levied a fine of $200,000 on the city, which was promply paid with borrowed money. The loan was not finally paid off until 1951.

THE STAR-SPANGLED BANNER

EARLY IN THE morning of September 13, 1814, during the War of 1812, a British fleet sailed into Chesapeake Bay to attack Baltimore, which was guarded by Fort McHenry. A young Washington lawyer named Francis Scott Key boarded one of the British ships under a flag of truce to secure the release of a friend. The release was promised, but since the attack was about to begin, Key was detained.

The bombardment lasted for 25 hours. British warships hurled more than 1,800 shells, each weighing over 200 pounds, at the ramparts of Fort McHenry.

At dawn Key saw that Fort McHenry had survived. Flying over the ramparts was a huge American flag. He was so moved that he wrote the first stanza of a poem, beginning, "O say can you see, by the dawn's early light. . . ."

The next day, released and back in Baltimore, Key finished the poem. His brother-in-law suggested that the poem be set to music, and had it printed on broadsides. A week later it was published in a Baltimore newspaper, and it soon became the unofficial national anthem. Congress finally made it official in 1931.

The flag Key saw flying above Fort McHenry, 30 by 42 feet, was made expressly for the fort by Mary Pickersgill of Baltimore. Her home, called the Flag House, exhibits a duplicate of the flag. The original is in the Smithsonian Institution.

In 1843, after a distinguished legal career, Francis Scott Key died. By congressional decree the Stars and Stripes flies day and night over his grave in Mt. Olivet Cemetery, in Frederick, Maryland.

In the same cemetery is the grave of a woman whose name is linked with a Civil War legend, which goes like this: When Stonewall Jackson was marching his army north through Frederick, all Union flags along the line of march had disappeared except one. This flew from the upper window of Barbara Fritchie's glove shop. Barbara defied Jackson with these words, later immortalized in a poem by John Greenleaf Whittier:

> "Shoot if you must this old gray head,
> But spare your country's flag," she said.

Barbara's home on Patrick St. is Frederick's chief tourist attraction today.

Fort McHenry National Monument and Historic Shrine is a familiar historical landmark and was the birthplace of the Star-Spangled Banner in 1814.

The Pimlico Race Course, in Baltimore, has been the home of the Preakness, one of the oldest thoroughbred races in the country, since 1873.

The supposed scene of a Civil War incident which historians doubt ever happened gives Frederick its chief point of interest, the

Barbara Fritchie House, 154 W. Patrick St., a reconstruction of the home of Barbara Fritchie, who ran a glove shop on the first floor and lived on the second. The legend, immortalized by the poet Whittier, describes the confrontation of Barbara and General Stonewall Jackson, who was riding through the city at the head of his troops. As the poem goes, Barbara thrust a Union flag from an upstairs window and shouted to the passing general:

"Shoot if you must this old grey head,
But spare your country's flag," she said.

Gallant Jackson is supposed to have responded with:

"Who touches a hair of yon grey head
Dies like a dog. March on," he said.

The house is open daily, 9 a.m. to 5 p.m. (Admission: adults 50¢, children 35¢.)

To pursue the legend to its logical conclusion, go to

Mount Olivet Cemetery, south end of Market St., where the grave of Barbara Fritchie is located. Coincidentally, there is another grave here of a person who was intimately associated with the flag Barbara Fritchie defended—Francis Scott Key, who

died in 1843. The grave is surmounted by an impressive monument and a statue of Key pointing to a nearby flagpole on which the Stars and Stripes flies night and day.

From Frederick it is about 16 miles northwest on US 40A to Boonsboro, then seven miles southwest on Maryland 34 to the site of Maryland's most important Civil War battle:

Antietam National Battlefield Site, marking the bloodiest single battle of the Civil War, which began on September 17, 1862, when Lee tried to invade the North, and was stopped by McClellan's overwhelmingly superior force.

The best place to begin exploring the battlefield is at the Visitor Center, one mile north of Sharpsburg on Maryland 65. Open daily, 8:30 a.m. to 5 p.m.; in summer until 8 p.m. In the battle Lee had about 41,000 men, McClellan about 87,000. At the end of a single day of intense fighting their combined losses amounted to about 23,000. Six generals were killed. Among the Union troops was Sgt. William McKinley, who later became president.

The tourist will see Sunken Lane (also known as Bloody Angle), where 4,000 men died, and Burnside Bridge, where a few hundred Confederate riflemen, under the bewhiskered General Burnside, held off four Union divisions. McClellan failed to follow up his victory at Antietam, and Lincoln removed him from command.

About 15 miles north of Frederick on US 15, then three miles west of the village of Thurmont, on Maryland 77, is

Catoctin Mountain Park, a rugged tract of 5,765 wooded acres, ranging in elevation from 700 to 1,800 feet. The park has an unusually rich variety of plants, trees, and wildlife. Just south is Catoctin Furnace, a picturesque ruin, which produced iron and steel for many years, including the iron for the battleship *Monitor.* On the slope of Catoctin Mountain is Camp David, an occasional wilderness hideaway for United States presidents. Franklin Roosevelt called it his Shangri-la.

From Frederick the roughly parallel routes of US 40 and Interstate 70 lead northwest about 25 miles to Hagerstown, an important manufacturing center, where one factory makes more pipe organs than any other in the world. US 40 and Interstate 70 continue northwest through the narrow panhandle that separates West Virginia and Pennsylvania. Interstate 70 diverges north into Pennsylvania, US 40 continues west. The chief community, about 65 miles west of Hagerstown, is

5. CUMBERLAND, population 32,000. It was settled in 1750 and became an outfitting base for westward migration through the Allegheny Mountains. The first route led through a mountain gap just west of the city. George Washington surveyed the first military road through the town. Cumberland was a supply center for the National Road, also called the Cumberland Trail. This was the first national highway, which eventually became US 40. The country's first railroad, the Baltimore and Ohio, reached Cumberland in 1842. A few years later the Chesapeake and Ohio Canal was extended west from Washington, and Cumberland became its western terminus.

Cumberland today is an important man-

Through the Cumberland Narrows passed the first pioneer trail to the Ohio Valley, the first federal highway, and the first railroad.

ufacturing center. Products include glass, fabrics, tires, and chemicals. West of town on US 40 is

Cumberland Narrows, a pass through the mountains where cliffs rise on either side of Will's Creek to about 1,000 feet. Near the gorge is one of the original toll houses on the National Road, built in 1833. Another relic of the road, about 25 miles west of Cumberland, is Cassleman River Bridge, built in 1813, the longest single-arch stone bridge in the country. About six miles west of the bridge, US 219 leads south through the mountains, into the heart of a popular Maryland vacation area:

Deep Creek Lake, a strikingly beautiful mountain lake with 65 miles of shoreline. The lake provides swimming and boating during summer months, and fishing year-round. Near the lake, on Marsh Mountain, is Wisp, one of the few ski areas south of the Mason-Dixon line. The largest commu-

nity in the area is Oakland, ten miles south, population 2,000, which has adequate accommodations and service facilities. About eight miles south of Oakland, at the southwestern tip of Maryland's panhandle, is Backbone Mountain, 3,360 feet, highest point in the state.

The Eastern Shore of Maryland can be reached by taking US 50-301 from Annapolis over the

Chesapeake Bay Bridge, one of the longest steel bridges in the world over salt water, 4.3 miles shore to shore. About ten miles east of the bridge US 301 swings northeast into Delaware and US 50 angles southeast, then south. About five miles southeast of the point where the two highways diverge, near the village of Wye Mills, is

Wye Oak State Park, a 21-acre tract around a tremendous white oak tree, the official tree of Maryland, said to be more

The Chesapeake Bay Bridge links Maryland's eastern and western shores and is the longest all-steel, over-water bridge in the world.

than 400 years old. The oak is almost 100 feet high and 27 feet around the trunk. About 15 miles south of the park on US 50 is

Easton, population 6,300, noted for antique shops, sport fishing facilities, and one historic building:

Third Haven Meeting House, on S. Washington St., built in 1682 by the Society of Friends (Quakers). It is one of the oldest frame churches in the country. William Penn occasionally attended meetings here. Ten miles west of Easton on Maryland 33, near the village of St. Michaels, famed for shipbuilding, is the

Chesapeake Bay Maritime Museum, just off Maryland 33, with a cluster of buildings overlooking the shore, exhibiting maps, ship models, a lightship, and a wooden lighthouse. Open Tuesday through Sunday, 10 a.m. to 5 p.m. in summer; until 4 p.m. in winter. (Admission: adults $1, children 25¢.)

From Easton US 50 leads south about 15 miles to

Cambridge, population 12,000, on the south shore of the wide Choptank River, with a fine harbor—the second largest deepwater port in Maryland. Seven miles south of Cambridge, in Church Creek, is

Old Trinity Church, a historic building of great charm, beautifully restored, said to be the oldest American Protestant church building still in use. Graveyard buffs will delight in the old churchyard.

Blackwater National Wildlife Refuge, five miles southeast of Church Creek on Maryland 335, is an 11,000-acre tract of marshland cut with saltwater channels, a sanctuary for the greatest concentration of waterfowl in the country. In the visitor center are wildlife displays.

At Cambridge US 50 turns sharply southeast. After 20 miles it passes just south of the Delaware border where, on Maryland 467, is the first of a series of stone markers that established the Mason-Dixon line, set in 1763. From the square granite marker, the transpeninsular line extends east to the ocean, and the Mason-Dixon line extends north, separating Maryland and Delaware, then turns west to mark the border between Maryland and Pennsylvania.

About ten miles southeast of the marker US 50 enters

6. SALISBURY, population 15,800, largest city on the Eastern Shore, one of Maryland's largest ports, and the center for a rich agricultural district—particularly the big poultry industry of the region. Several factories turn out boats, including Chris Craft. Salisbury is also a base for duck hunting and sport fishing. About 17 miles south of Salisbury, Maryland 143 diverges southwest from US 13, leads after 15 miles to

Crisfield, population 3,500, at the tip of a slender peninsula thrusting into Chesapeake Bay. Crisfield is Maryland's largest seafood-producing center and is famous for crabs, oysters, clams, and fish. The bays around Crisfield are said to yield the most productive seafood harvest in the country. The town is also a sport fishing center and has an excellent marina. Seafood processing plants welcome visitors.

From Salisbury, US 50 leads east to

Ocean City, population 1,000. Dominating the southern tip of a narrow island with ocean beaches on the east and a wide protected channel on the west, Ocean City is Maryland's only developed seashore resort. 200,000 or more visitors descend upon the town on weekends during the peak season. Ocean City has a boardwalk, an excellent beach, and facilities for deep-sea fishing. Ocean Downs, a harness racing track five miles northwest on US 50, operates during July and August.

From Ocean City, linked to it by Maryland 611, Assateague Island, a 35-mile-long barrier beach, extends south. Along with several smaller islands nearby, it has been reserved for development as

Assateague Island National Seashore, 39,500 acres, half land and half water. The Seashore, with splendid beaches, primitive marshland areas, and dunes, is being developed both to preserve its natural features, including wildlife, and to provide public recreation—swimming, boating, and fishing. Wildlife includes waterfowl of all types, the all but extinct falcon, and the famed wild ponies which are rounded up each year from islands just south, in Virginia. Roads on the island are not suitable for standard automobiles.

In Washington, D.C. a city filled with memorials, none is more impressive, more majestic, or better known than the massive, brooding Lincoln.

DISTRICT OF COLUMBIA.

WASHINGTON, D.C., is a splendid city, one of the few world capitals built to a definite plan. It has more trees, parks, and monumental buildings than any other large city in the world. It has little industry and is one of the cleanest cities in the East. Notwithstanding its recent tremendous growth, it has no tall buildings.

In 1790 Congress authorized the selection of a site for the new nation's capital not exceeding ten miles square, somewhere, in the Potomac region. President George Washington chose a square of land near the head of navigation on the Potomac River. The original ten-mile square included areas of both Maryland and Virginia.

To help develop the site and plan the new capital, Washington chose Pierre Charles L'Enfant, a protégé of Lafayette. L'Enfant went to work on his extraordinary plan, projecting a city like none the world had ever seen. L'Enfant's grand design was

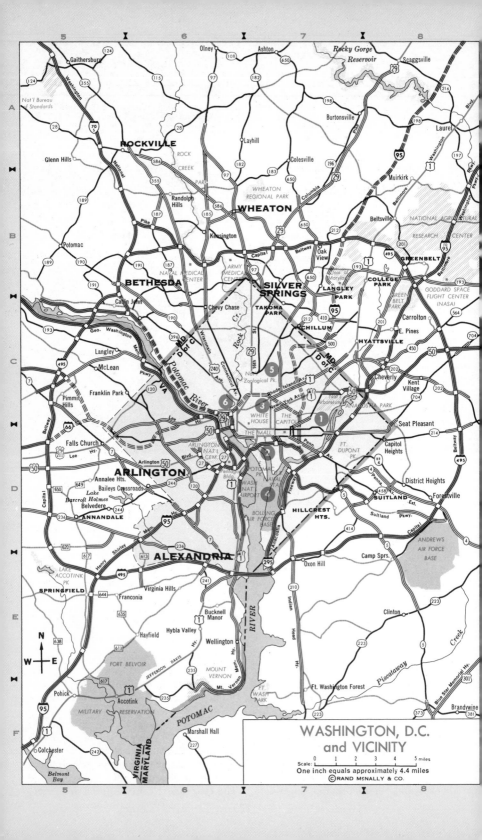

WASHINGTON, D.C.
and VICINITY

Scale:
0 1 2 3 4 5 miles

One inch equals approximately 4.4 miles

©RAND McNALLY & CO.

at first adopted only in part. It was almost 100 years later before its unique virtues were fully realized and it was used as the basic pattern for the growing city.

In getting around Washington some knowledge of the street pattern is helpful. The base from which streets are named and numbered is the Capitol. Starting from that center the city is divided into four sections: Northwest, Northeast, Southwest, and Southeast. Only the Northwest section is important to most visitors. Numbered streets run north and south, lettered streets east and west. House and building numbers for each section start from the base lines of the section. For example, 1450 G St. is on G St. be'ween 14th and 15th streets.

In the following text points of interest are described in sections designated by number in the text and on the map on the opposite page. Unless otherwise noted, all buildings and monuments are open free. In most sections places of interest are close enough together to walk to.

1. CAPITOL HILL is dominated by

The Capitol, which was a long time getting itself built. George Washington laid the cornerstone in 1793. Seven years later, when the government moved to Washington, the building was only partly finished. By 1830 it was completed essentially as planned. In 1863 the original low dome made of wood and covered with copper was replaced by the present cast-iron dome, topped by a statue of Freedom, 19½ feet tall. The last important change occurred in 1958, when the central portion of the eastern facade was extended 32 feet.

The Capitol is open from 9 a.m. to 10 p.m., Easter through Labor Day; 9 a.m. to 4:30 p.m., rest of the year. Conducted tours 9 a.m. to 5:25 p.m., Easter to Labor Day; to 3:55 p.m., rest of the year. (Fee: 25¢.)

The enormous building covers almost four acres. The most impressive single area is the **Rotunda,** a vast circular room about 100 feet in diameter, rising more than 280 feet to the dome, circled with eight enormous paintings showing scenes of American history. It is the best place to begin a tour, either with guides or on your own. Other rooms of special note include **National Statuary Hall,** south of the Rotunda. The galleries of the House and Senate chambers are open to the public by special pass when Congress is in session. Near the **Senate Chamber** is the ornate **President's Room,** with a gold-plated chandelier.

East of the Capitol, between Independence and Constitution avenues, is the

Library of Congress, Italian Renaissance in design, completed in 1897, housing more than 14 million books, many more millions of pamphlets, maps, prints, and historic documents, including the rough draft of the Declaration of Independence and the first and second drafts of Lincoln's Gettysburg Address. Open free, 9 a.m. to 10 p.m., Monday through Saturday; 11:30 a.m. to 10 p.m., Sunday and holidays. Behind the main building of the Library of Congress is the

Folger Shakespeare Library, 201 E. Capitol St. A handsome building, it contains the largest Shakespeare collection in the world and a model of the Globe Theater.

North of the Library, facing the Capitol from the east, is the

Supreme Court Building, which many regard as the most beautiful government building in Washington. The white marble building is a nearly perfect adaptation of classic Roman architecture. **Memorial Hall,** immediately inside the entrance, is frequently crowded with visitors waiting to enter the handsome courtroom. The building is open Monday through Friday from 9 a.m. to 4:30 p.m.; Saturday to noon. There are tours every 15 minutes except when court is in session, which occurs every other Monday October through April, and every Monday May through mid-June.

North of the Capitol grounds, on N. Capitol St., is the **Government Printing Office,** which has a bookstore where all government publications available for public distribution are displayed and sold.

2. THE MALL, gracious and impressive, sweeps from the west edge of the Capitol grounds to 14th St. On the north side of the Mall, facing Constitution Ave., is the

National Gallery of Art, between Fourth and Seventh streets and Constitution Ave. and Madison Dr. The main entrance is at Sixth St. The gallery, erected with funds made available by Andrew Mellon, was dedicated in 1941. It ranks near the top on any list of the world's great museums. Open free Monday through Saturday, 10 a.m. to 5 p.m. weekdays; 2 p.m. to 10 p.m. Sunday. The summer hours, April 1 through Labor Day, are 10 a.m. to 9 p.m. weekdays; noon to 10 p.m. Sunday.

West of the National Gallery, on Constitution Ave. facing Tenth St., is the

Museum of Natural History, with notable exhibits in the fields of natural history and anthropology, many in realistic dioramas and habitat groups. The collection of gems and minerals includes the celebrated 44-carat Hope Diamond and a 330-carat star sapphire. The museum is open free daily from 9 a.m. to 4:30 p.m.

Filling the area between Constitution Ave., 12th St., Madison Dr., and 14th St. is the massive new

Museum of History and Technology. The main entrance is at 13th St. Dramatic exhibits illustrate the cultural development of the country: military history, ships, transportation, printing, stamps, the history of machinery, agriculture from colonial days. One gallery exhibits gowns worn by the wives of United States presidents. The museum is open free daily from 9 a.m. to 9 p.m. in summer; rest of the year until 4:30 p.m.

On the opposite side of the Mall, between 9th and 12th streets on Independence Ave., are four buildings maintained by the

Smithsonian Institution, a most unusual organization. In 1829 the government was notified that an Englishman named James Smithson had left about $500,000 to the United States for the establishment of an institution for "the increase and diffusion of knowledge among men." The bequest was not accepted until 1846. Since that time the resources of the Institution have grown enormously. The most famous building is an architectural oddity, sometimes described as Victorian-Renaissance-Gothic. Of red sandstone, it is a fascinating clutter of towers, pinnacles, arches, and medieval elements, and houses the Smithsonian's administrative offices. Facing Independence Ave. at 9th St. is the

Arts and Industries Building. Most exhibits relate to aviation and transportation, including the Wright brothers' *Kitty Hawk,* the first successful airplane, and Lindbergh's *Spirit of St. Louis.* Next door is the Air and

Space Building, displaying aircraft, rockets, space capsules, and aeronautical models.

Just west of the Air and Space Building, facing Independence Ave., is the

Freer Gallery of Art, noted for its collections of Asiatic art and the works of James McNeill Whistler, including Whistler's Peacock Room, designed for a London shipbuilder. All of the four Smithsonian museums are open free daily, 9 a.m. to 4:30 p.m.

On the south side of the Mall along Independence Ave., from 14th St. to 3rd St., in a row of government buildings, is the

Bureau of Engraving and Printing, at 14th and C streets, entrance at 14th St., a huge building of no architectural distinction. Here all the United States paper money, stamps, and bonds are printed. Free tours Monday through Friday, 8 a.m. to 2:30 p.m.

On the north side of the Mall, beginning at 6th St. and extending to 15th St., is the

Federal Triangle, a right-angled triangle with Pennsylvania Ave. on the north, Constitution Ave. on the south, and 15th St. on the west, filled with government buildings. Of special interest is

The National Archives, one of the handsomest buildings in Washington, between Pennsylvania and Constitution avenues, Seventh and Ninth streets. It is the official depository of government records of permanent value. Superbly displayed in the exhibit hall are the Declaration of Independence, the Constitution, and the Bill of Rights. Open Monday through Saturday, 9 a.m. to 10 p.m.; Sunday, 1 p.m. to 10 p.m. To the west is the huge Department of Justice Building, between Ninth and Tenth streets, entrance at Ninth St. This is the headquarters of the FBI. The FBI tour draws swarms of visitors; it includes a museum of crime, a visit to the FBI laboratory and the reference library of guns, and a shooting demonstration. Free tours start every 30 minutes between 9:15 a.m. and 4:15 p.m., Monday through Friday.

The huge Post Office Department, between 12th and 13th streets on Pennsylvania Ave., has an excellent collection of United States stamps on exhibit in Room 1315.

North of the Federal Triangle is

Ford's Theater, at 511 Tenth St., where Abraham Lincoln was shot by John Wilkes

Booth while Lincoln was watching a play on April 14, 1865. The theater has been completely restored to its aspect on the night of the tragedy. In the basement is the Lincoln Museum, with exhibits illustrating Lincoln's life and death. Just across the street is the

House Where Lincoln Died, at 516 Tenth St., the home of William Petersen, a tailor who lived there at the time Lincoln was shot. In three rooms the story of Lincoln's last hours is vividly re-created. The Lincoln Museum and the House Where Lincoln Died are open daily, 9 a.m. to 9 p.m. During the theater season Ford's Theater is open Monday through Saturday, 9 a.m. to noon; Sunday, 9 a.m. to 9 p.m. Rest of the year the theater is open the same hours as the museum and the Petersen House. (Admission to all three places: adults 50¢, children free.) Between Seventh and Ninth streets and F and G streets are

The National Collection of Fine Arts and the **National Portrait Gallery,** housed in the old Patent Office Building, regarded as one of the most perfect examples of Greek architecture in Washington. The National Collection of Fine Arts covers American art from colonial times. The National Portrait Gallery traces the history of America through portraits, sculpture, and photographs of presidents, scientists, scholars, military leaders, and others. Both museums are open free daily except Monday, 9 a.m. to 4:30 p.m.

West of the Mall and extending south of Constitution Ave. to the Potomac River and three miles along the shore, is a section of the city called

3. POTOMAC PARK. In a triangular area south of Constitution Ave. and west of 14th St. is the

Washington Monument, completed in 1884, tallest masonry structure in the world and Washington's most famous landmark, an obelisk rising 555 feet above the crest of a low hill. Most visitors ride to the top in an elevator that whisks them to the 500-foot level in one minute. Some walk the 898 steps of a stairway spiraling around the elevator shaft.

The dimensions of the Washington Monument are impressive. Each side of the base is 55 feet wide, with 15-foot thick walls.

The gradual tapering makes walls at the top of the shaft 18 inches thick, and 34 feet wide. One can see a distinct change of color about one-third of the way up the monument, showing where construction stopped for more than 20 years because of lack of funds. Open March 20 through Labor Day, 8 a.m. to 11 p.m.; rest of the year, 9 a.m. to 5 p.m. (Elevator: adults 10¢, children free.)

The Monument grounds are the best place in Washington to view the

Lincoln Memorial, completed in 1922, a little less than a mile west of the Monument, its gleaming image reflected in a long, narrow pool which stretches between.

The Memorial has the general form of a Greek temple. Inner walls are surrounded by a colonnade of 36 Doric columns representing the 36 states of the Union at the time Lincoln was president. The interior has an overwhelming majesty which seems almost to animate the gigantic seated figure of Lincoln, by Daniel Chester French.

From the wide steps of the Lincoln Memorial, it is possible to look southeast across the Tidal Basin to the low white dome of the

Thomas Jefferson National Memorial, completed in 1943, built in the circular Pantheon style used by Jefferson in several buildings he designed, particularly his home at Monticello. The central feature is a standing bronze statue of Jefferson, 19 feet high, under a vaulted dome. Each spring, hopefully during the Cherry Blossom Festival, the Japanese cherry trees which line the Tidal Basin in front of the Memorial are in bloom.

Memorials to two other presidents are linked to West Potomac Park by parkways and bridges west and northwest of the Lincoln Memorial. One is the

Theodore Roosevelt Memorial, on Theodore Roosevelt Island in the Potomac, just northwest of the Lincoln Memorial, off the George Washington Memorial Parkway. The island is a wooded patch of wilderness, laced by foot trails. In a clearing near the center is a statue of Theodore Roosevelt in a characteristically dynamic pose, flanked by tablets carved with Roosevelt's best known comments on nature and government. Open daily, 9:30 a.m. to 5:30 p.m.

Northeast of the Lincoln Memorial, overlooking the Potomac, is the

John F. Kennedy Center for the Performing Arts, to be completed during 1970. The huge building will house an opera house, concert hall, theater, and a smaller studio playhouse.

Extending about seven blocks north from Constitution Ave., bounded by 15th and 17th streets, is a lovely area that can best be described as

4. THE WHITE HOUSE AREA, a complex of parks and buildings, curving drives and tree-shaded streets. Pennsylvania Ave. passes in front of the splendid mansion:

The White House, official residence of every president except George Washington. Washington himself selected the site. The cornerstone was laid in 1792 and eight years later President and Mrs. John Adams moved in. Between 1948 and 1952 the building was virtually rebuilt from the inside, at a cost of nearly $6 million. When finished, the White House had 132 rooms, 20 baths and showers, five elevators. The wife of the late President John F. Kennedy supervised a superb redecorating of the interior.

Visitors enter the White House through a special entrance on E. Executive Ave. opposite the Treasury Building. Open Tuesday through Saturday, 10 a.m. to noon; 10 a.m. to 2 p.m. Saturday during summer.

Rooms open to the public include the East Room, the largest and most famous, the Green Room, the Blue Room, regarded by many as the most beautiful, the Red Room, and the State Dining Room. Across Pennsylvania Ave. from the White House is

Lafayette Square, named for the Marquis de Lafayette. There is a statue of him in the park, as well as an impressive equestrian statue of Gen. Andrew Jackson cast from bronze cannon captured by Jackson in the Battle of New Orleans. Other statues are of Rochambeau, von Steuben, and Kosciuszko, all of whom aided the American cause in the Revolutionary War.

Just north of the park, at 16th and H streets, is

St. John's Episcopal Church, erected in 1816, and often called the Church of Presidents because so many have attended services here, starting with James Madison. Ever since, his pew, No. 54, has been re-served for presidents. The building has a mellow dignity and charm.

West of the White House is the most rapidly changing area of Washington, bounded by Pennsylvania and Constitution avenues, 17th and 23rd streets. Points of interest are described from east to west. At the north end of 17th St. is the

Corcoran Art Gallery, 17th and E streets, completed in 1879. Exhibit rooms are devoted to American painting and sculpture. Open Tuesday through Friday, 10 a.m. to 4:30 p.m.; Saturday, 9 a.m. to 4:30 p.m.; Sunday, 2 p.m. to 5 p.m. (Admission Thursday through Sunday: adults 50¢, children free. Free rest of the week.)

At 17th St. and Constitution Ave. is the

Pan American Union, headquarters for 21 American republics and the Organization of American States, built in a combination of French and Spanish Renaissance styles. Worth seeing is the Hall of Heroes. Opening from it is the Hall of the Americas, a superb ballroom, and the Blue Aztec Garden, with its statue of the Aztec God of Flowers. Open 8:30 a.m. to 4 p.m., Monday through Saturday. (Admission: 15¢.)

At 18th St. and New York Ave. is one of the most charming buildings in Washington, the

Octagon House, 1735 New York Ave., national headquarters for the American Institute of Architects. Octagon House, a fine example of late Georgian design, is actually six-sided, broken by a semicircular tower at the entrance. President Madison lived here for about a year after the British burned the White House in 1814. Here the treaty which ended the War of 1812 was signed. Several rooms, beautifully restored and authentically furnished, are open to the public. There are also exhibits of architectural interest. Open free, Tuesday through Saturday, 9 a.m. to 5 p.m.; Sunday, 2 p.m. to 5 p.m.

The enormous headquarters of the Department of State fills a two-block area around 21st and D streets. Along 18th St., north of C St., is the Interior Department, which has a notable museum and a craft shop where American Indian products are exhibited and sold.

South of Pennsylvania Ave. and east of 23rd St. is the growing campus of

George Washington University, the largest institution of higher learning in Washington, with about 13,000 students. The university began when George Washington left 50 shares of stock in the Potomac Canal to found it. Lisner Hall, 2033 G St., has a replica of Houdon's statue of Washington. The original is in the rotunda of the Virginia State Capitol at Richmond.

For about a mile north of Lafayette Square 16th St., Washington's most important north-south street, leads through what for want of a better name might be called the

5. EMBASSY AREA, with dozens of luxury hotels and apartment houses, foreign embassies, and many fine shops. Important avenues that cut through the district are Connecticut, Vermont, and Massachusetts. The shopping and hotel section is in the southern part of the district. Embassies and legations representing nearly every country in the world are scattered through the section, with many concentrated on both sides of Massachusetts Ave. northwest of Dupont Circle. Many are housed in former mansions. Of special interest is the strikingly handsome headquarters of the

National Geographic Society, at 17th and M streets. The Society, the world's largest nonprofit scientific and educational institution, produces maps, globes, atlases, television programs, and the *National Geographic* magazine, all financed by the dues of more than six million members. Explorers Hall in the headquarters building has dramatic exhibits relating to research, exploration, and geography. Open free, Monday through Friday, 9 a.m. to 6 p.m.; Saturday and holidays until 5 p.m.; Sunday, noon to 5 p.m.

One of the most remarkable buildings in Washington is the

Islamic Center, at 2551 Massachusetts Ave., the cultural and religious home of several thousand Moslem Americans. Special features include a mosque with a minaret rising 160 feet. Open daily, 10 a.m. to 6 p.m. There is a service at noon on Friday to which the public is invited. As with mosques everywhere, all visitors must remove their shoes before entering. A colonnade and cloister of white marble inlaid with blue tile links the mosque with the

Islamic Institute, which has a library, classrooms, and an auditorium.

The oldest section of Washington is

6. GEORGETOWN, extending north about two miles from the Potomac River, west from Rock Creek Park for about a mile. Places of interest include

Old Georgetown, filling the southeast corner of the section. The main east-west street is M St., an extension of Pennsylvania Ave.; the main north-south street is Wisconsin Ave. More than 200 years ago Georgetown was a wealthy little city at the head of navigation on the Potomac. It had the finest gun factories in the area and the biggest flour mill. It was the home port for a fleet of ships that carried Virginia tobacco all over the world. Georgetown citizens built fine houses in the wooded hills above the Potomac.

When the government moved to Washington in 1800 the only suitable houses were in Georgetown. Those who could not rent or purchase them built new ones, with the result that the narrow, tree-lined streets were soon lined with pleasant dwellings ranging from cottages to mansions. This was Georgetown's first golden age. The second was during the First World War, when hundreds of thousands of people swarmed into Washington. Many could not find houses in Washington so they looked west to Georgetown and discovered its fine old houses. A second housing boom began when the old houses were remodeled and modernized and new ones built.

Places of interest outside Old Georgetown include the

Chesapeake & Ohio Canal, west of 30th St. and south of M St., starting point for mule-drawn barge trips. Canal boats pulled by plodding mules provide barge riders with a bucolic trip past Georgetown's backyard.

A few blocks north is

Georgetown University, at 37th and O streets, overlooking the Potomac from a high bluff. The university, established in 1789, with about 7,500 students, is the oldest Catholic university in the country. It is noted for its School of Foreign Service, the first in the country, and also has a famous seismological laboratory.

North of downtown Georgetown is

Georgetown Heights, with several famous houses. The most notable is

Dumbarton Oaks, 1703 32nd St., a splendid Georgian mansion built about 1801, set in a grove of great oak trees and surrounded by magnificent formal gardens. In 1940 its owners gave the mansion and their notable collection of Byzantine and early Christian art to Harvard University, which now maintains the house as a center of medieval studies.

In 1944 Dumbarton Oaks gained world-wide renown as the setting for an international meeting which led to the founding of the United Nations. Open free, Tuesday through Sunday, 2 p.m. to 5 p.m.

From Dumbarton Oaks, R St. leads west about two blocks to an intersection with Wisconsin Ave., on which, about a half-mile northwest, is the entrance to the

U.S. Naval Observatory, one of the finest astronomical facilities in the world. Open free Monday through Friday; conducted tours at 2 p.m. Night tours are available the week before each full moon, on Tuesday, Wednesday, and Thursday, 8 p.m. to 9 p.m.

From the Observatory, Wisconsin Ave. climbs to the crest of Mount Saint Alban, the highest point of natural land in Washington. Just beyond 36th Pl. on Wisconsin Ave. is the main entrance to

Washington National Cathedral, officially the Cathedral Church of St. Peter and St. Paul, a great Gothic cathedral that, when completed, will rank among the ten largest churches in the world.

Under construction since 1907, the Protestant Episcopal cathedral is expected to be completed sometime within the next ten or twelve years. Much of it, including the soaring central nave and two transepts extending from it, is already completed. The stained-glass rose windows in the transepts are regarded as some of the finest in the world.

Famous Americans buried in the cathedral include Woodrow Wilson, Admiral Dewey, and Cordell Hull. President Eisenhower's funeral took place here. Tours every day, 9 a.m. to 4:30 p.m.; after 11 a.m. on Sunday.

The eastern limit of the Georgetown area is

Rock Creek Park. The largest park in Washington, it covers more than 1,800 wooded acres. The park takes its name from Rock Creek, which flows through the center. The creek bed is very rugged, strewn with gigantic fragments of rock, and its steep bank is heavily wooded. Rock Creek Parkway threads the whole park, and there are more than 30 miles of bridle paths, dozens of foot trails, and two nine-hole golf courses. The most popular facility is the

Washington Zoo, officially the National Zoological Park, with about 3,000 animals. The bird house is notable. The zoo is open free daily from daylight to dark.

Among widely separated points of interest in northeast and east Washington the following are noteworthy:

National Shrine of the Immaculate Conception, largest Roman Catholic church in the country, dedicated in 1959. One of the world's great basilicas, its striking design is a combination of Romanesque and Byzantine styles. It is crowned by a dome faced with brightly colored tiles and a cross that rises 235 feet above the ground. The shrine is associated with the Catholic University of America, one of the most important Catholic educational centers in the country. CU's extensive campus is adjacent to the shrine.

About three miles southeast of the shrine is the

National Arboretum, on the east bank of the Anacostia River, with an entrance from Maryland Ave. at M St., N.E. The arboretum is threaded with roads and foot trails, and has an experimental forest and the biggest collection of azaleas in the country. Associated with the arboretum, across the river, are the remarkable

Kenilworth Aquatic Gardens, with an entrance from Douglas St., off Kenilworth Ave. Approximately 14 acres of ponds are planted with some of the most colorful displays of water lilies, lotus, iris, and sub-aquatic plants in the world.

The National Park Service recommends that the tourist visit the gardens as early in the day as possible since water plants tend to close their blooms as the day advances. Best blooming seasons are mid-June and late July or early August.

Forlorn in its abandonment, many a crumbling homestead portrays the courage necessary for those who settled the American frontiers.

WEST VIRGINIA.

WEST VIRGINIA is remarkable for several things: its immensely rugged character, with wild, steep-sloped, forested mountain ranges; its irregular shape; its origin as a state, having split off from Virginia during the Civil War; its huge mineral wealth, particularly coal and natural gas; and the abject poverty of some of its remote mountain communities.

Within its irregular boundaries, West Virginia covers 24,181 square miles; it is 41st in size in the country. It is 245 miles north to south, 275 miles east to west. Mountain ranges fill the whole eastern two-thirds of the state, with some crests rising almost 5,000 feet above narrow valleys cut with ravines and gorges. From the mountains, three rivers flow in three directions. The Kanawha flows northwest into the Ohio River, which forms the northwest border of the state; the Monongahela flows north into Pennsylvania, becoming part of the Ohio River at Pittsburgh; and the Potomac flows east to Washington, D.C., forming West Virginia's irregular northeast border.

Very little of West Virginia is worth farming. The only farms of any size are in the Ohio River valley and in the western part of the state. Small farms produce fruit, sheep, poultry, and subsistence crops. Forests, covering 60 percent of the state, are an important commercial resource.

WEST VIRGINIA FACTS

Name. So named during the Civil War when Virginia's western counties rejected secession and were admitted to the Union.

Nickname. Mountain State.

Area. 24,181 square miles, 41st in the United States.

Population. 1,791,000, 1969 estimate, 30th in the United States.

Admitted as a state. 1863, following secession from Virginia, 35th state.

Capital and largest city. Charleston, population 82,000.

State tree. Sugar maple.

State flower. Rhododendron.

State bird. Cardinal.

Industry. Bituminous coal, 30 percent of United States production; natural gas, leads the country; chemicals, glass, pottery, steel.

Agriculture. Small farms producing subsistence crops, apples, peaches, tobacco.

Odds and Ends. Site of Harpers Ferry National Historical Park, where abolitionist John Brown staged his famous raid; some of the oldest mineral spring spas in the country, and the first salt well west of the Alleghenies.

Most of the state's wealth derives from vast mineral resources—coal, natural gas, and salt—in which it surpasses all other states in the East. A huge industrial concentration around Charleston turns out plastics, glass, and chemicals. Other areas specialize in steel and pottery.

Though the first settlement of West Virginia occurred in the eastern panhandle in 1726, substantial settlement awaited completion of roads through the mountains, particularly the National Road to Wheeling, opened in 1818. The first census, taken after the Civil War, gave West Virginia a population of about 450,000. It is now estimated at about 1.8 million.

Not on main routes of travel and isolated by its mountainous character, West Virginia can claim few important events of history. One exception occurred at Harpers Ferry, on the edge of the eastern panhandle. There, just before the Civil War, the firebrand abolitionist John Brown seized a federal arsenal in an attempt to arm the slaves. The event helped trigger the Civil War. The site is now being restored as a national memorial.

West Virginia has no large cities. The largest is the capital, Charleston, and the second largest is Huntington, both relatively close together in the western part of the state. The third largest is Wheeling, in the northern panhandle, on the Ohio River. There are no cities of any size in the mountains, though the valleys are studded with tiny, often desolate villages.

West Virginia's highway pattern is irregular. Main roads follow the river valleys, except in the east and southeast, where they twist through the mountains. Interstate highways converge at Charleston. North-south Interstate 77 becomes West Virginia's only toll road, south of Charleston. Interstate 64, slowly extending northwest across the state from White Sulphur Springs, has been completed between Charleston and Huntington. Interstate 79 will eventually link Charleston with Clarksburg, extend north to Pittsburgh. The chief east-west route is US 60, extending from Huntington and Charleston over the mountains to White Sulphur Springs.

Many of the mountain districts of West Virginia are highly scenic, but visitors will find that facilities are limited and frequently inaccessible.

In the text that follows points of interest

are indicated by number on the maps on pages 138-139 and 140-141 and described in associated text, starting in the west with

1. HUNTINGTON, population 80,000, one of the most attractive and best planned of West Virginia's larger cities. Huntington has a commanding setting on the south bank of the Ohio River, a few miles east of the Kentucky border. Two main highways, Interstate 64 and US 60, lead through it east and west. US 52 leads south along the western edge of the state.

Founded in 1871, Huntington is named for Collis P. Huntington, president of the Chesapeake & Ohio Railroad. The C & O is still one of Huntington's largest industries. The city is an important shipping point for coal, which is barged down the Ohio River. The International Nickel Co. has a large refinery and rolling mill in Huntington. Points of interest in the city include

Huntington Galleries, 3065 Eighth Street Rd., at the crest of Park Hills. Both a museum and a producing craft center, it has wide-ranging collections of paintings, prints, firearms, pottery, and tapestry. Open free, Tuesday through Saturday, 11 a.m. to 5 p.m.; Sunday, 1 p.m. to 5 p.m.

Two plants producing fine glass in or near Huntington are worth visiting. One is the

Rainbow Art Glass Co., where visitors can watch craftsmen blowing colored glass. Rainbow's glass is widely used in churches. A more famous glass factory is 14 miles east of Huntington in the village of Milton, the

Blenko Glass Co. A wide variety of glass products, including stained glass, is exhibited in a visitor center. One can buy glass here, and watch the glass blowers from an observation gallery. The factory is open free Monday through Saturday, 8 a.m. to 5 p.m.; Sunday, noon to 5 p.m.

About 50 miles east of Huntington on Interstate 64 is

2. CHARLESTON, population 82,000. On the north bank of the Kanawha River, Charleston dominates the river valley, which extends several miles in either direction. Sometimes called the Miracle Valley, it is one of the world's largest districts for the production of industrial chemicals, glass,

natural gas, and coal. Huge, modern plants line the banks of the river. Charleston is the center of the largest gas field in the East.

One of the oldest settled communities in West Virginia, Charleston was founded in 1794. An early resident was Daniel Boone, who served as a member of the Virginia legislature. The town remained relatively small and unimportant until about 1825, when the development of salt deposits began.

Charleston became the capital of West Virginia in 1885. During the First World War the manufacture of explosives became an important industry, which is now centered in a suburb of Charleston called Nitro. The enormous development of other chemical resources came after the war.

Charleston's main point of interest for visitors is the

State Capitol, within handsomely landscaped grounds facing the Kanawha River a few blocks east of the downtown area. Huge and ornate in the classic Italian Renaissance style, the capitol is generally regarded as one of the most beautiful in the country, the masterpiece of the architect Cass Gilbert. Completed in 1932, it has a spectacular gold and blue dome rising 300 feet.

From the interior of the dome, hanging 180 feet above the central rotunda, is a spectacular rock crystal chandelier made of more than 6,000 pieces. The capitol is open free Monday through Saturday, 9 a.m. to 5 p.m.; Sunday, 1 p.m. to 5 p.m. Guided tours are available.

From Charleston two main highways lead south and east into the mountains. One is the

West Virginia Turnpike, a toll road that cost more than $133 million. It extends south 88 miles into and through the mountains to the coal mining town of Princeton, and is occasionally dubbed "the toll road that leads nowhere" since its southern terminus links with no important highway. The turnpike will eventually meet Interstate 77 leading north from Charleston and south into Virginia. The drive is pleasant and highly scenic, but there are no developed recreation areas close to the highway. The only community of importance on the toll road is

Beckley, population 17,000, in a mining district that calls itself the Smokeless Coal Capital of the World. Many small mining and farming towns are nearby. A point of interest in Beckley is the

Beckley Exhibition Coal Mine, on N. Oakwood Ave., in New River Park. An old mine used to demonstrate mining equipment, it is open Monday through Saturday, 10 a.m. to 5 p.m., Sunday, noon to 7 p.m. between May 1 and October 31. (Admission: adults $1, children 35¢.)

The second important east-west highway leading through Charleston is US 60, which twists southeast through the mountains for about 90 miles to the border of Virginia. At its eastern end US 60 merges with the developing route of Interstate 64. A completed section of Interstate 64 leads through

3. WHITE SULPHUR SPRINGS, population 2,700, altitude 1,923, an attractive little city on the Greenbrier River, one of the oldest communities in West Virginia. It was settled in 1750 because of nearby mineral springs which were said to have curative properties. The most famous was White Sulphur Spring, which became the center for a growing resort area that drew people from all parts of the East and Europe.

A famous hotel called Old White was built near the spring. In 1913 it was replaced by the splendid

The Greenbrier in White Sulphur Springs is surrounded by a 6,500-acre estate, the perfect setting for golf, tennis, horseback riding, and other resort activities.

Greenbrier Hotel, one of the great resorts of the country. The Greenbrier dominates the whole White Sulphur Springs region. The 6,500 acres of grounds and many historic buildings are worth seeing. The original White Sulphur Spring is supplemented by an extensive diagnostic center. The first golf course in the country was laid out in 1884 in the nearby village of Oakhurst.

About 30 miles south of the Pennsylvania border, at the junction of US 19, Interstate 79, and US 50, is

4. CLARKSBURG, population 25,000, altitude 1,007, established in 1773, chief community in an industrial district producing glass, coal, and natural gas. Clarksburg was the birthplace of Gen. Thomas J. "Stonewall" Jackson, one of the great military leaders of the Confederacy. His home, which stood at 326 W. Main St., is marked by a bronze plate. There is a statue of Jackson at the northeast corner of the courthouse square.

About 12 miles east of Clarksburg, just south of US 50, is

Tygart Lake State Park, a wooded, rugged tract of about 1,800 acres around Tygart Lake. The lake has a 70-mile shoreline; fishing and boating are available.

About 40 miles northwest of Clarksburg is West Virginia's curious northern panhandle, which extends 60 miles north between Ohio on the west and Pennsylvania on the east, ranging in width from five to 15 miles. The Ohio River forms the western edge. In the center of the panhandle is

5. WHEELING, population 48,000, strategically located on the east bank of the Ohio River. A relatively old city, Wheeling was established in 1769 by two brothers, Ebenezer and Silas Zane. Fort Henry, site of present-day Wheeling, was the setting for the last battle of the American Revolution, in September 1782. The site is marked by a monument in the center of town.

There is little of special interest for visitors in Wheeling. The city is an industrial center, particularly for steel. Most visitors now pass through on Interstate 70 or the parallel route of US 40. Until the recent completion of Interstate 70, Wheeling was a serious traffic bottleneck dreaded by motorists. North of Wheeling is

Oglebay Park, two miles northeast on West Virginia 88. Handsomely landscaped, the park has about 1,200 acres, extensive gardens and greenhouses, and many recreational facilities, including golf, boating, and winter sports. Historic Mansion House in the park has period rooms furnished to suggest the history of the area from 1835 to the present. The house is open Monday through Saturday from 9 a.m. to 8 p.m. during July and August, rest of the year until 5 p.m. (Admission: adults $1, children free.)

West Virginia's eastern panhandle is a mountainous, rugged, picturesque area. Its northern border is the Potomac River. At the extreme eastern corner of the panhandle, just west of the Virginia border, is

6. HARPERS FERRY, population 600, one of the most dramatically picturesque villages in the East, in the heart of a rugged, scenic area where three states, West Virginia, Maryland, and Virginia, and two rivers, the Shenandoah and Potomac, come together in a scenic gorge.

Harpers Ferry, less than 60 miles northwest of Washington, has been a strategic spot for more than 200 years. In 1747 the ferry was built which gave the city its name. George Washington surveyed the area, and Thomas Jefferson, standing on a crest named for him, described the view as "one of the most stupendous scenes in nature." Soon after the end of the Revolutionary War the United States government built an arsenal at Harpers Ferry. Then the Chesapeake and Ohio Canal was built through the mountain pass on the Maryland side of the Potomac River. The abandoned route is visible today.

The next event made Harpers Ferry famous. During the night of October 16, 1859, John Brown, the fanatical Kansas abolitionist, with 18 followers, attacked and seized the arsenal in an attempt to arm slaves for rebellion. John Brown and his band locked themselves in the armory to prepare for a siege. The next day marines from Washington, commanded by Col. Robert E. Lee and Lt. J. E. B. Stuart, stormed the arsenal and killed ten of John Brown's men, including two of his sons. John Brown and six of his followers were promptly tried for treason and hanged within a few days at nearby Charles Town.

During the Civil War Harpers Ferry, regarded by both sides as a key to the city of Washington, was repeatedly fought over.

This peaceful setting with its quaint covered bridge and pleasant shade trees was the scene on June 3, 1861, of the first land battle of the Civil War.

Beautiful throughout the year is Blackwater Falls, in Blackwater Falls State Park, which tumbles 60 feet to begin its twisting journey through the rugged Blackwater Canyon.

During the Antietam campaign in 1862, Stonewall Jackson destroyed most of the village in a terrific bombardment, capturing more than 12,000 prisoners. The town changed hands at least eight times during the war. At war's end it was a ghost town.

In 1963 Harpers Ferry became a National Historical Park, with 1,500 acres in West Virginia and Maryland within the gorge of the rivers and on the surrounding heights. Restoration of Harpers Ferry is expected to take several years.

The only satisfactory way to fully explore the park is to walk, stopping first at the Visitor Center on Shenandoah St., where one can get a map and study the exhibits. The center is open free daily from March through October; closed rest of the year. A marked walking tour of a little more than half a mile covers most places of interest. The tour starts with the

Master Armorer's House Museum, on the site of the old armory. Relics connected with the violent history of Harpers Ferry are exhibited.

Next the tour leads off Shenandoah St. under a railroad trestle to

The Point, a scenic promontory thrusting between three states and two rivers. Back in town on Potomac St. at Old Arsenal Square is John Brown's Fort, the brick engine house where Brown and his men took refuge, and where those not killed were captured.

The tour then leads along several streets in the old town, passing houses built before 1859. Several are now restored. One open to visitors is

Harper House, off High St., built between 1775 and 1782 by the town's founder. It is furnished in mid-19th century style, and adjoins a handsome garden. House and garden are open free daily, 10 a.m. to 5 p.m., mid-June to Labor Day; rest of the year on weekends by appointment.

On High St., but not within the historical park, is the

John Brown Wax Museum, privately owned, housed in a building more than 115 years old. Open daily, April through November, closed rest of the year. (Admission: adults 65¢, children 35¢.)

At the crest of a hill above High St. is the scenic overlook called

Jefferson Rock, where, in 1783, Thomas Jefferson stood, and called the view of the gorge one of the most stupendous in nature.

About seven miles southwest of Harpers Ferry on US 340 is

Charles Town, population 3,300, county seat of Jefferson County. Charles Town (often confused with Charleston, the capital of West Virginia), one of the oldest towns in the state, was laid out in 1786 by Charles Washington, George Washington's brother, and named for him. Many streets are named for members of his family. Charles Town's greatest claim to fame is that it was the setting for the trial and hanging of John Brown. The trial occurred in the

Jefferson County Courthouse, at the corner of George and Washington streets, a handsome red brick building built in 1836. The gallows site is nearby, at the corner of Samuel and Hunter streets, marked by a pyramid of stones. A tablet on the post office wall marks the site of the jail where Brown was imprisoned prior to his trial.

Worth seeing in Charles Town are some fine old houses, none of them open to the public, built between 1820 and 1850.

Charles Town Race Course and Shenandoah Downs are both east of town on US 340. About 30 miles northwest of Charles Town, linked to it by West Virginia 9, is

Berkeley Springs, population 1,100. In a picturesque mountain setting on the south bank of the Potomac River, Berkeley Springs is said to be the oldest health spa in the country. George Washington bathed in the springs while surveying the area in 1748. The town, originally called Bath, after the English resort, reached the height of its fame after the Revolutionary War. The springs, which flow 2,000 gallons a minute at a constant temperature of 74 degrees, are still in use. A modern bathhouse near the center of town is open year-round.

Nine miles south of Berkeley Springs on US 522 is

Cacapon State Park, a tract of almost 6,000 acres, including the crest of wooded Cacapon Mountain, 2,300 feet high, reached by a gravel road. Park facilities include cabins and a lodge, fishing, swimming, and boating in a six-acre lake, horseback riding and tennis.

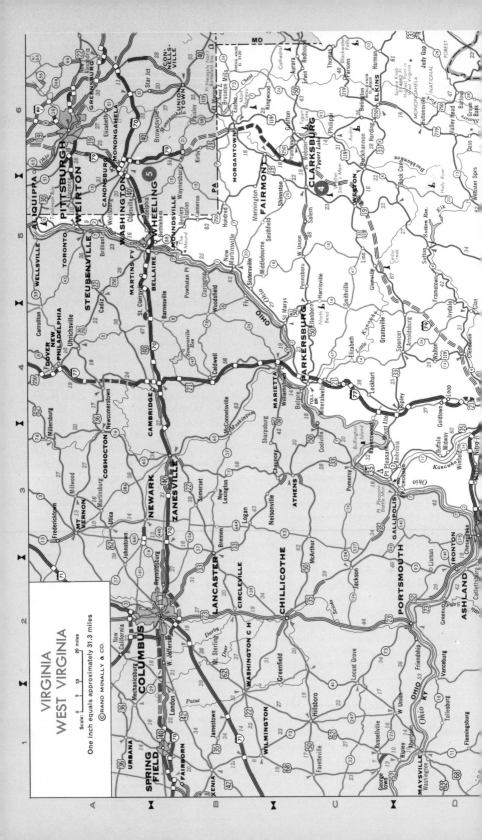

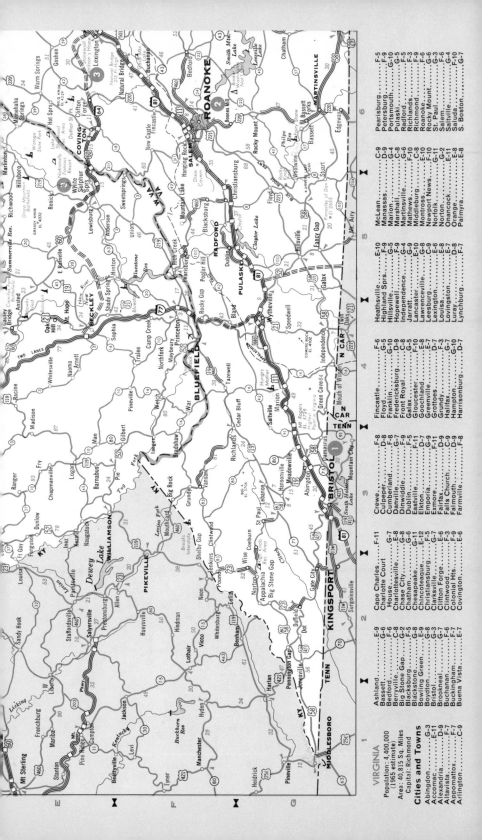

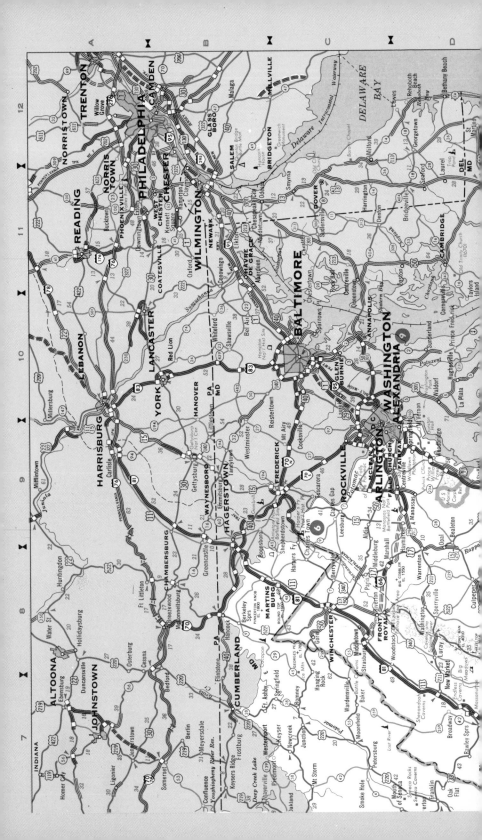

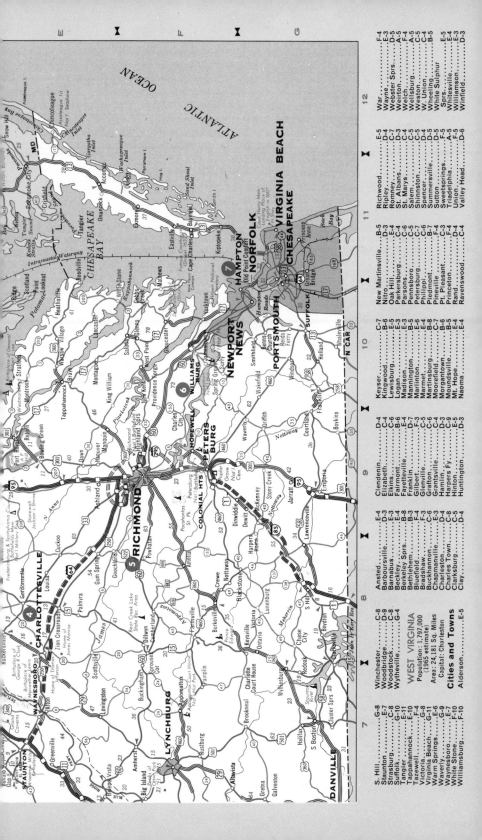

Thomas Jefferson designed and began to build Monticello in Charlottesville in 1768. No other house in America so completely reflects its builder's ingenuity as does this one.

VIRGINIA.

VIRGINIA claims the first legislative assembly in the western world, the first public Thanksgiving celebration, the first whiskey distilled in the New World, the first slaves brought to work on plantation land, the first president of the United States (who would be followed by seven other Virginia presidents), the first oil well, the first iron works, and the first college fraternity.

The state was once many times greater than it is now. It is shaped like a rough triangle, 425 miles east to west and 200 miles north to south. It is bordered on the east by the Atlantic Ocean, on the northeast by Maryland and the District of Columbia, on the northwest and west by West Virginia, and on the southwest by Tennessee and North Carolina. Few states have more neighbors.

Within its present limits Virginia has 40,817 square miles, of which nearly 2,365 square miles are water, making it 36th in size among the states.

Virginia's diverse topography begins in the east with a slender finger of land on the east side of Chesapeake Bay, an almost orphan area called the Eastern Shore. Beyond Chesapeake Bay is the main body of the state. Virginia's four famous rivers create a series of irregular land fingers that form the historic Tidewater region. The rivers from north to south are: the Potomac, the Rappahannock, the York, and the James.

West of the Tidewater, which has most of Virginia's famous mansions and historic homes, is the Piedmont Plateau, a heavily cultivated region, Virginia's most productive farmland. West of the Piedmont begins the rolling, partially wooded foothills of Virginia's historic mountains. The most famous are the lovely Blue Ridge Mountains, named for the blue haze that almost always envelops the forested slopes. Behind the Blue Ridge is a valley variously called the Valley of Virginia or the Shenandoah Valley, with the Shenandoah River flowing north through it, to join the Potomac. The valley is one of Virginia's most famous agricultural regions, renowned for apples. West of the valley rise the more rugged, tumbled slopes and crests of the Appalachian ranges. Here are primitive, isolated areas and much of an important resource, coal.

Virginia began as a part of a business deal, when, an enormous and completely unknown region, it was granted to the London Company by Queen Elizabeth. In 1606 the company sent an expedition to colonize the new land, which was called Virginia, after Elizabeth, the Virgin Queen. The grant was vague and included all of the land in the New World north of the Spanish settlements. In time, huge chunks of the original grant were ceded to other areas.

The colonists came ashore on the north bank of the James River on May 17, 1607, and so established Jamestown, the first English colony in the New World. After a difficult start, Jamestown began to develop as a successful community. It accounted for many Virginia firsts, including the first slaves, the first tobacco, the first glass. The whole Tidewater area grew up around Jamestown. Great plantations were based on the hugely profitable tobacco crop.

Virginia's most important contribution to the Revolutionary War was its leader, George Washington. The war ended in Virginia, when the British surrendered at Yorktown.

Virginia was the chief battleground of the Civil War. Bitter contests were fought in many parts of the state. Richmond was the capital of the Confederacy, and several of the South's greatest military leaders were Virginians. This war too ended in Virginia, at the farm village of Appomattox, in April, 1865, and Virginia returned to the Union.

In the meantime, a considerable area of Virginia had become a new state, now called West Virginia, a cluster of mountain counties that had refused to join the Confederacy.

Though the scars left by the Civil War are still visible, Virginia has long since recovered. It has become prosperous again, both in agriculture and industry. Its 16 million acres of farms, none large in the West-

ern sense, grow a diversity of products. Virginia ranks high in tobacco, apples, sweet potatoes, and peanuts. A famous Virginia farm product is ham, produced from peanut-fed pigs.

Virginia ranks high in lumber and wood products, chemicals, processed foods, textiles, and ships. A third type of product is seafood, for which some Virginia communities are famous. The state's most important mineral product is coal, mined in the western mountains.

Virginia's cities are chiefly in two areas, along the eastern tidal rivers and in the Shenandoah Valley. The state's largest city is Norfolk, with a population of 300,000. The next largest is Richmond, the capital, with 221,000. Norfolk is the central community of a cluster of cities around the great harbor of Hampton Roads, with a total population of about a million. Only 30 cities in the state exceed 10,000 in population. In addition to the coastal area, a chain of cities stretches up the Shenandoah Valley between mountain ranges. Of these, Roanoke, the largest, has about 99,000 people. Many of Virginia's cities grew from colonial towns and have historic associations that draw thousands of visitors, particularly Williamsburg and Fredericksburg.

Virginia communities are linked by a network of excellent highways, including several important Interstate routes. The whole eastern portion of the state is served by Interstate 95, which links Washington with Richmond. The Valley of Virginia is served by Interstate 81. An east-west Interstate route which will be under development for several years is Interstate 64. It will eventually link Richmond with Charleston, the capital of West Virginia. Other main highways from east to west include US 13, threading the Eastern Shore, tunneling under and hopping over the mouth of Chesapeake Bay into Norfolk. To the west is US 17. US 301 roughly flanks Interstate 95, as does historic US 1, which Interstate 95 has almost replaced as a main route of travel. Main east-west routes include US 50 in the north, US 60 through the center of the state, and US 58 along the southern edge.

Points of interest in Virginia are indicated on the maps on pages 138-139 and 140-141 by numbers, and described after those numbers in associated text. Secondary places of interest are described following numbered points.

VIRGINIA FACTS

Name. For Elizabeth I, the Virgin Queen.

Nickname. Old Dominion State.

Area. 40,817 square miles, 36th in the United States.

Population. 4,648,000, 1969 estimate, 14th in the United States.

Admitted as a state. 1788, 10th among the 13 colonies, seceded in 1861, readmitted in 1870.

Capital. Richmond.

Largest City. Norfolk, 300,000.

State flower. American dogwood.

State bird. Cardinal.

Industry. Shipbuilding, textiles, cigarettes, wood products (including furniture, paper), coal mining, commercial fishing.

Agriculture. Tobacco, apples and other fruits, peanuts.

Odds and Ends. Jamestown, 1607, was the first settled area in the colonies. Virginia was the scene of the first representative legislature; was the birthplace of eight presidents; was the scene of General Lee's surrender to General Grant, which ended the Civil War; and has more historic shrines, homes, and battlefields than any other state.

---

1. BRISTOL, population 16,200, but actually much larger, since the larger part of the city, population about 20,000, is in Tennessee. Now essentially an industrial community, Bristol began in 1771 as a frontier outpost. It is a hub of main highways, with Interstate 81 coming in from the northeast intersecting US 58, which extends west to the sharp southwestern tip of Virginia. Nearby is

South Holston Lake, created by a TVA dam in the Holston River about six miles southeast of Bristol. The lake, 25 miles long, with a shoreline of 168 miles, is surrounded by wooded hills. It offers fishing, boating, camping, and swimming.

About 15 miles northeast of Bristol, off Interstate 81, is the famous community of

Abingdon, population 4,700, altitude 2,057, a summer resort and Virginia's largest burley tobacco market. It is better known as a craft center, and sponsors an arts and crafts festival each summer. Factories produce fabrics, china, and furniture. Abingdon's most celebrated institution is the

Barter Theatre, which started during the Depression, when a gifted entrepreneur named Robert Porterfield persuaded a group of Broadway actors to move to the community and accept their pay in locally grown and packaged foods. The Barter has since become the state theater of Virginia, open from mid-April to mid-October, Tuesday through Saturday, performances at 8:15 p.m., Sunday at 7 p.m. Matinees are Wednesday at 2 p.m., Saturday at 5 p.m. (Admission: $3.50, matinees $3.)

About 90 miles west of Bristol on US 58, in the heart of a scenic area, is

Cumberland Gap National Historical Park, a tract of about 20,000 mountain acres in Virginia, Tennessee, and Kentucky, which preserves the historic Wilderness Road. Daniel Boone led a group of hunters and trappers through the Gap in 1769, and in 1775 blazed the Wilderness Road. Until 1775 the Alleghenies had barred westward migration. The Gap, now threaded by US 58 and a rail line, crosses the mountains at an elevation of 1,700 feet. In the visitor center near the Middlesboro entrance in Kentucky is a museum with exhibits that tell the story of the route. The park has excellent campgrounds and picnic areas. Trails lead to a number of scenic overlooks.

From Bristol, Interstate 81 and the parallel route of US 11 lead about 140 miles northeast to

2. **ROANOKE,** population 99,000, largest community in western Virginia. Though settled as early as 1740, Roanoke was a wilderness outpost until the establishment of the Norfolk and Western Railway, for which it is the headquarters. Now an industrial center and a hub of main highways, Roanoke is a convenient base for visiting several worthwhile sights and facilities. The most famous is the

Blue Ridge Parkway, a unique and beautiful mountain boulevard that stretches about 473 miles along the ridge of the mountains, with an entrance six miles east of Roanoke on US 460.

The parkway links the Shenandoah National Park in northern Virginia with the Smoky Mountains National Park in North Carolina. Beautifully engineered, it twists and turns along the crests of mountains ranging from 2,000 to 6,000 feet high. 215 miles of the parkway are in Virginia, the rest in North Carolina. The parkway bypasses all towns. Police vigorously enforce a speed limit of 45 miles per hour. At various points there are facilities for dining, camping, and picnicking (limited accommo-

dations). Visitor centers along the way interpret typical aspects of the mountain region and issue helpful maps. Mabry Mill Visitor Center has a restored waterpowered gristmill that grinds cornmeal and buckwheat flour, a blacksmith shop, sawmill, and still, open May through October.

The parkway as a whole is open year-round, but winter driving can be hazardous, and some sections are closed completely in winter.

A place of historic interest easily reached from Roanoke is

Booker T. Washington National Monument, reached by Virginia 116 south from Roanoke 18 miles, then Virginia 122 east six miles. The monument covers a little more than 200 acres, approximately the area of the original Burroughs plantation, where Booker T. Washington was born a slave in 1856 and where he spent about ten years of his childhood. Freed in 1865, he left the plantation with his family. Later he was to become one of the most famous members of his race. He was the founder of Tuskegee Institute in Alabama, which trains Negroes in business, trades, and professions. The monument includes a replica of the log cabin where Washington was born. A visitor center provides information on Washing-

The beauty of winter along the Blue Ridge Parkway is missed by the traveler because the parkway is closed to traffic during the winter months.

ton's life and a map of a self-guiding trail.

About 30 miles northeast of Roanoke on Interstate 81 is Virginia's most celebrated natural oddity:

Natural Bridge, a limestone arch spanning a gorge, one of the seven natural wonders of the world. It is 215 feet high, 90 feet long, and varies in width from 50 to 150 feet. Across the arch runs US 11.

Famous since colonial days, Natural Bridge and the gorge it spans were bought by Thomas Jefferson in 1774 for 20 shillings. Later Jefferson established facilities for visitors, who soon flocked to see this odd creation of nature. Over the years a somewhat honky-tonk collection of establishments has grown up around Natural Bridge.

About 13 miles north of Natural Bridge on US 11, at the intersection with US 60, is

3. **LEXINGTON,** population 8,500, one of the most attractive and interesting towns in

Natural Bridge near Lexington towers 215 feet high, 90 feet in length. Carved by a mountain stream over countless centuries, it is one of the seven wonders of the world.

the Shenandoah Valley. Lexington was established in 1777 as a frontier town in the foothills of the mountains, and it developed as a trading center for a rich agricultural district. It has become famous because of its association with two of the great leaders of the Confederacy, Stonewall Jackson, who lived here for many years, and Robert E. Lee, who lived here after the Civil War.

Lexington has several places of interest for visitors. The Visitor Center at 401 S. Main St. has maps of a self-guiding tour of the town. Washington and Lee University, with an extensive and beautiful campus on W. Washington St., has handsome Colonial buildings. The university has about 1,400 students, all men, and was founded in 1749. It flourished after George Washington endowed it in 1782, when it was called Washington Academy. Closed during the Civil War, it reopened after the war with Gen. Robert E. Lee as president, a position he held until his death in 1870, when the name was changed to Washington and Lee University. Of high interest on campus is the

Lee Chapel, containing the Lee family tomb and a famous reclining figure of Robert E. Lee. Lee and several members of his family are buried here, including his father, "Light Horse Harry" Lee. There are portraits of Washington and Lafayette and the art collections of both the Washington and Lee families. An unusual exhibit is Lee's office, maintained just as he used it. Open free daily, 9 a.m. to 4 p.m.

Near the center of town, off US 11, is the campus of

Virginia Military Institute (VMI), founded in 1839 as a state engineering and arts college. Students have included some of the greatest military leaders of the South. Stonewall Jackson was a member of the faculty. Gen. George C. Marshall, Army Chief of Staff during the Second World War, was a VMI graduate. A point of special interest on the campus is the George C. Marshall Research Library, completed in 1964, at the west end of the parade ground. It houses many of Marshall's personal and official papers. There is also a museum with an electric map telling the story of World War II, and an exhibit relating to the Marshall Plan, developed when Marshall was Secretary of State. The library is open Monday through Saturday, 9 a.m. to 5 p.m.;

Sunday, 1 p.m. to 5 p.m. (Admission: adults 50¢, children free.) An exhibit in Lexington relating to Stonewall Jackson is the

Stonewall Jackson Memorial, 8 E. Washington St., one block east of Main St. The only home Jackson ever owned, it is furnished with his possessions and contains relics of his life. Open free daily, 9 a.m. to 5 p.m. Jackson is buried in a small cemetery on the east side of Main St., along with other Confederate soldiers.

From Lexington US 60 leads west through the mountains 45 miles to Covington. Here US 60 intersects US 220, leading north through a beautiful valley. In that valley, 15 miles north of the junction, is a chain of historic thermal springs, Healing Springs, Hot Springs, and Warm Springs, popular spas since Colonial days. The most important is now Hot Springs, central feature of

The Homestead, at an elevation of 2,195 feet, a 17,000-acre estate, one of the most famous luxury resorts in the country. The Homestead controls two springs, maintains three championship golf courses and private trout fishing streams, and offers almost every conceivable activity from skiing on Warm Spring Mountain to trap shooting. The Homestead has more than 500 rooms and suites in the main hotel and additional facilities in a celebrated Colonial inn at Healing Springs, just north.

About 40 miles southeast of Lexington, 22 miles on US 60, then 18 miles south on US 29, is

Lynchburg, population 55,000, in the eastern foothills of the Blue Ridge Mountains, on the James River. Lynchburg has been a tobacco center since the founder, John Lynch, built the first tobacco warehouse in the country here about 1790. It is the home of several small colleges. The best known is Randolph-Macon Woman's College, with about 900 students and a handsome campus overlooking the river. Lynchburg itself played a very small part in the Civil War; however, it is the closest town to

Appomattox Court House National Historical Park, about 15 miles east of Lynchburg on US 460. Here, on April 9, 1865, Gen. Robert E. Lee surrendered his army to Gen. Ulysses Grant. The famous meeting occurred in the parlor of the Mc-Lean House, where generous surrender terms were offered by Grant. Visitors should go first to the restored courthouse, now a visitor center, with an excellent museum and an audiovisual slide program that tells the story of the surrender and events leading to it. One exhibit is a familiar but inaccurate painting showing the surrender meeting. A self-guiding tour starts from the courthouse. The most important stop on the tour is the historic McLean House, carefully reconstructed to its presumed appearance at the time the surrender occurred. (Admission: $1.) Several village buildings, including a country store, a law office, and the county jail, have been well restored and are worth seeing. A point of historic interest just east of the courthouse is the Surrender Triangle, the place where about 30,000 Confederate soldiers stacked their arms following the surrender. The park is open daily from 8:30 a.m. to 5 p.m., September through June; until 7 p.m. during summer months.

About 35 miles northeast of Lexington on Interstate 81 and the parallel route of US 11 is

Staunton, population 25,000, altitude 1,382. A prosperous, handsome city, Staunton is a manufacturing and trading center for a rich agricultural district. Settled in 1736, it is one of the oldest towns in the valley. Visitors find interest in one house:

Birthplace of Woodrow Wilson. A handsome, three-story Colonial house where Wilson was born, in 1856. It contains much of the Wilson family furniture and possessions. There is a pleasant garden in the rear. The house is open from 9 a.m. to 5 p.m. (Admission: adults $1, children 35¢.)

From Staunton US 250 leads 35 miles east through the mountains and the town of Waynesboro, crosses the crest of the Blue Ridge Mountains and drops down the eastern slopes to historic

4. CHARLOTTESVILLE, population 39,000. In the eastern foothills of the Blue Ridge Mountains, Charlottesville is the seat of Albemarle County, famed for fine homes and estates scattered through the hills nearby, for horse breeding and fox hunting, and for fruit orchards, including the renowned Albemarle pippin apple.

But more than anything else it is famous because of one man who was born nearby and lived in the county most of his life. He had a hand in planning or developing most of the things which make Charlottesville so fascinating. The man was Thomas Jefferson. At the crest of a high hill just east of Charlottesville Jefferson designed and built Monticello, the remarkable mansion that was his home for many years. On the western edge of Charlottesville Jefferson designed the buildings of the University of Virginia, some of the most beautiful and admired college buildings in the country.

Routes To and Through. Charlottesville can be bypassed on either the north or south. US 29 and US 250 loop around the main business district to the north, US 29 continuing north and US 250 east. Interstate 64 completely bypasses the city on the south. The main street through the town is also US 250.

Monticello is three miles southeast of downtown Charlottesville on Virginia 53. The name of the extraordinary house means "little mountain" in Italian. It stands at the crest of one of the highest hills in the area, 857 feet above sea level, and commands spectacular views in all directions, including a clear view of Charlottesville and the campus of the University of Virginia to the northwest. Jefferson was 25 years old in 1768 when he decided to build Monticello, on land inherited from his father. He cleared a flat area at the top of the hill. The lower slopes were heavily forested, and still are. Building continued until 1809. Jefferson supervised every stage of the planning and building. Special architectural features in the design, a classic adaptation of Greek and Roman styles, include a flat octagonal dome rising above the east and west porticos, framed by Doric columns. The whole effect is one of striking beauty and perfect symmetry. The house is flanked on either side by L-shaped promenades that lead to smaller houses. One served as a honeymoon cottage for Jefferson and his bride while the main house was being built. The promenades also link with rows of service quarters, including kitchens, ice house, carriage house, and stable. More than 650 acres of grounds surround the house; the central sections are beautifully landscaped.

For most visitors the fascination of Monticello is not so much the exterior beauty of the house and grounds, but the interior, distinguished by beauty of woodwork and decoration. Monticello is filled with evidence of Jefferson's ingenuity. He loved gadgets and invented many: dumbwaiters, disappearing beds, unusual lighting effects, special folding doors, and a huge, extraordinary clock with weights and pulleys that disappear in the walls and tell the day of the week by their position. No other house in America so completely reflects the taste, talents, and character of its owner as Monticello, the home of one of the few geniuses this country has produced.

The house and gardens are open daily, March through October from 8 a.m. to 5 p.m.; November through February to 4:30 p.m. (Admission: adults $1.25, children 50¢.)

Many visitors to Monticello also stop at

Ash Lawn, on Virginia 53, about two miles southeast of the entrance to Monticello. The house, which takes its name from great ash trees on the long front lawn, was the home of James Monroe, a neighbor and close friend of Jefferson, and president of the United States from 1817 to 1825. Jefferson designed the house, but it was not completed as originally planned. Now, adequately restored and furnished with many of Monroe's possessions, Ash Lawn is open daily from 7 a.m. to 7 p.m. (Admission: adults $1, children 50¢.)

Next on the tourist's list should be the

University of Virginia, on the west side of Charlottesville. The plan which Jefferson made for the university was to be an adaptation of the English system of colleges, where a small group of students live in close association with a member of the faculty, who serves both as proctor and teacher. Jefferson designed an imposing Rotunda at the north end of a central terraced quadrangle, flanking about 100 smaller buildings in four parallel lines, separated by lawns and gardens. The architectural style was classical Roman. Dominating the whole is the striking and beautiful Rotunda, an adaptation of the Pantheon in Rome. The whole superb complex is now maintained as Jefferson originally planned it, as university and home for about 40 students. Many of the student rooms are still in use. Edgar Allan Poe and Woodrow Wilson lived here. Dozens of serpentine brick walls frame the gardens and drives leading to the central lawn.

New buildings have been built in harmony with the original classic design, with the exception of an architectural tragedy,

Curving brick walls serve as frames for the many gardens and drives leading to the central lawn on the campus of the University of Virginia, Charlottesville.

northeast of the Rotunda, called **The Brooks Museum.** Built in 1877, it is an example of the worst period of Victorian design.

The best way to see the university is to take one of the free tours offered during the school year, starting from the Rotunda at 11 a.m., 2 p.m., and 4 p.m.

From Charlottesville, US 250 and the partially completed route of Interstate 64 parallel each other, extending southeast about 60 miles to

5. **RICHMOND,** population 221,000. At the head of navigation on the James River, Richmond spreads over a cluster of hills. The capital of Virginia since 1779, Richmond is now a prosperous center for manufacturing and commerce. It has several big cigarette factories. Captain John Smith noted the site of Richmond as early as 1607, the same year Jamestown was founded. In 1644, after an Indian massacre, a frontier fort was erected. William Byrd, whose vast holdings in Virginia included the site of Richmond, set aside an area which was named Richmond in 1742. It remained little more than a village until 1779, when the capital was moved from Williamsburg to Richmond. Richmond then began to grow steadily, was the most important city in Virginia when the Civil War started, and became the capital of the Confederacy. During the tense four years of the war, the city was in constant peril. Seven different drives against Richmond were launched by Union forces. Twice, in 1862 and 1864, Union forces came dangerously close to capturing the city.

As the end of the war came near as a result of the siege of Petersburg to the south, General Lee abandoned Richmond and led his exhausted army southwest to final defeat and surrender at Appomattox Court House, but not before setting fire to Richmond warehouses full of supplies. The fire spread, destroying much of the city. Fortunately, many historic buildings were spared.

Following the Civil War, Richmond slowly regained population and prosperity, and has in recent years enjoyed a solid boom in industry and manufacture.

Routes To and Through. North-south Interstate 95 links near the center of the city with Interstate 64. Other main routes include north-south US 1, east-west US 60.

Points of Interest—City Center.

It is almost impossible to get around here except on foot. A good place to start is

Capitol Square, a beautifully landscaped, 12-acre slope framed by 9th and 12th streets and Capitol and Bank streets, with winding walks and huge old trees. Dominating the square is the

State Capitol, superbly set at the crest of Capitol Hill, facing southwest toward the James River. The capitol, classic in design, is generally regarded as one of the most beautiful in the country. Its design, an adaptation of the Maison Carrée, a Roman temple at Nimes, France, was suggested by Thomas Jefferson. The central building was completed about 1788. The building is famous as the place where the world's oldest continuous English-speaking legislative body still meets.

The capitol's most famous feature is in the rotunda, a superb white marble statue of George Washington by Jean Antoine Houdon. The capitol is open free Monday to Friday, 8:15 a.m. to 5 p.m.; Saturday and holidays, 9 a.m. to 5 p.m.; Sunday, 1:30 p.m. to 5:30 p.m.

Among the many statues and monuments scattered over the grounds of Capitol Square the most famous and imposing is the

Washington Monument, at the northwest corner of the square, generally regarded as Richmond's finest sculptural group. The central figure of the 60-foot-high bronze monument is an equestrian statue of George Washington, flanked by figures of famous Virginians. The sculptor was Thomas Crawford.

At the northeast corner of the square, not open to the public except during Garden Week (last week in April), is the

Governor's Mansion, a two-story, Federal-style brick house, painted white, with a Doric portico, completed in 1813. It has been the home of Virginia governors ever since.

Facing Capitol Square, at Ninth and Grace streets, is

St. Paul's Episcopal Church. Completed in 1845, it became known as the Church of the Confederacy. Jefferson Davis and Rob-

George Washington, *by Jean Antoine Houdon, stands in the rotunda of the state capitol in Richmond. It is the only statue of the first president made while he lived.*

ert E. Lee regularly attended services here. A notable feature is a Lee memorial window.

Three historic houses are within easy walking distance of Capitol Square. The most celebrated is the

Confederate Museum, at 12th and Clay streets, also known as the White House of the Confederacy, since it was the residence of Jefferson Davis during the Civil War. It is crowded with exhibits relating to the Civil War, including paintings, documents, weapons, uniforms, battle flags, and the sword and uniform worn by Lee when he surrendered. Open Monday through Saturday from 9 a.m. to 5 p.m.; Sunday, 2 p.m. to 5 p.m. (Admission: adults 50¢, children 25¢.)

About a block north of the Confederate Museum, on Clay St., is the

Valentine Museum, 1015 E. Clay St., a handsome mansion completed in 1812, a fine example of the Federal period, with a spiral stairway, exhibits of period furniture, costumes and various collections relating to Virginia and Richmond history. Open Monday through Saturday, 10 a.m. to 5 p.m.; Sunday, 2:30 p.m. to 5 p.m. (Admission: adults $1; students over 12, 25¢; under 12 free.)

A third historic house, about three blocks west of the Valentine Museum and one block south, is the

John Marshall House, 818 E. Marshall St., a fairly simple house built in 1789 from designs made by Chief Justice John Marshall, who lived here for many years. Many of Marshall's furniture, books, papers, and pictures are exhibited. Open Monday through Saturday from 10 a.m. to 5 p.m.; Sunday, 2 p.m. to 5 p.m. (Admission: adults 75¢, children free.)

Several points of interest in Richmond are close together on North Blvd., about two miles northwest of the downtown area. They include

Battle Abbey, headquarters for the Virginia Historical Society, at 428 North Blvd., corner of Kensington Ave. Surrounded by beautiful gardens, the Abbey is a windowless building of white marble housing a collection of manuscripts, Civil War records, uniforms, portraits, and weapons. It is particularly noted for a series of splendid murals of Civil War battles. The Abbey is open Monday through Friday, 9 a.m. to 5 p.m.; Saturday and Sunday after 2 p.m. (Admission: adults 50¢, children free.) Just south of Battle Abbey is the

Virginia Museum of Fine Arts, at the corner of Grove Ave. and North Blvd., with wide-ranging collections of paintings, jewelry, prints, and decorative arts. A famous exhibit is a collection of the Crown Jewels of Russia and Russian Easter eggs. Open from mid-September to mid-June, Tuesday through Saturday, 1 p.m. to 5 p.m., and 8 p.m. to 10 p.m.; rest of the year, 11 a.m. to 5 p.m. (Admission: weekdays adults 50¢, children free; Saturday and Sunday no admission charge.)

Monument Ave., a continuation of Franklin St. in the business section, extends several miles to the outskirts of the city. One

The Richmond home of sculptor Edward V. Valentine, now a museum, is elegantly furnished with pieces from the 18th and 19th centuries.

of the handsomest streets in America, with a landscaped central strip, it derives its name from the statues placed at important intersections. The most famous is the Lee Monument, at Allen Ave. Others include monuments to J. E. B. Stuart, Jefferson Davis, Stonewall Jackson, and Matthew Maury. For many years a section of Monument Ave. was Richmond's most fashionable residential district.

Richmond's East Side, once a pleasant residential area, now rather shabby and rundown, has several points of historic interest. The most famous is

St. John's Episcopal Church, at 24th and Broad streets, at the crest of Church Hill. One of the oldest churches in Richmond, built in 1741, it is a simple white frame building with a three-tiered square tower.

Here, on March 20, 1775, during a meeting of the Second Virginia Convention, Patrick Henry made his famous "Liberty or Death" speech. In the graveyard of St. John's are buried many famous Virginians, including George Wythe, the country's first professor of law, and Elizabeth Poe, mother of Edgar Allan Poe. A few blocks southwest of St. John's Church is the

Edgar Allan Poe Museum, at 1914 E. Main St., a tiny gray stone cottage built in 1686, the oldest house in Richmond. Poe lived in Richmond for about 26 years. Next to the museum is a delightful, old-fashioned garden, and a carriage house with displays of drawings inspired by Poe's poem, "The Raven." The house itself has many of Poe's possessions and belongings. Open Tuesday through Saturday, 10 a.m. to 4:30 p.m.; Sunday and Monday, 1:30 p.m. to 4:30 p.m. (Admission: adults $1, children 25¢.)

About 70 houses built before 1861 in the Church Hill district around St. John's Church are being restored. Many will be open to the public.

Two miles south of St. John's Church, Broad St. becomes Government Rd., then Williamsburg Rd., which angles sharply east. At the angle is

Chimborazo Park, at the crest of a promontory overlooking an industrial district along the James River. During the Civil War the park was the site of a military hospital, said to have been the largest in the world. Now it is a part of the

Richmond National Battlefield Park, with a visitor center and a museum at 3215 E. Broad St., on US 60. The museum has information and exhibits relating to the seven attempts by Union forces to seize Richmond during the Civil War. A self-guiding tour map to the battlefields is available.

From Richmond, Interstate 95, a toll road, and the parallel route of US 1 lead south 23 miles to

Petersburg, population 38,000, on the Appomattox River, a brisk commercial center with factories producing cigarettes, optical equipment, and luggage. Petersburg is also a peanut market.

Petersburg's part in the Civil War was strategic: it controlled the Confederate supply lines into Richmond. When Grant failed to take Richmond in the summer of 1864, he decided to move south and cut the supply lines through Petersburg. The siege lasted for ten months, and resulted in the collapse of Lee's army. History is re-created in

Petersburg National Battlefield, with about 100 miles of well-preserved earthworks, both Union and Confederate. At the Visitor Center, off Virginia 36, about two miles east of Petersburg, is a "war room" with a map and audiovisual exhibits. A self-guiding route leads to historic points:

Patrick Henry gave his famous "Give me liberty or give me death" speech in St. John's Church. Built in 1741, it is the oldest church in Richmond.

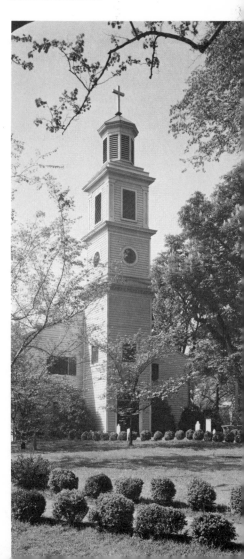

1. Battery 5, where Grant installed "The Dictator," the 17,000-pound mortar with which he shelled Petersburg. A replica of the mortar is displayed.

2. Fort Stedman, where Lee's last attempt to break the siege failed.

3. The Crater, where Union troops tunneled under Confederate lines and exploded four tons of powder, creating a hole 107 feet long, 60 feet wide, and 30 feet deep.

A famous memorial, about midway between Petersburg and the Crater, at 319 S. Crater Rd., is

Old Blandford Church, built in 1735. Since the Civil War the church has become a memorial to the Confederacy, with 15 Tiffany stained glass windows dedicated to the Southern states. The cemetery contains the graves of 30,000 Confederate soldiers. The church is open free May through October, 10 a.m. to 4:30 p.m., Monday through Saturday; Sunday from 3 p.m. to 5:30 p.m.; closed rest of the year.

From Richmond three highways lead southeast between the James and York rivers to Williamsburg, Yorktown, and Jamestown, and the complex of communities that surround the great harbor of Hampton Roads. The three highways are US 60, the developing route of Interstate 64, and, about eight miles to the south, closely following the James River, Virginia 5, the historic river road that links famous plantations on the river. If the motorist is not in a hurry to reach Williamsburg, traveling that route is worthwhile. He can stop at several of the

James River Plantations. All the plantations have entrances from Virginia 5, though most of the houses face the river. In the order in which they are met proceeding east from Richmond on Virginia 5, they are

Shirley Plantation, one of the largest of the Tidewater mansions, built between 1720 and 1740. Its architectural charm is marred by 19th-century additions. The house has been owned for many generations by members of Virginia's celebrated Carter family, one of whom married the father of Robert E. Lee. The grounds and first floor are open to visitors. Notable features are the superbly paneled walls and an unusual hanging staircase, family portraits, and silver. Open daily, 9 a.m. to 5 p.m. (Admission: adults $1.50, children 60¢.)

About three miles farther east on Virginia 5 is

Berkeley, home of two presidents, William Henry Harrison and Benjamin Harrison. The first Thanksgiving is said to have been held

"Shirley," on a plantation owned and operated by the same family since 1660, is one of the largest of the 18th-century mansions on the lower James River in Virginia.

on the grounds in 1619. At about the same time the first whiskey distilled in the United States was made at Berkeley by an English preacher. During the Civil War it was a headquarters for General McClellan. The house has been restored and furnished with pieces typical of the period of its use. House and grounds are open daily from 8 a.m. to 5 p.m. (Admission: adults $1.50, children 75¢.)

About a mile beyond Berkeley a road leads off Virginia 5 to

Westover, built around 1730 by William Byrd II, founder of Richmond. The house, one of the most elegant of the great plantation homes, is not open to visitors, but you can tour the grounds, see one of the finest boxwood gardens in Virginia. Open daily from 9 a.m. to 5 p.m. (Admission: adults $1, children free.)

Virginia 5 leads east to

6. **WILLIAMSBURG,** population 11,000, which includes a modern community and the Historic Area, generally referred to as Colonial Williamsburg, a reconstruction of the colonial capital of Virginia between 1699 and 1780. Since the restoration began, more than 40 years ago, Williamsburg has drawn nearly 20 million visitors. More than a million a year flock to it now.

Routes To and Through. The highway pattern of Williamsburg is fairly complex. US 60 bypasses the center of town on the north, but from it US 60Z diverges southeast into the heart of town. At the west end of the Historic Area US 60Z is joined by Virginia 31, called the Jamestown Road, leading southwest to Jamestown. Various routes into and skirting the city intersect with the Colonial Parkway, linking Jamestown and Yorktown.

The story of Williamsburg goes back to the early years of the 17th century. Its settlement and development derived in part from an Indian massacre at Jamestown in 1622, which drove settlers to higher ground in the center of the peninsula. About 1633 the colonists erected a palisade across the narrow peninsula to protect themselves from Indians. A few scattered homes, an inn, two mills, a blacksmith shop, and a church were built, all within the area called Middle Plantation. In 1693 Middle Plantation was chosen as the site for a free school and

college which became known as the College of William and Mary, the second oldest college in the country. In 1698 the State House at Jamestown was destroyed by fire. A year later the legislators voted to move the capital to the higher ground of Middle Plantation, which they named Williamsburg, in honor of William III, reigning king of England.

Williamsburg in the 18th century ranked with Boston, Philadelphia, and New York as a city of charm and elegance. The man most responsible for this was Governor Francis Nicholson. He laid out a broad central avenue 99 feet wide, named it Duke of Gloucester Street. At one end were the grounds of the College of William and Mary and at the other end was the capitol. Two parallel streets, Nicholson and Francis, preserved the governor's name. He planned the new community as a "green country town" with every house allotted at least half an acre of land. Intersecting the main east-west streets was the Palace Green, which led to the gardened grounds around the Governor's Palace. Thanks to the College of William and Mary, Williamsburg was an important educational center. Many leaders of the Colonial era were students, including Thomas Jefferson. One of its great teachers was George Wythe, the country's first professor of law.

Williamsburg also became the setting for great events. At the handsome capitol the Virginia General Assembly met for almost 75 years. Here, over the years, the principles of democracy and freedom that were to be expressed in the Declaration of Independence and the Constitution slowly evolved. Here Patrick Henry made his famous speech defying the Stamp Act of England.

But the stirring days ended in 1780 when, for reasons of convenience and safety, the capital was moved to Richmond. Williamsburg became a sleepy college town. Many of its great and handsome buildings were destroyed by fire or vandalism. Others fell into disuse, or were disfigured by tasteless false fronts and additions.

Williamsburg's modern life began in 1926, when the Reverend W. A. R. Goodwin exhibited the quiet community to John D. Rockefeller, Jr., and persuaded him that Williamsburg was worth preserving and restoring.

Now an exhibition building in Colonial Williamsburg, the colonial capitol has been carefully reconstructed to its appearance of the early 1700s.

Colonial Williamsburg has been developing ever since. About $81 million has been spent on restoration and reconstruction. The Historic Area now covers about 170 acres, and extends a mile in length from the Wren Building of the College of William and Mary to the capitol. Eighty-five of Williamsburg's 18th-century houses, shops, taverns, and public buildings have been restored to their original condition. In addition 50 important buildings and a number of small structures have been rebuilt on original sites after careful archaeological, architectural, and historical research. They include the two most important buildings of Williamsburg, the Governor's Palace and the capitol. More than 90 acres of gardens and greens have been restored to their 18th-century character.

The collection of furniture, pictures, art, and accessories with which the buildings are equipped constitute the most outstanding collection of English and American antiques in the country, ranging from the simplest kitchen and farm tools to the most elegant pieces in the Governor's Palace. In all, there are more than 200 furnished exhibition rooms in 45 separate buildings. Williamsburg's gardens have been called the greatest gardens of the western world. No two

are alike. About a hundred are open to the public, from simple kitchen gardens to the splendid formal gardens of the Palace. Another element of high appeal is the growing number of craft shops including an apothecary, bakery, blacksmith, bookbinder, bootmaker, cabinetmaker, clockmaker, gunsmith, and silversmith.

Information centers, free bus transportation, costumed guides, convenient parking areas, fine restaurants, and excellent accommodations combine to make a trip to Williamsburg enjoyable. First stop by the

Information Center, Virginia 132 and the Colonial Parkway. Here you can purchase tickets and plan your tour, obtain a very complete official guidebook and detailed map, see an orientation film, and begin the free bus ride that leads to all parts of the restored area.

Though a number of the main streets of the Historic Area are barred to automobile traffic, it is possible to make a reasonably satisfactory tour using your own car. There are several parking areas, most of them close to points of interest. The recommended procedure, however, is to park your car near the Information Center, hop in the free bus, and make a complete circuit of the

Historic Area, The bus makes 15 stops. This will give you a good idea of what you might want to go back to.

Many places of interest, such as Bruton Parish Church, the craft shops, and several notable restaurants, are not classified as exhibition buildings, but are very much worth seeing.

The Motor House, near the Information Center, has 314 rooms, a big cafeteria, and a handsome restaurant called the Cascades.

In the following text, buildings of special interest are described in three groups. All buildings are within easy walking distance of each other. We begin with

The Capitol, east end of Duke of Gloucester Street. Architecturally distinctive, it is designed in the shape of the letter "H," with rounded ends, and set on landscaped grounds. The style is basically Georgian. The present building is a reconstruction of the original 1705 capitol destroyed by fire in 1747. Each Saturday evening the capitol is exhibited by candlelight.

Just east of the capitol, across Waller St., is one of Williamsburg's most interesting restaurants:

Christiana Campbell's Tavern, famous during Colonial days for fine food, and a favorite gathering place for legislators. The menu features dishes popular during the Colonial period.

North of the capitol, across Nicholson St., is the

Public Gaol. Stocks and pillories in front of the building are a favorite with photographers. Prisoners ranged from obscure debtors to famous pirates, including 15 of Blackbeard's men. The jail also served as a madhouse and a military prison.

Duke of Gloucester Street extends west from the capitol to the College of William and Mary. It was the main street of 18th-century Williamsburg and is the community's widest and most famous street today. Three important buildings along it are about two blocks east of the capitol. On the north side is

Raleigh Tavern, a white frame building with 31 dormer windows. Built about 1740, it was the most famous inn in Colonial Williamsburg.

Across the street is

Wetherburn's Tavern, which opened around 1738, has been in continuous use for more than 200 years, as a private home, a tavern, a store, a boardinghouse, and a girls' school. The bedrooms, kitchens, dining rooms, and the original gardens behind the inn have all been restored. On the same side of the street, opposite Raleigh Tavern, is another of Williamsburg's notable restaurants, the

King's Arms Tavern, a favorite restaurant of colonial days. Its menu also features dishes popular during the Colonial period.

A second group of Williamsburg buildings, just south of the Historic Area, is the

Craft House Group. This includes the Craft House itself, the luxurious Williamsburg Inn, Williamsburg Conference Center, and the Williamsburg Lodge.

Especially popular with most visitors to Williamsburg is the

Craft House, where many reproductions of Williamsburg antiques are on sale, including furniture, glass, silver, pewter, china, fabrics, wallpaper, lighting fixtures, all faithful copies of items in the Colonial Williamsburg collection. There are also associated collections of paintings, books, and needlework. The Craft House has mail order catalogues available. Immediately south of Craft House is the

Abby Aldrich Rockefeller Folk Art Collection, a comprehensive collection of American folk art assembled by the late Mrs. John D. Rockefeller, Jr. Probably the most notable collection of its type in the country, it displays about 1,500 examples of American folk art. It is open free.

Of the three major groups of exhibits described in this text, the following, in the northwest section, is probably the most splendid and interesting. It is the

Palace Green Area, including the Governor's Palace, the big, handsomely landscaped Palace Green, and several important houses that flank the Green, as well as historic Bruton Parish Church. They are described separately, starting with

Bruton Parish Church, at the northwest corner of Duke of Gloucester Street and Palace Green. The present building, one of great charm and high architectural interest, was completed about 1715 and has been in continuous use as a church ever since. The original parish which the church served was established in 1674. It was the church's rector, the Reverend Goodwin, who interested John D. Rockefeller, Jr., in the restoration of Colonial Williamsburg. The church is in regular use today, the bell in the tower still summoning the congregation to attendance. The building is open daily from 10 a.m. to 5 p.m. Special candlelight concerts are given each Tuesday and Saturday at 8 p.m.

On the west side of Palace Green, a short distance north of the Bruton Parish Church, is one of the finest private dwellings in Colonial Williamsburg, the

Wythe House, for many years the home of one of Williamsburg's most famous residents, George Wythe, built about 1775 by Richard Taliaferro, one of the best architects in Williamsburg. Taliaferro left the house in 1775 to his son-in-law, George Wythe, the first professor of law in America and the teacher of such famous Americans as Thomas Jefferson, John Marshall, and Henry Clay. Wythe was a signer of the Declaration of Independence and an active delegate to the Constitutional Convention. The house was Washington's headquarters before the siege of Yorktown. It has been beautifully restored, and the adjoining gardens form a plantation in miniature.

One block north of the Wythe House is

The Governor's Palace, facing the Palace Green from the north behind ornate entrance gates, easily the most elegant building in Williamsburg. The original palace, completed in 1720, was designed in classic Georgian style. It dominated very extensive gardens stretching behind it and on either side, the largest and most interesting of all the many gardens of Williamsburg. The original Palace building was destroyed by fire in 1781. Thomas Jefferson helped plan the reconstruction. The sumptuous furnishings, nearly all antiques

The beauty and fascination of the ten acres of gardens at the Governor's Palace in Colonial Williamsburg may be enjoyed the year round.

acquired in England, closely follow inventories for the original Palace.

The only exhibition not within the restored area is the

Wren Building, on the campus of the College of William and Mary, west end of Duke of Gloucester Street. The oldest academic building in continuous use in English-speaking America, it is also the only building in America believed to have been designed by Christopher Wren, for whom it is named. It was also the first of the Williamsburg buildings to be restored by Mr. Rockefeller. Several rooms, including the chapel, are open to the public from 9 a.m. to 5 p.m. The College of William and Mary claims several collegiate firsts: the first use of the honor system, the first School of Law, and the first Phi Beta Kappa Fraternity.

Combination tickets which you can buy at the Information Center admit you to all exhibit buildings. Adults $4.50, students and military $2, children 7 to 11 $1, under 7 free. A family admission plan offers tickets for large families for a $12 maximum charge.

Williamsburg is a convenient base for visiting several historic places nearby. The nearest is

Carter's Grove, a James River plantation six miles southeast of Williamsburg on US 60, managed by Colonial Williamsburg. The great 20-room house stands at the crest of a bluff overlooking the James River. The 400-acre estate is part of an original 1,400-acre tract bought by Robert "King" Carter, who at his death is said to have owned 300,000 acres of land and 1,000 slaves. The house, superbly restored and refurnished, is open 10 a.m. to 5 p.m., March through November; closed rest of the year. (Admission: adults $1.75, children free.)

Two places of high interest are reached from Williamsburg on the Colonial Parkway, which extends from the James River on the west, through Williamsburg, to the York River on the east. The most celebrated is

Jamestown Island, ten miles west on the Colonial Parkway. Now a part of Colonial National Historic Park, Jamestown is the site of the first permanent English settlement in North America. There, on May 13, 1607, 13 years before the Pilgrims landed

at Plymouth, Massachusetts, three ships brought about 140 settlers sent out by the London Company. At that time Jamestown was an island in the James River, so the site seemed a safe one for a colony. It proved to be not only unsafe but extraordinarily unhealthy. Colonists died like flies from disease and were massacred by Indians. Two years after the settlement began only 60 settlers out of 500 survived, following a winter of starvation. Notwithstanding hardships and calamities the colony grew slowly. By 1622, it had about 1,250 members. Tobacco made the colony prosper, and became so popular and valuable that it was grown in the streets and in the graveyards. Two famous Jamestown citizens were the redoubtable Captain John Smith, who is alleged to have escaped killing by the Indians through the intervention of Pocahontas, daughter of the chief, Powhatan. In 1614 Pocahontas married the second most important member of the colony, John Rolfe.

Jamestown continued to have its troubles. It became a royal colony in 1624 under a British governor whose high-handed methods so provoked the colonists that in 1676 they revolted, and later burned the town. It was partially rebuilt, but in 1698 the State House burned and the government decided that Jamestown was not a fit place for the capital of the growing colony. It was moved to Williamsburg, and almost immediately Jamestown began to decline. At the beginning of the Civil War it had almost completely disappeared. Only ruins of old buildings were left.

The obvious beginning to any exploration of Jamestown Island is the

Visitor Center, open daily, where the story of Jamestown is dramatically recreated by models, dioramas, and relics. Additional places of interest on Jamestown Island include the

Old Church Tower, the only standing ruin of the original 17th-century town. The tower is all that is left of the first brick church, begun in 1639 and in use until about 1750. Foundations of an earlier church are visible. There Pocahontas was married and the first legislative assembly in North America met. Nearby are three monuments: a statue of John Smith, a statue of Pocahontas, and a towering Tercentenary Monument, erected in 1907 to commemorate the 300th anniversary of the founding of Jamestown. None of the original houses and buildings of Jamestown has been restored and probably never will be. But many foundations have been uncovered through recent excavations. In the excavated area are markers and paintings that re-create the buildings. Not a reconstruction, but a reproduction of a Jamestown industry, the first glassmaking factory, is the

Glass House, where appropriately costumed workers demonstrate their glassblowing skill.

Not connected with the park, but quite close to it, is the recently developed

Jamestown Festival Park, built in 1957. Exhibits include reconstructions of a fort and several houses. Two pavilions show the achievements of early settlers and examples of Old World culture which they hoped to transplant in North America. Full-scale copies of the three vessels, *Susan Constant, Godspeed,* and *Discovery,* which brought the settlers to Jamestown in 1607, are afloat in the James River and can be boarded. Festival Park is open daily, 9 a.m. to 5:30 p.m., June through Labor Day; rest of the year to 5 p.m. (Admission: adults $1, children 25¢.)

Jamestown is the western terminus for the

Colonial Parkway, a 23-mile scenic boulevard maintained by the National Park Service linking Jamestown with Yorktown. Much of the route follows the shores of two famous rivers, the James in the west and the York in the east. Markers along the way explain historic events. At its eastern end, 13 miles southeast at Williamsburg, is

Yorktown, population 310. Yorktown faces the York River, which is spanned by a high bridge carrying US 17. Yorktown was settled in 1691 when the Virginia Assembly chose the site as an ocean port. It was soon a busy transfer point for the tobacco crop that was making planters rich throughout the Tidewater. In 1781 Cornwallis captured and fortified Yorktown as a base for the British fleet. Soon the French fleet, in close association with Washington, bottled up the British in Yorktown. American and French troops under Washington's command encircled the town on the land side and laid a siege which lasted about two weeks. On October 19 the British marched out and laid down their arms, and the Revolutionary War was over.

The picturesque town, with narrow streets climbing the bluff above the river,

The world's largest private shipyards are operated by the Newport News Shipbuilding and Dry Dock Company. Its huge docks serve the city's many industries.

has some fine old houses. Several bear scars of the 1781 siege. The battlefield surrounds the town. The Visitor Center on the southeast side of town offers movies, slides, and literature on Yorktown history, and a map for a self-guiding battlefield tour. On the edge of the battlefield is

Moore House, where the surrender terms were made, about one mile east of town at the end of Virginia 238.

From Williamsburg, three parallel main highways lead southeast down the center of the narrow peninsula between the James and York rivers to

7. HAMPTON ROADS, Virginia's great ocean harbor and the center of a cluster of communities that make up her largest urban concentration and most important commercial and industrial district. The communities that fringe the harbor are Newport News and Hampton at the tip of the peninsula, Norfolk and Virginia Beach to the east, facing the open ocean, and Portsmouth to the southeast. In Newport News is the country's largest shipbuilding yard, which turns out both naval and commercial craft. The largest naval base in the world is in Norfolk. Points of interest in the area are widely scattered, often buried in commercial and industrial districts. They are described in following text in relation to the communities where they occur, starting with

Newport News, population 138,000, essentially an industrial city. The world's largest private shipyards are operated by the Newport News Shipbuilding and Dry Dock Company. One of the world's largest railway yards is here. Its huge docks are used for shipping coal, tobacco, grain, and other products.

Newport News was one of the first communities in Virginia to be settled, in 1619, 12 years after the establishment of Jamestown. Its name has a curious origin. One of the ships that brought colonists and supplies to Jamestown had a captain named Christopher Newport. When his ship arrived it was "good news," and the landing place was called Newport News by happy colonists. The city is served by two main highways, US 17 and US 60. US 17, joined by US 258, leads west over the James River on a towering new toll bridge. The most interesting place in Newport News is the

Mariners Museum, just west of US 60 in an 880-acre park overlooking the James River. The museum's enormous collections include many ships' figureheads and ship models. There is a fine research library, with thousands of books and documents. The museum is open Monday through Saturday, 9 a.m. to 5 p.m.; Sunday, noon to 5 p.m. (Admission: adults 50¢, children 25¢.)

Also reached from US 60, southeast of the museum, is the

War Memorial Museum of Virginia, about one-half mile north of the James River Bridge on US 60, exhibiting weapons, uniforms, and other relics, chiefly from World Wars I and II. Open free Monday through Saturday, 9 a.m. to 5 p.m.; Sunday, 2 p.m. to 5 p.m. Though the docks and shipyards of Newport News are not generally open to visitors, glimpses of both can be seen by taking the Newport News Harbor Cruise. From June 15 through Labor Day cruises leave at 10 a.m., noon, 2 p.m., and 4 p.m. Twilight cruises nightly at 7:30 p.m. during July and August. The dock is at Jefferson Ave. and 12th St., in the southern end of the city. The cruise lasts an hour and a half. (Fare: adults $2, children $1.)

From Newport News, US 258 and US 60 lead east into

Hampton, population 122,000. Settled in 1610, Hampton claims to be the oldest continuously occupied English settlement in the New World. But its existence was threatened several times. It was attacked by pirates, shelled during the Revolutionary War, burned by the British in 1813, and burned again in 1861 by Confederates to keep it out of the hands of Union forces. Later during the Civil War it was a Union base. Hampton today is the largest center in Virginia for commercial fishing, with the emphasis on oysters. It is also an important military base. Langley Air Force Base, headquarters for the Tactical Air Command, just north of the city, is the site of NASA's Langley Research Center.

The chief point of interest is actually outside Hampton:

Fort Monroe, dominating a point of land southeast of the city proper, reached by US 258. Though an active military base, headquarters for the United States Continental Army Command, Fort Monroe is

MEN OF VIRGINIA

FEW STATES in the Union can top Virginia's list of famous men. A complete list would be far longer than the brief alphabetical one which follows.

George Rogers Clark (1752-1818). Born near Charlottesville. Revolutionary War general and conqueror of the Northwest Territory. Defeated the British in various engagements, including the capture of Vincennes, Indiana. Older brother of:

William Clark (1770-1838). Born in Caroline County. Appointed by President Thomas Jefferson as co-leader with Meriwether Lewis of the famed Lewis and Clark Expedition to the Pacific Northwest. Became governor of Missouri Territory and superintendent of Indian Affairs.

Patrick Henry (1736-1799). Born in Hanover County. Became a lawyer and Revolutionary patriot, famed for his eloquence. Some of his phrases, like: "If this be treason, make the most of it," and "Give me liberty, or give me death," are widely familiar. As governor of Virginia during the Revolutionary War, Henry sent George Rogers Clark to conquer the Northwest Territory. Two of his Virginia homes, Scotchtown, in Hanover County near Ashland, and Red Hill, at Brookneal, where he is buried, are historic shrines.

Thomas Jefferson (1743-1826). Born at Shadwell, near Charlottesville. He drafted the Declaration of Independence, was governor of Virginia and the third president of the United States, 1801 to 1809, during which time he negotiated the Louisiana Purchase and sent the Lewis and Clark Expedition to explore the newly acquired lands. A many-sided genius, Jefferson designed and built Monticello, his beautiful hilltop home, established the University of Virginia, and designed its first buildings. Impressive monuments to his memory are in Washington, D.C., and at Mount Rushmore in South Dakota. His grave is at Monticello.

Robert E. Lee (1807-1870). Born at Stratford Hall, the ancestral Lee family plantation in Westmoreland County. He became an officer in the United States Army; but refused command of the Union forces on the eve of the Civil War to lead the Confederate Army of Virginia. Following his surrender to Grant at Appomattox, Lee became president of Washington College (now Washington and Lee University) at Lexington, Virginia, where his grave is a national shrine.

open to visitors and very much worth seeing. Designed as a seven-pointed star, rising above a wide, deep moat, the picturesque old fort has through the years resisted all attacks. The present fort, completed in 1834, was held by Union forces throughout the Civil War, one of the few Southern forts not surrendered to the Confederacy. In 1862 the Confederate ironclad *Merrimac*, built in nearby shipyards, unsuccessfully attacked the fort and later became engaged with the Union ironclad *Monitor* in the middle of Hampton Roads. Areas of the fort are open free between 8 a.m. and 5 p.m. Of particular interest is the Casemate Museum, with the cell where Jefferson Davis was a prisoner two years, charged with plotting against Abraham Lincoln.

From Hampton, US 60 and Interstate 64 cross the wide channel between Hampton Roads and Chesapeake Bay by a combination of bridge and tunnel, south into

Norfolk, population 300,000, Virginia's largest and most complicated city. Norfolk began in 1682 when the General Assembly of Virginia, needing an ocean port, bought the site from a settler for 10,000 pounds of

Meriwether Lewis (1774-1809). Born near Charlottesville. He was a friend and neighbor of Thomas Jefferson, who as president made him his private secretary, and co-leader, with William Clark, of the Lewis and Clark Expedition.

James Madison (1751-1836). Born in Port Conway, King George County. He helped frame the Constitution and was fourth president of the United States, 1809 to 1817, during which time the War of 1812 was fought with England. Montpelier, Madison's plantation in Orange County, Virginia, where he is buried, is a national shrine.

John Marshall (1755-1835). Born in a log cabin in Fauquier County on the Virginia frontier, Marshall became one of the country's greatest jurists. As fourth chief justice of the Supreme Court, from 1801 to 1835, he established the court's influence and broadened its powers. His home in Richmond is a popular shrine.

James Monroe (1758-1831). Born in Westmoreland County. Governor of Virginia, fifth president of the United States, 1817 to 1825, during which time he purchased Florida from Spain and proclaimed the Monroe Doctrine. His two Virginia homes, Oak Hill in Loudon County and Ash Lawn in Albemarle County, and his law office in Fredericksburg, are historic shrines. Monroe is buried in Hollywood Cemetery in Richmond.

Booker T. Washington (1856-1915). Born a Negro slave in Franklin County, where his log-cabin birthplace is now a national shrine. Educated at Hampton Institute, Hampton, Virginia, Washington founded Tuskegee Institute in Alabama to train Negroes for meaningful careers. Gained fame as a botanist, agricultural innovator, public speaker, and writer.

George Washington (1732-1799). Born at Wakefield Plantation in Westmoreland County. Renowned both as a soldier and a statesman, Washington became the most famous of all Virginians. He led American troops throughout the Revolutionary War. First president of the United States, from 1789 to 1797, he chose the site of the capital and helped plan it. His Virginia home, Mount Vernon, is one of the most visited shrines in the country.

Thomas Woodrow Wilson (1856-1924). Born at Staunton, where his family home is a national shrine. Law graduate of the University of Virginia. Successively president of Princeton University, governor of New Jersey, 28th president of the United States, 1913 to 1921. Following the First World War, Wilson became the chief sponsor of the League of Nations. He is buried in the National Cathedral in Washington.

tobacco. By 1740 Norfolk was Virginia's largest community and one of the chief seaports in the colonies. At the beginning of the Revolutionary War Norfolk was shelled by British ships. Later the whole town was burned by American troops to prevent its capture. Only one building, St. Paul's Church, was left intact. In 1882 the Norfolk and Western Railroad brought the first carload of coal into the city for ocean shipment. Since that time Norfolk has become the most important coal-shipping port in the United States. It is also the world's largest naval base. Its port facilities, combined with

Newport News, make it the sixth largest seaport in the country.

Much of the older section of the city is being rebuilt. The handsome new Civic Center dominates the area. But Norfolk remains a difficult city to visit.

Routes To and Through. Norfolk is a hub of main highways converging from all directions, their routes controlled by the unusual geographic position of the city, with the James River and Chesapeake Bay merging just north in Hampton Roads. The open ocean is on the east, and the whole city is laced by channels from the sea and rivers flowing out of the Dismal Swamp to the south. Until the recent construction of bridges and tunnels over and under water areas, travel through Norfolk was difficult. But now through traffic moves quickly and easily, on Interstate 64, US 60, and US 17. US 13, coming down the Eastern Shore, enters Norfolk via a remarkable system of tunnels and bridges extending nearly 20 miles across the mouth of Chesapeake Bay. The toll is $4 for driver and car and 85¢ for each additional passenger.

Two parallel main highways lead east from the center of the city to link with the Norfolk-Virginia Beach Toll Road. Bridges and tunnels on the south edge of Norfolk link it with adjoining Portsmouth. The chief route is US 58, which tunnels under the Elizabeth River.

Points of interest in Norfolk are widely scattered. In the downtown area is the

General Douglas MacArthur Memorial, at City Hall Ave. and Bank St., in the former city hall, built in 1852. Souvenirs and relics of the life and achievements of General MacArthur are displayed. The MacArthur tomb is in the rotunda. A continuous film in an adjoining auditorium tells the story of the general's life. The memorial is open free, April 1 to Labor Day, Monday through Saturday, 10 a.m. to 5 p.m.; Sunday, 11 a.m. to 6 p.m.; rest of the year, noon to 5 p.m.

A short distance from the MacArthur Memorial, at the corner of St. Paul's Blvd. and City Hall Ave., is historic

St. Paul's Episcopal Church, the oldest public building in Norfolk. Built in 1739, it stands within a walled graveyard. One headstone is dated 1673. Modified Georgian in design, the ivy-covered old church is a building of great charm. Imbedded in one wall is a cannonball fired from a British warship during the Revolutionary War. St. Paul's is open daily from 10 a.m. to 4:30 p.m. A museum has relics of local history.

Northeast of St. Paul's, at the corner of Yarmouth St. and The Hague, is the

Norfolk Museum of Arts and Sciences, with collections of American glass, European and American paintings, and the natural history of Norfolk and the Tidewater area. Open free daily, noon to 5 p.m.

There are several things worth seeing in the northern section of the city, along and near the shore of Chesapeake Bay. The most famous is the

Norfolk Naval Base and Naval Air Station, east of Interstate 64 and US 60, with an entrance at Hampton and Admiral Taussig boulevards. The docks are usually lined with aircraft carriers, atomic submarines, and assorted fighting ships. A one-hour bus tour of the base leaves the main gate April 1 through Labor Day, starting at 10 a.m., and at approximately 45 minute intervals thereafter, until 2:30 p.m. (Fare: adults $1, children 50¢.)

Filling an extensive area just north of the Municipal Airport is the

Norfolk Botanical Gardens, also called Gardens-by-the-Sea. The displays are regarded as some of the finest in the East, particularly the azaleas, of which there are more than 250,000, camellias, flowering shrubs and trees. The garden covers more than 100 acres, and is threaded with canals. Special features include a Japanese garden and a fragrance garden for the blind. In addition to canal boat trips (Fare: 75¢, $1 in the evening) and miniature train rides (Fare: 50¢), there is a pirate ship which takes visitors to Treasure Island. The gardens are open free daily, sunrise to sunset.

US 60 leads east from the Naval Air Station along the shore of Chesapeake Bay to link Norfolk with Virginia Beach. About midway is the region's most historic house:

Adam Thoroughgood House, 1636 Parrish Rd., just south of the junction of US 60 with US 13. Called the oldest brick residence in the country, the tiny, charming house was built about 1640. Only 45 feet long and 22 feet wide, with a high pitched roof between massive chimneys, the house is a fine example of an early plantation house. Partially restored, with a small garden behind, it is open April 1 to Labor Day, 10 a.m. to 5 p.m.; noon to 5 p.m. rest of the year. (Admission: adults 50¢, children 25¢.)

From the Thoroughgood House, US 60 swings around a sandy point of land, historic

Cape Henry, where, on April 26, 1607, the first English settlers in America landed briefly before sailing on to Jamestown. The site is marked by a great stone cross. The Old Lighthouse, near the memorial, built in 1791, was the first lighthouse authorized in the United States. Nearby is another lighthouse, built in 1879, rising 157 feet, visible from 20 miles at sea.

From Cape Henry, US 60 extends south, closely following the Atlantic shore, to

Virginia Beach, population 149,000, Virginia's largest and most popular resort. It is linked with downtown Norfolk by US 58 and the Norfolk-Virginia Beach Toll Road. The district includes about 30 miles of Atlantic shoreline, two miles of concrete boardwalk, eight miles of public beach, and a full range of facilities, including opportunities for fishing and beach buggy rides. Proximity to Norfolk keeps most of these facilities constantly busy. There is a wide range of accommodations.

West of Norfolk, on the west bank of the Elizabeth River, is the last of the cluster of five cities that surround the great harbor of Hampton Roads and Chesapeake Bay:

Portsmouth, population 120,000, a satellite of Norfolk, to which it is linked by tunnels and bridges. From its beginning Portsmouth has been a naval and shipbuilding city. Its largest installation is the Norfolk Naval Shipyard, closely associated with the Naval Air Station in Norfolk. The yard has been building ships since 1767. One was the *Chesapeake,* sister ship of the *Constitution.* The *Merrimac* was built and launched here. The yard's drydock, still in use, was first opened in 1831. Also in Portsmouth is the oldest naval hospital in the country. Visitors with a high interest in naval history may want to visit the

Portsmouth Naval Shipyard Museum at 2 High St., overlooking the Elizabeth River. Ship models, uniforms, weapons, and flags are displayed. Open free, 10 a.m. to 5 p.m.; Sunday, 2 p.m. to 5 p.m.

Portsmouth's most historic church is

Trinity Episcopal, Court and High streets, built in 1762. There is an interesting Confederate memorial window. In the churchyard are graves of many prominent Virginians.

Portsmouth has fine old Colonial, Revolutionary, and pre-Civil War houses, some of them well restored. They are widely scattered, however. The Chamber of Commerce issues a walking tour of the older part of town where the houses are located.

From Norfolk US 13 leads northeast, linking the city with the Eastern Shore peninsula along the eastern side of Chesapeake Bay. The peninsula, referred to as the Eastern Shore or the Delmarva Peninsula, is shared by three states: Virginia in the south, Maryland and Delaware in the north. The Virginia end extends southwest from the Maryland border for about 70 miles, a slender finger of land no more than 15 miles wide at its widest point, its shore fringed by islands. The combination of Chesapeake Bay on the west and the open ocean on the east provides a unique opportunity for sport and commercial fishing. The only highway of importance on the peninsula is US 13. Along and near it are dozens of tiny, often primitive villages whose residents are dedicated to fishing.

The only place of interest on Virginia's Eastern Shore is

Chincoteague Island, a few miles south of the Maryland line, about ten miles east of US 13 on Virginia 175. One of the oldest settled places in Virginia, first established in 1662, the island, quaintly primitive in character, almost wholly devoted to fishing and oystering, has changed little in more than 100 years. Though Chincoteague's oysters are famous, more famous are their wild horses, believed to be descendants of horses that strayed from their owners during Colonial times, who have lived ever since in the nearby salt marshes. Many are no larger than a pony. A famous annual event is the Pony Penning, staged the last Wednesday and Thursday in July. The ponies are rounded up and forced to swim the channel to the village of Chincoteague, where they are auctioned. Those not sold return to their pastures.

About 50 miles north of Richmond on Interstate 95 is

8. FREDERICKSBURG, population 14,700, a prosperous manufacturing and trading center for a wide area. Its historic buildings, monuments, and battlefields go back to colonial days.

At the head of navigation of the Rappahannock River, Fredericksburg was once a busy ocean port, the fourth largest in the

Every July during Pony Penning Week, wild ponies from Chincoteague Island are forced to swim the channel to the village of Chincoteague, where they are auctioned.

country. During Colonial days and through the Revolutionary period, it was a strategic political and cultural center. Civil War battles surged around it. Few cities in Virginia have more historic houses and monuments, and none is a better center from which to understand the Civil War.

Fredericksburg is closely identified with George Washington and his family. He was born on a farm overlooking the Potomac some distance east, spent his boyhood just across the Rappahannock River from Fredericksburg, and attended school in Fredericksburg. His only sister, Betty, and his mother lived in Fredericksburg. Fredericksburg was also the home of President James Monroe. Points of interest start with

Mary Washington College, Women's Branch of the University of Virginia, on Marye's Heights at Sunken Rd. and Monroe St., northwest edge of the city. Named for George Washington's mother, the college was founded in 1908, and has about 2,000 students. The campus, with handsome Georgian buildings, spreads over rolling, wooded hills. Four blocks east, at the corner of Washington Ave. and Pitt St., is the

Grave of Mary Washington, who died in Fredericksburg in 1789, soon after her son became president. The grave is marked by a 50-foot obelisk.

Four blocks south of the monument, with an entrance from Amelia St., is the

Confederate Cemetery, a nostalgic graveyard with old trees and mossy tombstones enclosed by a brick wall. Buried here are 2,640 Confederate soldiers and officers who died on nearby battlefields. If you have driven this far, this would be a good place to park and make the rest of your tour on foot. Stop first at historic and beautiful

Kenmore, 1201 Washington Ave., just northeast of the Confederate Cemetery. The mansion, begun in 1752, was the home of Washington's sister, Betty, wife of Fielding Lewis. One of the finest Colonial homes in America, Kenmore is beautifully furnished. Some rooms have carved and molded woodwork and ceilings. Washington's sister and her family lived here more than 40 years. Her husband, Fielding Lewis, called the Gunsmith of the Revolution, supplied arms for his brother-in-law's troops. The house, with its spacious grounds, has a fine boxwood garden. There is a separate 18th-century kitchen where you'll be served tea and gingerbread. Kenmore is open daily, March to November, 9 a.m. to 5 p.m., rest of the year until 4:30 p.m. (Admission: adults $1, children 50¢.)

One block east, with an entrance on Prince Edward St., is

Stoner's Store Museum, 1202 Prince Edward St., an authentically furnished and equipped country store, stocked with food and accessories typical of 19th-century rural America. Open daily, 9 a.m. to 5 p.m. (Admission: adults $1, children free.) One block east is the

Mary Washington House, corner of Lewis and Charles streets, a Dutch Colonial cottage where Washington's mother lived from 1772 until her death in 1789. Washington visited his mother here many times. The house is authentically restored and has a charming English garden behind. House and garden are open daily, 9 a.m. to 5 p.m. March to November; rest of the year until 4:30 p.m. (Admission: adults 50¢, children 25¢.)

Two blocks east and a block and a half north is the

Rising Sun Tavern, 1306 Caroline St., built about 1760 by Charles Washington, brother of George. For many years the tavern was a stage stop and a social and political center. The tavern is open daily, 9 a.m. to 5 p.m. (Admission: adults 50¢, children 25¢.) About two blocks south on the same street is the

Hugh Mercer Apothecary Shop, at the corner of Caroline and Amelia streets, established in 1761 by Dr. Mercer, a friend of Washington. The shop displays pillboxes, carboys, bottles, and medical and surgical accessories used by Mercer, who served under Washington as a brigadier general during the Revolutionary War. The shop is open daily, 9 a.m. to 5 p.m. (Admission: adults 50¢, children 25¢.)

At the corner of William and Charles streets is the Old Slave Block, a circular stone block, three feet high, which served as a mounting block for ladies about to ride horseback and the place where slaves were exhibited for auction. Across the street is the

James Monroe Law Office, at 908 Charles St., a low brick building set in handsome Colonial gardens, little changed since Monroe practiced law there between 1786 and 1790. In it are furnishings Monroe bought in France and later used in the White House, including a desk on which the Monroe Doctrine was written. The house is open to visitors, 9 a.m. to 5 p.m. (Admission: adults 50¢, children 25¢.)

About two blocks southeast, facing each other across Princess Anne St., the main street of Fredericksburg, are two churches. On the east side is

St. George's Church, Protestant Episcopal. The church, architecturally undistinguished, is the third built on the site. Built in 1849, it has a memorial window to Mary Washington. It is of interest for its churchyard, with the graves of many distinguished Virginians. Diagonally across the street is the Presbyterian church. Two cannonballs that struck the front portico during the Civil War bombardment are still imbedded in the wall. Clara Barton, the organizer and first president of the American Red Cross, used the church as a temporary hospital during the Civil War.

About a mile southwest of the center of town, on US 1, at the corner of Lafayette Blvd. and Sunken Rd., is the best place in Virginia to get a comprehensive understanding of several important battlefields. It is the Visitor Center for the

Fredericksburg and Spotsylvania National Military Park, consisting of four battlefields covering about 3,600 acres around Fredericksburg. The Visitor Center has a big relief map of the battlefields, and displays of photographs, military relics, charts, and maps, which give a graphic picture of what happened. You can get a map of a self-guiding tour of all the battlefields. The four battles were Fredericksburg, fought in 1862 in the area adjoining the Visitor Center, particularly to the south and west; Chancellorsville, fought in 1863, ten miles west on Virginia 3; Wilderness, about five miles beyond the Chancellorsville Battlefield on Virginia 3; and Spotsylvania Courthouse, south of Fredericksburg on Virginia 208. The last two were fought in May 1864.

The four great battles involved the heaviest and bitterest fighting and the greatest loss of life ever to take place in this country. Union forces lost 17,000 men, Confederate forces about 13,000, including their great commander, Stonewall Jackson, who was killed at Chancellorsville. The first two battles resulted in resounding defeats for the Union. The last two were indecisive.

To see all four fields takes at least a day, but the Fredericksburg field alone, perhaps the most interesting, can be seen in an hour or two. Near Fredericksburg is

Ferry Farm, on Virginia 3, just across the Rappahannock River, about two miles east of Fredericksburg. Washington, who spent a good deal of his boyhood on the farm, learned surveying here. The farm is the place where the legend of the cherry tree began. Of greatest interest to visitors is a working reproduction of a Colonial ferry over the river on which you can ride. Ferry Farm is open daily from 9 a.m. to 5 p.m. (Admission: adults 50¢, children 25¢, including the ferry ride.) About 35 miles east of Fredericksburg on Virginia 3 is

George Washington Birthplace National Monument, covering a substantial part of the Tidewater plantation where the original birthplace stood. The present house, however, is neither a restoration nor a reconstruction, but a handsome Georgian Colonial cottage, furnished with pieces typical of the period.

Washington's great-grandfather, father, and 28 other members of the Washington family are buried near the house. Worth seeing is a gristmill, half a mile beyond the house, built in 1713.

A much more imposing house than the Washington Birthplace, and in many ways more rewarding to visitors, is just east, with an entrance gate on Virginia 3. It is

Stratford Hall, the family estate of the Lees of Virginia, of whom Robert E. Lee, born at Stratford, was the most celebrated member. Completed in 1727, Stratford Hall is a superb example of a great Colonial manor house. Massive, almost fortresslike, it dominates 1,200 acres of grounds and gardens overlooking the Potomac River. In addition to the mansion itself, beautifully restored and furnished with many Lee family possessions, the grounds contain the buildings, shops, and dwellings of a complete working plantation. Open daily, 9 a.m. to 4:30 p.m. (Admission: adults $2, children 50¢.)

From Fredericksburg the parallel routes of Interstate 95 and US 1 lead northeast to a cluster of communities on the west bank of the Potomac, opposite Washington, D.C. Of these, the most important is

9. ALEXANDRIA, population 115,000, a city which leads a double life. It is a booming suburb of Washington and a hub of main highways, but it is also one of the oldest, most historic cities in the East.

Founded in 1749, Alexandria soon became a prosperous tobacco port, carrying on a lucrative trade with the colonies and abroad. It was also a fashionable city, the shopping and social center for plantations along the Potomac.

Alexandria today preserves some of the fine old Colonial houses typical of her prosperous early years. Some have historic associations, but many are simply charming and picturesque, lining narrow, tree-shaded, cobbled streets. Points of interest in Alexandria begin in the north with

Robert E. Lee Home, at 607 Oronoco St., a small, attractive, Georgian Colonial house where the Lee family moved in 1818 when Robert was four years old. Nearby is the Lloyd House, at 220 Washington St., built in 1793. It is regarded as one of the finest examples of formal domestic architecture in Alexandria. There Lee received his commission as general in the Confederate Army. A block south and a block east, at the corner of Cameron and Columbus streets, is Alexandria's most famous church:

Christ Church, a handsome building of late Georgian Colonial design, built between 1767 and 1773. George Washington was a vestryman and regularly attended services. His funeral was held here. Lee was also a member of the congregation. The interior has a handsome pulpit and a big Palladian window. The most distinctive feature is a fine brass and crystal chandelier. A block west and half a block south of Christ Church is

Friendship Fire Engine House, at 107 S. Alfred St., a small, red brick building which housed the local fire company, organized in 1774. George Washington was once the company's honorary captain. Early fire-fighting equipment is exhibited, including a fire engine donated by Washington.

A monumental building commemorates Washington's association with the Masons. Built in a style completely alien to Colonial Alexandria, it is the

George Washington Masonic National Memorial, on King St., at the crest of Shooter's Hill, a site once suggested for the national capitol. The most visible landmark in Alexandria, the memorial is a massive

The Friendship Fire Engine House in Alexandria, now exhibiting early fire-fighting equipment, once housed the local fire company organized in 1774.

gray tower built in three stages, topped by a pyramid modeled after the ancient lighthouse of Alexandria, Egypt. Visitors without Masonic affiliations are welcome. Many exhibits are related to Washington, who was Master of the Alexandria-Washington lodge. A portrait, completely unretouched, is supposed to show Washington as he really looked. Open free daily, 9 a.m. to 5 p.m. East of Washington St. is

Gadsby's Tavern, 132 N. Royal St. Built in 1752, it was one of the most popular meeting places in Colonial America. Washington recruited two companies here in 1754 and marched them off to the French and Indian War. He attended his last birthday party at the tavern in 1799 and ended his military career with a review of Alexandria's troops. Part of the original tavern has been authentically restored and is open to the public. Rooms of special interest include the ballroom, kitchen, and bar. The tavern is open daily, 10 a.m. to 5 p.m. (Admission: adults 25¢, children free.) A block east of the tavern, at 121 N. Fairfax St., is historic

Carlyle House, one of the finest Georgian Colonial houses in Alexandria and one of the few open to the public. Built in 1752,

the home of a Scottish merchant, it has been beautifully restored and furnished with fine Colonial pieces. Many Virginia leaders, including Washington and Jefferson, were frequent visitors. The house is open daily, 9:30 a.m. to 5:30 p.m. (Admission: adults 50¢, children 30¢.) South of the Carlyle House is the

Stabler-Leadbeater Apothecary Shop, at 107 S. Fairfax St., restored and maintained as a pharmaceutical museum. One of the oldest drugstores in the country, it opened in 1792. Famous customers included Washington, Daniel Webster, Henry Clay, and John C. Calhoun. One exhibit is a note from Martha Washington ordering a quart of castor oil. The building is open free Monday through Saturday.

Closely associated with Alexandria, linked to it by scenic Mount Vernon Memorial Highway, is

Mount Vernon, on the Potomac, nine miles south of Alexandria. Visitors enter at the rear of the house, across a wide stretch of lawn, with gardens and outbuildings on either side. Mount Vernon has been restored to look as it did during the last years of Washington's life. The development of the estate began in 1674 when John Washing-

By car, visitors approach Mount Vernon from the rear. The front of the house overlooks the Potomac. Alexander is to the north.

ton acquired 5,000 acres. Over the next 80 years the estate was controlled by a succession of Washingtons, including George Washington's father and his half-brother Lawrence, who died in 1752, leaving Mount Vernon to George. In 1759 Washington married Martha Dandridge Custis, a young, well-to-do widow with two children. Then Washington began enlarging Mount Vernon, continued to do so over more than 30 years. It was his home until his death in 1799.

Mount Vernon was the headquarters out of which Washington rode to inspect his productive estate holdings. At a time when most wealthy Americans were farmers, Washington was one of the wealthiest. At his death Mount Vernon was one of the finest and best run farms in the country. Vivid evidence of Mount Vernon's wealth can be seen today in the superbly planned mansion with its cluster of outbuildings, shops, gardens, all joined by graceful arcades. Washington was buried, as he had requested, on the estate grounds. In 1802 Martha Washington died and was buried beside her husband. The burial vault is on the slope of lawn by the Potomac River.

In 1856 ownership of Mount Vernon passed to the Mount Vernon Ladies Association, which had raised $200,000 to buy the estate and make it a national shrine. Over the years, the association has succeeded in superbly restoring the estate and grounds, now about 500 acres, approximately the area of the original estate. By searching the country, the ladies acquired hundreds of Washington's personal possessions. The admission fee of $1, probably the best investment in sightseeing you can make, is entirely devoted to keeping up the estate and grounds.

The outbuildings include a smokehouse, wash house, greenhouse, coach house, spinning house, and the slave quarters, where about 60 of Washington's 200 slaves lived.

The rooms are full of Washington relics, ranging from the simplest candle snuffer to a harpsichord for which he paid 1,000 pounds, famous portraits, and the key to the Bastille, given to Washington by General Lafayette.

Mount Vernon is open every day between 9 a.m. and 5 p.m., March to September; rest of the year until 4 p.m. (Admission: adults $1, children and servicemen free.) Near the entrance gate is a museum displaying many possessions and relics that could not be exhibited in the house, and an attractive restaurant and souvenir shop where you can buy potted boxwood shrubs and vines grown in the Mount Vernon garden.

Two historic buildings are about three miles west of Mount Vernon on Virginia 235. One, just south of US 1, east of the junction with Virginia 235, is

Washington's Grist Mill, authentically restored, once a busy mill, the center for a blacksmith shop, cooper shop, and distillery, all part of Washington's plantation. Built by Washington's father, the mill was later enlarged and improved by Washington himself, who claimed that the flour ground at the mill and whiskey distilled there were equal to any.

Nearby, west of the junction of US 1 and Virginia 235, is a handsome mansion called

Woodlawn Plantation, built in 1805 on land that was once part of Mount Vernon, willed by Washington to his wife's granddaughter, Eleanor Custis. The mansion was designed by William Thornton, first architect of the Capitol in Washington, D.C., in classic Georgian style. It is open the same hours as Mount Vernon. (Admission: adults $1, children 50¢.)

North of Alexandria is

Washington National Airport, one of the two commercial airports serving Washington, both owned and operated by the federal government. (The other, huge Dulles Airport, is some distance northwest.) National Airport, one of the busiest in the country, handles domestic flights for most major and regional airlines, including frequent shuttle flights to New York and Boston. The terminal, constantly being rebuilt and extended, is linked to downtown Washington by bus and taxi.

North of the airport, on the west side of US 1, is

The Pentagon, world's largest office building, with 3.7 million square feet of office space, 17½ miles of corridors. Constructed during World War II at a cost of $83 million, the building houses personnel of the Department of Defense, including the Secretary of Defense and the secretaries of the Army, Navy, Air Force, as well as the Chiefs of Staff. Its daytime population is 27,000, 60 percent of whom are civilians.

The building's unusual name derives from its five-sided shape. Its total area is over 34 acres surrounded by 200 acres of grounds, including 67 acres of parking lot with space for nearly 10,000 vehicles. Visitors are admitted from 8 a.m. to 6 p.m., Monday through Friday. There are no escorted tours.

Overlooking the Pentagon are the partially wooded slopes of

Arlington National Cemetery, the largest cemetery in the country and one of the most beautiful. It fills a roughly semicircular tract of about 500 acres, rising from the river in beautifully landscaped hills. The cemetery has about 143,000 graves—soldiers, sailors, and marines of every rank from the humblest private to the most distinguished officer.

Except for the graves of famous individuals all the graves are of two types. Headstones rounded on top are for known dead, inscribed with name, state, dates of birth and death. Flat-topped headstones mark graves of unknown dead and are carved only with a grave number.

A famous house in the cemetery is the

Custis-Lee Mansion, often called Arlington House. From its hilltop setting the mansion commands a superb view of Washington across the river. The lawn is now studded with graves, including those of former President Kennedy and his brother Robert.

The classically perfect mansion was built in 1802 by George Washington Parke Custis, grandson of Martha Washington. It was the scene of the marriage between Mary Ann Randolph Custis, daughter of the builder, and Lt. Robert E. Lee, in 1831. Thereafter, more than any other place in the country, Arlington was Lee's home as he rose through the ranks of army service.

At the beginning of the Civil War, Lee was called to Washington for a secret meeting with an emissary of President Lincoln and offered the command of the Union forces. After two days of consideration Lee refused the offer. He soon left Arlington to accept the command of the Confederate Army, never to return.

Toward the end of the Civil War the grounds of Arlington House began to be used as a burial ground, which grew into Arlington Cemetery. Many years later Custis Lee, who inherited the property, sold Arlington House to the government for $150,000.

Entrance is usually from the rear, where limited parking facilities are available. On the grounds are a smokehouse, summer kitchen, ice house, toolhouse, and stable. Just north is a small but excellent museum. In front of the main portico is a monument shaped like a classic bench marking the grave of Pierre L'Enfant, who laid out the plans for the city of Washington. A little down the slope are the two Kennedy graves.

Visitors go through the house in small groups, with a guide. It is open from 9:30 a.m. to 6 p.m., April through October; rest of the year until 4:30 p.m. (Admission: adults 50¢, children free.)

Nearby is the

Tomb of the Unknowns, south of Lee Mansion, at the approximate center of the cemetery. The simple tomb, a gigantic block of white marble, stands on a terrace commanding a view of the cemetery and Washington across the river. Two armed sentries pace the terrace with clocklike precision. In a crypt beneath the marble block are the bodies of three soldiers, all unknown, killed in three wars, World Wars I and II and the Korean War. The inscription reads: "Here rests in honored glory an American soldier known but to God." This refers to the body of an unknown soldier of World War I placed in the tomb November 11, 1921. The guard is changed every hour on the hour during the day, every other hour at night.

Adjoining the tomb is the Arlington Memorial Amphitheater, surrounded by an impressive colonnade. At the east end is a trophy room, with displays of decorations conferred on the unknown soldiers by foreign governments.

Adjoining Arlington Cemetery on the north is the dramatic

U.S. Marine Corps War Memorial, a heroic-size bronze reproduction of a famous World War II event: the raising of the American flag on Mount Suribachi, Iwo Jima. Almost everyone who sees the memorial for the first time is astonished at its size and dramatic detail.

The story behind the memorial is this:

172

In February, 1945, after 72 days of bombing, U.S. Marines stormed Iwo Jima, held by 23,000 Japanese troops. During the assault Company E of the 28th Regiment of the Fifth Marine Division managed to reach the crest of Mount Suribachi, accompanied by a news photographer named Joe Rosenthal. There, five members of the troop and a medical corpsman raised a flagpole with the American flag. As they did so Rosenthal made his photograph. It became the most widely published photograph of the war. A sculptor, Felix W. de Weldon, determined to translate the photograph into bronze. Completed in plaster, the statue was cast in bronze, cut into pieces, and brought to Washington, where it was erected and dedicated in 1954. The monument is an exact reproduction of the photograph in every detail, except the size. Each man is 32 feet high, the rifle carried by one is 16 feet long, and a canteen carried by another, if filled, would hold 32 quarts of water. At the base is carved a moving tribute from Admiral Nimitz: "Uncommon valor was a common virtue." Marines paid the entire cost of the memorial, $850,000. By presidential proclamation the flag over the monument is never lowered.

South of the Marine Memorial is the

Netherlands Carillon, a square, 127-foot, open tower with a 49-bell carillon, a gift from the people of Holland in appreciation of aid received from the United States during and after World War II. The biggest bells are six feet in diameter and weigh over 12,000 pounds. In spring the grounds blaze with thousands of tulips, also a gift from Holland. Concerts are given each Sunday, April through September, at 3 p.m.

From Arlington County, main highways lead west to two points of special interest. Most important are the

Bull Run Battlefields, officially called Manassas National Battlefield Park, about 2,500 acres, twice the scene of major Civil War battles. The First Battle of Bull Run was the first large-scale test of Union and Confederate strength. The park is linked to Arlington, about 20 miles to the east, by Interstate 66 and the parallel route of US 29-211. The Visitor Center, the best place to start from, is just off Virginia 234, about midway between the two express highways. First Manassas (the First Battle of Bull

Run) was fought on July 21, 1861. Union forces, numbering about 35,000, engaged about 32,000 Confederate troops. Union leaders expected an overwhelming victory and a possible end to the young war. Both armies were green and untried, and the whole battle action was one of high confusion. The Union forces were badly beaten and retreated to Washington a few miles away, after losing nearly 3,000 men. Gen. Thomas J. Jackson stood his stand during the height of the fighting at the crest of a hill and refused to budge. A Southern officer, seeing him there, rallied his retreating troops with the cry, "Look! There stands Jackson like a stone wall. Rally behind the Virginians." Jackson, one of the greatest of the Confederate leaders, was "Stonewall" ever after. A gigantic equestrian statue of Jackson is the area's most notable memorial.

Second Manassas was fought a little more than a year later, August 28-30, 1862. Its object was the same as the first: to gain control of a railway junction. The result is generally regarded as a draw. The northern general, John Pope, lost about 14,000 men out of a force of 73,000. Gen. Robert E. Lee, who opposed him, lost about 9,000 out of 55,000. From the Visitor Center, where there is an excellent museum, a self-guiding tour leads over the battlefield area, links most important sites and memorials, including Henry Hill, the center of fighting during both battles, and a reconstruction of an old stone bridge over Bull Run, where an overturned carriage blocked the bridge, causing chaos among retreating Union forces. The park is open free daily, 8 a.m. to 9 p.m. (Museum admission: adults 50¢, children free.)

About ten miles north of the park on Virginia 28 is

Dulles International Airport, opened in 1962, built and operated by the Federal Aviation Agency as a prototype of jet-age airports. Twice the size of Kennedy International Airport in New York, Dulles spreads over 10,000 acres. Each of its three runways is two miles long. Eero Saarinen designed the terminal building, 600 feet long, and control tower, 177 feet high. The striking terminal has slanting walls of steel and a sweeping curved roof supported by massive stone piers. Big mobile lounges carry passengers to and from planes that may be parked as far as half a mile away.

Accommodations & Restaurants.

THE PAGES that follow present a selective list of hotels, motels, and restaurants in the Mid-Atlantic states. We have tried to list the most appealing places to stay and the most interesting restaurants in every city or region covered in the guide. In large cities or important resort areas we give you a wider selection.

Listings are presented by state from north to south: New York, Pennsylvania, New Jersey, Delaware, Maryland, District of Columbia, West Virginia, and Virginia. Within each state the sequence is alphabetical by town. Following the name of the town is a brief description of its distance from the nearest larger city or natural feature, and the chief highways serving it.

The hotel and motel descriptions omit mention of such practically universal features as air-conditioning or telephones, but do say whether rooms have dressing area, balcony or patio, kitchen, or fireplace. Rate descriptions are intended only as a general guide.

Since rates are subject to frequent changes, dollar figures would, in many cases, be out of date before this book is published. Therefore, in this volume we have used comparative descriptions only. They may be interpreted roughly as follows (all dollar figures refer to minimum rates for a double room, as of press time):

Inexpensive: Under $14
Reasonable: Between $14 and $18
Moderately expensive: Between $18 and $23
Expensive: $23 or more

The phrase "Special family rate" means that children under 12 are accommodated free in the same room as their parents.

All of the restaurants described have some feature which makes visiting them worthwhile. We give some indication of the size and style of the establishment, the type of food served, whether there is a bar or cocktail lounge, and wine selection, and an indication of the cost of a complete dinner without wine or liquor. Thus, for restaurants, Inexpensive means under $3, Reasonable, $3 to $6, Moderately expensive, $6 to $9, and Expensive, over $9.

Restaurants associated with hotels and motels in most cases are not described separately, even though many of them would rank high.

New York.

ALBANY — east central section, on the Hudson River and the New York State Thruway, junction of US 20.

Tom Sawyer Motor Inn
1444 Western Ave., four miles west of city center on US 20 (Tel. 438-3594). Eighty-eight ground-floor rooms, all with parking at door, in pleasant, English-inn type motel, back from highway. Landscaped grounds. Guest lobby, three meeting rooms. Pool, wading pool, sun patio, playground. Restaurant open after 6:30 a.m. Cocktail lounge.
Reasonable

Restaurant.
Jack's Oyster House
42 State St., downtown, near the capitol (Tel. 465-8854). Seats 150 in an elegant, long-established restaurant. Menu features hearty American food, with the emphasis on seafood, steak, salads, sandwiches. Cocktail lounge. Open lunch, dinner.
Moderately expensive

ALEXANDRIA BAY — north central border, on the St. Lawrence River, junction of New York 12 and New York 26, just north of Interstate 81.

Capt. Thomson's Motor Lodge
Thomson Point, center of town, on the St. Lawrence (Tel. 482-9611). Two floors, 67 large, pleasant rooms, all with balcony or terrace, dressing area, and picture window overlooking the Seaway. Fishing pier, docks, launching ramp. Swimming and wading pools, sundeck. Restaurant adjacent. Motel is closed November through April.
Moderately expensive

Pine Tree Point Club
Pine Tree Point, one mile north of town cen-

ter (Tel. 482-9911). One and two floors, 48 rooms in main building and chalets, most with balcony or terrace. Well-equipped resort on the St. Lawrence in spacious, wooded grounds. Guest lobby, recreation room. Fishing pier, private beach, water skiing. Pool, patio, playground, skeet and trapshooting. Sauna. Restaurant open after 8 a.m. Cocktail lounge, piano bar, dancing. Resort closed November through April. Modified American Plan.
Moderately expensive

Restaurants.
Argonne Restaurant
15 Church St., downtown, on New York 26 (Tel. 482-2269). Seats 90 in three dining areas of a pleasant restaurant decorated in Victorian style. Fireplace. American menu, featuring shore dinners, roast beef, turkey, homemade bread and pastry. Cocktail lounge, wine selection. Open lunch, dinner, closed November through April.
Moderately expensive

Cavallario's Steak House
28 Church St., center of town (Tel. 482-9867). Seats 180 in two dining areas decorated in the style of King Arthur's Court. American and Italian food, featuring steak and lobster. Cocktail lounge, dancing and entertainment. Wine selection. Open dinner only, closed November through March.
Moderately expensive

BINGHAMTON — south central section, near the Pennsylvania border, junction of Interstate 81 and New York 17.

Schrafft's Motor Inn
65 Front St., two blocks west of city center on New York 12 (Tel. 724-2412). Three floors, 122 large, tastefully furnished rooms. Health lounge and recreation room, two saunas, indoor pool. Meeting rooms. Landscaped grounds, sun terrace. Restaurant open after 7 a.m. Cocktail lounge. Special family rate. *Reasonable*

Restaurant.
Scotch 'N Sirloin Restaurant
4700 Vestal Pkwy., Vestal Plaza, two miles west of city center on New York 17 (Tel. 729-6301). Seats 180 in two dining areas of an intriguing restaurant with sawdust on the floor, timbered walls. Steak and lobster only, also salad bar. Cocktail lounge, wine

selection. Open dinner only, closed Sunday.
Moderately expensive

BLUE MOUNTAIN LAKE — northeast section, junction of New York 28 and New York 30, in Adirondack Forest Preserve.

Hemlock Hall
Two miles northwest of village off New York 28N and New York 30 (Tel. 352-7706). Twenty-three rooms in main lodge and cottages, eight cottages with terrace and kitchen. All rooms furnished in comfortable Early American style. Main lodge has big lounge, three fireplaces, library, porch. Five acres of wooded and landscaped grounds, private beach on Blue Mountain Lake. Sailfish, canoes, and rowboats free. Diving float. Restaurant, open after 8:30 a.m. No bar. Modified American Plan. *Moderately expensive*

BUFFALO — southwest section, on Lake Erie, just west of the New York State Thruway (Interstate 90), junction of US 20.

Holiday Inn #2, Downtown
620 Delaware Ave., one mile north of city center on New York 384 (Tel. 886-2121). Eight floors, 168 large, nicely furnished rooms. Guest lobby, meeting rooms. Pool, sauna. Restaurant open after 6:30 a.m. Cocktail lounge. Special family rate.
Reasonable

Lord Amherst Motor Hotel
5000 Main St., five miles northeast of city center on New York 5 (Tel. 839-2200). Two floors, 100 large, attractively decorated rooms, most with dressing area. Colonial-style motel in quiet residential section, overlooking small lake. Guest lobby with stone fireplace. Meeting rooms, gift shop. Pool and sun patio, wading pool. Restaurant open after 7 a.m., noted for steak, roast beef. Cocktail lounge. *Reasonable*

Restaurants.
David's Table
675 Delaware Ave., one mile north of city center on New York 384 (Tel. 884-1100). Seats 120 in one main dining area decorated in colorful Mediterranean style. American and Continental menu, featuring Dover sole, beef Stroganoff. Nightly entertainment. Cocktail lounge, wine selection. Open dinner only. *Moderately expensive*

Oliver's Restaurant

2095 Delaware Ave., four miles north of city center on New York 384 (Tel. 877-9327). Seats 160 in two dining areas of a pleasant, modern restaurant. Varied menu, steak, chops, seafood are featured. Cocktail lounge, wine selection. Open lunch, dinner, also late supper, 10 a.m. to 1 a.m.

Moderately expensive

CATSKILL — southeast section, on the Hudson River and US 9W, just east of the New York State Thruway, about 30 miles south of Albany.

Catskill Motor Lodge

Two miles west of town center on New York 23, at Exit 21, New York State Thruway (Tel. 943-5800). Two floors, 42 nicely furnished rooms. Guest lobby. Landscaped grounds, mountain view. Pool and sun patio, playground. Restaurant open all meals after 7 a.m. except breakfast only Tuesday. Cocktail lounge. *Reasonable*

Restaurant.
Skyline Restaurant

One mile northeast of town center on New York 23, at the Rip Van Winkle Bridge Approach (Tel. 943-2550). Seats 135 in a handsome dining room with picture windows overlooking a wooded hillside. American and Continental food, featuring roast beef, lobster stuffed with crabmeat. Cocktail lounge, wine selection. Open dinner only, Sunday after 1 p.m. Closed Monday.

Moderately expensive

COOPERSTOWN — east central part of state, junction of New York 80 and New York 28, about 30 miles southeast of Utica.

Lake Front Motel

10 Fair St., on Otsego Lake, one block from Baseball Hall of Fame (Tel. 547-9511). One and two floors, 44 rooms, all with balcony or terrace. Guest lobby. Pleasant motel in wooded lakeshore grounds, large marina. Public beach one-quarter mile away. Waterskiing, fishing, boat trips available. Restaurant open after 7 a.m., specializing in fresh lake bass. Service bar.

Moderately expensive

CORNING — south central part of state, near the Pennsylvania border, on New York 17, about 20 miles northwest of Elmira.

Treadway Baron Steuben Motor Hotel

Centerway Square, center of town, on New York 414 (Tel. 936-4661). Five floors, 82 rooms, in pleasant, well-maintained hotel. Guest lobby, meeting rooms, barber shop, drugstore. Restaurant open after 7 a.m. Cocktail lounge. Special family rate.

Inexpensive

Restaurant.
Lodge on the Green Restaurant

About three miles west of town center, junction of US 15 and New York 17, in Painted Post (Tel. 962-2456). Seats 475 in three dining areas of an attractive restaurant serving a variety of American food. Cocktail lounge. Open all meals after 7 a.m.

Moderately expensive

ELMIRA — southern border, south central section, on New York 17.

Howard Johnson's Motor Lodge

Westinghouse Junction, four miles north of town center at junction of New York 17, 14, and 328 (Tel. 739-5636). Two floors, 76 spacious, attractively furnished rooms, all with balcony or terrace, some with dressing area. Extensive, landscaped grounds, pool and sun patio. Restaurant open after 7 a.m. Service bar. *Reasonable*

Restaurant.
Pierce's "1894" Restaurant

228 Oakwood Ave., three miles north of town center off New York 328, in Elmira Heights (Tel. 734-2022). Seats 350 in five dining areas 'decorated in lush Edwardian style. Restaurant managed by the same family for four generations. Varied menu, featuring Continental, Chinese, and American food. Seafood, lobster, veal, and roast beef are specialties. Cocktail lounge, entertainment. Wine selection. Open dinner only, Sunday brunch and dinner after 11 a.m. Closed Monday.

Moderately expensive to expensive

ITHACA — central section, southern end of Cayuga Lake, junction of New York 13 and New York 34.

Howard Johnson's Motor Lodge

N. Triphammer Rd., three miles north of city center on New York 13 (Tel. 273-6066). Two floors, 72 nicely furnished rooms, all with balcony or terrace, dressing area, in attractive motel opposite shopping center. Guest lobby, meeting room, pool and landscaped sun patio. Restaurant open after 7 a.m. No bar. Special family rate.

Reasonable

Restaurants.

Station Restaurant

806 W. Buffalo St., five blocks west of town center (Tel. 272-2609). Seats 270 in five dining areas of a delightful restaurant in a remodeled, late 19th-century railroad station. Menu features steak, beef Stroganoff, chicken, lobster tail. Cocktail lounge, wine selection. Open dinner only.

Moderately expensive to expensive

Taughannock Farms Inn

Ten miles north of city center on New York 89, in Trumansburg (Tel. 387-7711). Seats 130 in four dining areas of a beautiful 100-year-old white frame house overlooking a formal garden and Cayuga Lake. American menu, family-style service. Specialties include duck, lobster tail, roast beef, homemade desserts. Cocktail lounge, wine selection. Open dinner only, closed mid-November to mid-April.

Moderately expensive

LAKE GEORGE — village at southern end of Lake George, junction of Interstate 87 and US 9.

Depe Dene Motel

Three miles north of village center on New York 9N (Tel. 668-2788). Eighteen cottages, 11 with kitchen, 23 rooms in main lodge, decorated in Early American style. Wooded grounds on lake, with private beach, boating, sundeck, playground, lawn games. Restaurant open after 8 a.m.

Moderately expensive

Tahoe Motel

Lake Shore Dr., one-half mile north of village on New York 9N (Tel. 668-5711). Two floors, 73 spacious, attractively furnished rooms, most with balcony overlooking lake. Landscaped grounds, private beach, pool and sun patio. Coffee shop open after 7 a.m. No bar.

Expensive

LAKE PLACID — northeast section, junction of New York 86 and New York 73, in Adirondack Forest Preserve, about 70 miles south of the Canadian border.

Art Devlin's Olympic Motor Inn

350 Main St., three blocks south of town center (Tel. 523-3700). Two floors, 50 rooms, all with balcony or terrace, six two-bedroom suites. Handsome motor inn, large, attractively decorated rooms. Guest lobby. Landscaped grounds, swimming and wading pools, sun patio, playground. Coffee shop open after 7 a.m., breakfast and lunch only. Special family rate.

Reasonable

Mirror Lake Inn

35 Mirror Lake Dr., one-half mile west of town center (Tel. 523-2544). Four floors, 60 rooms, some with balcony or terrace, in main lodge, annex, and cottages. Guest lobby, recreation room. Seven acres of landscaped and wooded grounds, swimming and wading pools, patio, playground. Lake beach, boating. Skiing, free instruction. Restaurant open all meals after 8 a.m. Cocktail lounge. Special family rate. Modified American Plan.

Moderately expensive

LONG ISLAND.

AMAGANSETT (Long Island — near the southeast tip, on New York 27).

Restaurant.

The Inn at Napeague

Montauk Hwy., five miles east of Amagansett on New York 27 (Tel. 267-8103). Seats 60 in two dining areas of an intimate restaurant with redwood walls, fireplace. American and Continental menu, featuring beef Stroganoff, veal Marsala, lobster tails. Service bar. Open dinner only, closed mid-October through April, and Monday in off season. *Moderately expensive to expensive*

EAST HAMPTON (Long Island — near the southeast tip, three miles west of Amagansett).

East Hampton House

226 Montauk Hwy., one mile east of town center on New York 27 (Tel. 324-4300). Two floors, 40 spacious, handsomely furnished rooms, all with balcony or terrace, dressing area, front and rear doors, 22 with kitchen. Guest lobby, recreation room. Five acres of landscaped grounds, swimming and wading pools, sun patio, playground. Two tennis courts, golf driving net. Coffee shop open 9 a.m. to 3 p.m. No bar.

Expensive

GREENPORT (Long Island – near the northeast tip, on New York 25).

Sound Shore Resort Motel

Two miles west of town center on County Route 27A, in Southold (Tel. 477-1910). Two floors, 60 rooms, all with balcony or terrace and dressing area, 20 with kitchen, in attractive motel facing Long Island Sound. Guest lobby, recreation room, all-weather tennis court. Private beach, pool, sundeck, playground. Restaurant open after 7 a.m., featuring fresh fish and seafood. Cocktail lounge, wine cellar. *Expensive*

Restaurant.

Claudio's Restaurant

111 Main St., center of town, on New York 25 (Tel. 477-0627). Seats 300 in three dining areas of an attractive restaurant-marina, with a fine view of the harbor. Nautical decor, souvenirs of America's Cup races displayed. American and Continental cooking, specializing in seafood, lobster, frogs' legs, shish kebab. Cocktail lounge, wine selection. Open lunch, dinner, closed mid-November to mid-April, and Tuesday in off season. *Moderately expensive*

MONTAUK (Long Island – southeast tip).

Driftwood Motel and Cottages

Montauk Hwy., five miles west of town center on New York 27 (Tel. 668-5744). Sixty rooms in main lodge and four cottages, all with balcony or terrace, dressing area, most with kitchen. Well-equipped resort motel. Guest lobby, meeting and recreation rooms. Private beach, ten acres of landscaped grounds. Two all-weather tennis courts, shuffleboard, volleyball. Pool and sun patio. Restaurant two blocks away, open after 8 a.m. Closed November 1 to mid-April. *Moderately expensive*

RIVERHEAD (Long Island – east central section, junction of New York 24 and New York 25, on Flanders Bay).

Wading River Motel

Eight miles west of town center on New York 25 (Tel. 727-7700). Thirty-two ground-floor rooms, 15 with kitchen, in pleasant motel surrounded by lawns. Recreation room. Pool, sun patio, wading pool, playground. Free Continental breakfast. Restaurant two miles away. *Reasonable*

SAG HARBOR (Long Island – near the southeast tip on New York 114, overlooking Gardiners Bay).

Baron's Cove Inn

W. Water St., two blocks west of town center (Tel. 725-2100). Two floors, 52 rooms, 40 with balcony or terrace, 12 with kitchen, in attractive motel overlooking Sag Harbor. Own marina, boats for rent. Landscaped grounds, pool and sun patio. Restaurant open after 8 a.m. featuring steak, seafood. Cocktail lounge, wine selection, dancing. *Expensive*

SOUTHAMPTON (Long Island – southeast section, on New York 27A).

Restaurants.

John Duck, Jr. Restaurant

15 Prospect St., three blocks north of town center (Tel. 283-0311). Seats 225 in four dining areas, and an outdoor terrace in season, of a popular, long-established restaurant. Menu features American and German dishes, especially duck, seafood, steak, and sauerbraten. Bar, wine selection. Open lunch, dinner, closed Monday. *Moderately expensive*

Ridgely's Fabulous Steaks

Montauk Hwy., three miles east of town center on New York 27, in Water Mill (Tel. 726-9699). Seats 200 in three dining areas, one with a waterfall. Limited American menu, steak and lobster are specialties. Cocktail lounge, entertainment and dancing. Wine selection. Open dinner only, closed from late September to mid-May. *Moderately expensive*

MASSENA – northern border, on the St. Lawrence River, junction of New York 37 and New York 56.

Village Motel

One mile west of city center on New York 37B (Tel. 769-3561). Thirty-three ground-floor rooms. Pleasant motel in landscaped grounds, pool and sun patio, playground, lawn games. Village Inn Restaurant adjacent. Special family rate. *Reasonable*

NEW PALTZ – southeast section, junction of New York 299 and New York 32, just west of the New York State Thruway and the Hudson River.

Lake Mohonk Mountain House

Five miles northwest of town, Exit 18, New York State Thruway (Tel. 255-1000). Six-story, French chateau-type resort on glacier-fed mountain lake, 7,500 acres of grounds. Most of the 300 rooms have balcony or terrace, half have fireplace. Guest lobby, recreation room, library, music rooms. Swimming, riding, fishing, boating, skiing. Restaurant open all meals after 8 a.m. No bar. Special family rate. American Plan.

Expensive

MONTICELLO — southeast section, junction of New York 17 and New York 42.

Holiday Mountain Motor Lodge

In Rock Hill, four miles east of Monticello off New York 17 (Tel. 796-3000). One and two floors, 70 rooms, all with balcony or terrace. Attractively decorated motel in 200 acres of wooded, landscaped grounds. Guest lobby with fireplace. Pool, sun patio, playground. Hunting available. Restaurant open breakfast and dinner in winter, all meals in summer. Cocktail lounge.

Reasonable

NEW YORK CITY.

(For a more complete listing see separate Rand McNally New York City Guide.)

THE BRONX (New York City).

Town and Country Motor Lodge

2244 Tillotson Ave., Exit 5, New England Thruway, ten miles north of Times Square (Tel. 994-9000). Two floors, 65 rooms, in a pleasant motel with guest lobby, meeting rooms, pool and sun patio. Restaurant open after 7 a.m. Cocktail lounge, dancing.

Reasonable

Restaurant.
Lobster Box Restaurant

34 City Island Ave., 20 miles east of Times Square off the New England Thruway and Hutchinson River Pkwy., on City Island in Long Island Sound (Tel. 885-1952). Seats 550 in three dining areas, and an outdoor terrace in season, of a popular restaurant in a 156-year-old building overlooking Long Island Sound. Early American decor. Menu features 23 different lobster dishes, fresh fish, steamed clams, steak, chicken. Cocktail lounge, wine selection. Open dinner only.

Moderately expensive to expensive

BROOKLYN (New York City).

Golden Gate Motor Inn

3867 Shore (Belt) Pkwy., at Knapp St. (Tel. 743-4000). Three floors, 150 rooms, half with balcony or terrace, all with dressing area, in pleasant motel overlooking Sheepshead Bay. Guest lobby, meeting rooms, pool and sundeck. Restaurant open after 7 a.m. Cocktail lounge. *Reasonable*

MANHATTAN (New York City).

Algonquin

59 W. 44th St. (Tel. 687-4400). Just east of the theater district, a favorite with actors and writers. Two hundred rooms, both transient and residential. Two notable dining rooms: Oak Room and Rose Room. Cocktail lounge. Garage opposite.

Moderately expensive

Americana

Seventh Ave. and 52nd St. (Tel. 581-1000). New, strikingly designed, 50-story hotel, 2,000 rooms and suites, full range of convention facilities. Shopping arcade, garage. Four restaurants, including Royal Box Supper Club, with top entertainment, La Ronde Restaurant. *Expensive*

Barclay

111 E. 48th St., between Park and Lexington avenues (Tel. 755-5900). Fifteen floors, 800 rooms, many executive suites. Spacious, unusual lobby, cocktail terrace. Shopping arcade. Doorman garage service. Two restaurants. *Expensive*

Doral Park Avenue

70 Park Ave., at 38th St. (Tel. 687-7050). Small luxury hotel, recently converted from an apartment house; 17 floors, 200 rooms and suites. Dining room and cocktail lounge. *Expensive*

Essex House

160 Central Park S., between Sixth and Seventh avenues (Tel. 247-0300). Luxury hotel, 40 floors, 1,200 rooms and suites, many with pantry, Central Park view. Doorman garage service. Shopping arcade, banquet and meeting facilities. Casino-on-the-Park Restaurant. *Expensive*

Lincoln Square Motor Inn

155 W. 66th St., at Broadway (Tel. 787-

6800). Ten floors, 262 rooms. Restaurant, bar, cocktail lounge, roof garden and pool. Free indoor parking. *Reasonable*

New York Hilton
Sixth Ave., between 53rd and 54th streets, in Rockefeller Center (Tel. 586-7000). Strikingly designed, ultramodern hotel with over 2,000 rooms, 500 suites. Complete convention facilities, ballroom accommodates 5,000. Drive-in automobile registration and garage. Shopping arcade. Eight restaurants, several cocktail lounges. *Expensive*

Plaza
Fifth Ave. at 59th St., overlooking Central Park (Tel. 759-3000). A historic luxury hotel of the Continental type. Seventeen floors, 1,000 rooms and suites. Convention facilities. Several notable restaurants: Palm Court, Oak Room, Trader Vic's. Cocktail lounge. *Expensive*

Roosevelt
Madison Ave. at 45th St. (Tel. 686-9200). Commercial and transient, 18 floors, 1,000 rooms. Shopping arcade into Grand Central Terminal. Complete convention facilities, several dining rooms, coffee shop. Cocktail lounge. *Moderately expensive*

St. Regis-Sheraton
Fifth Ave. at 55th St. (Tel. 753-4500). A distinguished luxury hotel, transient and residential, with 600 rooms and suites. Three notable restaurants, celebrated King Cole Bar, with a famous Maxfield Parris painting. Doorman garage service. *Expensive*

Summit
Lexington Ave. at 51st St. (Tel. 752-7000). Colorful new hotel of unusual design, 21 floors, 800 rooms, most with refrigerator, bar, and dressing room. Some lanai suites. Two restaurants, cocktail lounge. Drive-in garage. *Expensive*

Restaurants.
Café Renaissance
338 E. 49th St., between First and Second avenues (Tel. 751-3160). Seats about 60 in two areas of an elegant, small restaurant decorated in Italian Renaissance style. Unusual menu features northern Italy, southern France, and Basque dishes. Bar, cocktail lounge. Open lunch, dinner; weekends dinner only after 6 p.m. *Moderately expensive*

Cattleman
5 E. 45th St., between Fifth and Madison avenues (Tel. 661-1200). Big, popular restaurant, seating about 400 in many distinctive, ornate dining areas, ranging from recreations of a Pullman Palace dining car to San Francisco during the days of the Barbary Coast. Big cocktail lounge. Menu features steak served in many ways. Free canapé chuck wagon after 5 p.m. Open lunch, dinner, Sunday after 2 p.m. Stagecoach at door for trips around block.
Moderately expensive

Fountain Café
Bethesda Fountain in Central Park, just north of 72nd St. Drive (Tel. 249-7332). Seats about 200 at tables both in the open and under shelter, at the foot of the Terrace steps, facing fountain and lake. Light, but varied menu, with the emphasis on cold plates, omelets, crepes, unusual desserts. No bar, but domestic and imported beer, wine by glass, carafe, or bottle. Open lunch, dinner between mid-May and mid-September. *Reasonable*

Italian Pavilion
24 W. 55th St., between Fifth and Sixth avenues (Tel. 586-5950). Seats about 110 in several areas of a handsome, spacious restaurant with a dining terrace in summer. Extensive North Italian menu. Bar, cocktail lounge. Open lunch, dinner, closed Sunday. *Moderately expensive*

Janssen's Steak Pub
430 Lexington Ave., at 44th St. (Tel. 532-5661). Seats 500 in several dining areas of a big, colorful, long-established restaurant. Decor features big collection of ship models. Wide choice of German dishes, some based on historic recipes from two-generation ownership. Complete steak dinner, all the beer you can drink, for about $6. Bar and cocktail lounge, wine, German beer. Open lunch, dinner, closed Sunday, and Saturday during July and August. *Reasonable*

La Fonda del Sol
123 W. 50th St., in Time-Life Building, between Sixth and Seventh avenues (Tel. 757-8800). Seats about 400 in seven dining areas of one of the city's most colorful and unusual restaurants, decorated with thousands of examples of art and ornament from every Latin American country. Big broiling

wall with three open fireplaces. Menu features authentic regional Latin American dishes. Bar, cocktail lounge, native drinks. Open lunch, dinner, Sunday after 1 p.m. *Moderately expensive*

Le Poulailler
43 W. 65th St., opposite Lincoln Center (Tel. 799-7600). Seats about 225 in several dining areas of a spacious restaurant decorated with lighthearted Gallic charm. Notable French menu, many gourmet dishes. Bar, cocktail lounge. Open lunch, dinner, late supper, closed Sunday. *Moderately expensive*

Luchow's
110 E. 14th St., between Third and Fourth avenues (Tel. 477-4860). Seats about 1,000 in several dining areas of a popular restaurant decorated with pictures and souvenirs of two generations of New York life. Extensive menu features German and Viennese dishes. Old-fashioned bar, wide choice of imported beer and wine. Open lunch, dinner. *Reasonable*

Marchi's
251 E. 31st St., just west of Second Ave. (Tel. 679-2494). Seats about 180 in several informal dining areas overlooking a garden. Unusual restaurant developed in the lower floors of several former town houses. Very fine North Italian food served family style. No menu, but a complete, five-course dinner, from antipasto to fruit and cheese dessert. Wine and beer. Open dinner only, closed Sunday. *Moderately expensive*

Pierre au Tunnel
306 W. 48th St., just west of Eighth Ave. (Tel. 265-9039). Seats about 150 in several dining areas of an informal, bistro-type French restaurant. Table d'hôte menu, typical French dishes. Bar, wine cellar, wine by the glass. Open lunch, dinner, closed Sunday during July and August. *Reasonable*

Rainbow Room
30 Rockefeller Plaza, 65th floor of the RCA Building (Tel. 757-9090). Seats 300 in several beautiful dining areas of the highest and one of the most colorful restaurants in New York. Many tables have a wonderful view of the city. Menu features international specialties in the gourmet range. Bar and big cocktail lounge. Table d'hôte menu, dinner one price, regardless of menu choice. Open dinner only, Sunday brunch. Associated Rainbow Grille, same management, features dancing, entertainment, after-theater supper. *Expensive*

Spats
35 W. 33rd St., between Fifth and Sixth avenues (Tel. 279-1934). Seats about 175 in two areas of a distinctive new restaurant with black marble and mirror decor, suggesting the 1930s. American menu, featuring steak, seafood, Southern specialties, also some notable Italian dishes. Bar, cocktail lounge. Open lunch, dinner, closed Sunday. *Moderately expensive*

QUEENS (New York City).

International Hotel
Belt Pkwy. and Van Wyck Expressway, entrance to JFK Airport (Tel. 995-9000). Six floors, 520 rooms, in handsome motor inn. Guest lobby, full convention facilities, barber and beauty shops. Free parking, free airport pickup. Restaurants open after 7 a.m. Cocktail lounge, wine celler. *Moderately expensive*

NIAGARA FALLS — western border, between Lake Ontario and Lake Erie, about 17 miles northwest of Buffalo on the New York State Thruway.

Treadway Inn
7003 Buffalo Ave., four miles east of city, Exit 50, New York State Thruway (Tel. 236-0272). Eight floors, 160 rooms, all with dressing area, a few with balcony. Handsome motor inn on the banks of the Niagara River. Landscaped grounds, pool, sun patio, marina. Restaurant, with view of river, featuring New England cooking. Cocktail lounge, wine selection. Special family rate. *Reasonable*

Restaurants.
Clarkson House Restaurant
810 Center St., seven miles north of city center on US 104, in Lewiston (Tel. 754-4544). Seats 90 in one main dining area of an early 19th-century house, decorated with oil lamps. Open-hearth cooking, featuring steak, lobster, roast beef, baked Alaska. Homemade salad dressings. Cocktail lounge, wine selection. Open dinner only. *Moderately expensive*

John's Flaming Hearth Restaurant

1965 Military Rd., five miles east of city center on New York 62 and New York 265 (Tel. 297-1414). Seats 385 in four elegant dining areas. Limited menu, steak, lobster, chicken, sandwiches, homemade bread, pumpkin ice cream pie are specialties. Cocktail lounge, entertainment. Wine selection. Open lunch, dinner.

Moderately expensive

PLATTSBURGH — northeast corner, on Lake Champlain and US 9, junction of New York 3, just east of the New York State Thruway, 20 miles south of the Canadian border.

Howard Johnson's Motor Lodge

One mile west of town center, junction of Interstate 87 and New York 3 (Tel. 561-7750). Two floors, 48 spacious, attractively decorated rooms, all with dressing area, balcony or terrace. Guest lobby, meeting rooms. Landscaped grounds, lawn games. Pool, playground, sun patio. Restaurant open after 7 a.m. Cocktail lounge. Special family rate. *Reasonable*

POUGHKEEPSIE — southeast section, on the Hudson River and US 9, junction of US 44, about halfway between Albany and New York City.

Po'Keepsie Motor Hotel

418 South Rd., one mile south of town center on US 9 (Tel. 452-5453). One and two floors, 115 rooms, 50 with color TV. Guest lobby, recreation room. Extensive wooded grounds, swimming and wading pools, sun patio, playground. Howard Johnson's Restaurant open all meals after 7 a.m. Cocktail lounge. Special family rate. *Reasonable*

Restaurant.
Treasure Chest Restaurant

568 South Rd., three miles south of town center on US 9 (Tel. 462-4545). Seats 110 in four dining areas, and an outdoor terrace in season. Pleasant restaurant in an 18th-century Colonial house. Menu features Rock Cornish hen, shish kebab, steak, roast beef. Cocktail lounge, piano music. Wine selection. Open lunch, dinner, closed Tuesday.

Moderately expensive

ROCHESTER — western section, just south of Lake Ontario, junction of Interstate 490, US 104, and US 15.

Downtowner Motor Inn

155 Broad St. E., downtown (Tel. 232-3600). Five floors, 237 rooms, oversize beds with vibrators. Nicely decorated downtown motor inn, free parking. Guest lobby, meeting rooms, barber and beauty shops. Swimming and wading pools, sun deck. Restaurant open after 8 a.m. Cocktail lounge, dancing and entertainment Friday and Saturday. *Reasonable*

SARANAC LAKE — northeast section, in Adirondack Forest Preserve, ten miles west of Lake Placid, junction of New York 86 and New York 3.

Gauthier's Motel

143 Lake Flower Ave., one mile south of town center on New York 86 (Tel. 891-1950). Two floors, 32 large rooms, in pleasant, comfortable lakefront motel. Eight rooms with balcony overlooking lake. Landscaped grounds, swimming and wading pools, sun patio. Playground, tennis courts. Restaurant and bar adjacent, open after 8 a.m. *Reasonable*

SARATOGA SPRINGS — east central section, on US 9 and New York 50, just west of the New York State Thruway, 23 miles north of Albany.

Grand Union Motel

92 S. Broadway, one mile south of town center on US 9 (Tel. 584-9000). Sixty-four spacious, nicely decorated rooms, a few with dressing area, some with parking at door. Guest lobby. Landscaped grounds, Victorian gazebo with mineral spring. Swimming and wading pools, sun patio, shuffleboard. Restaurants next door and across street. *Reasonable, except expensive during August racing season*

Restaurant.
Trade Winds Restaurant

S. Broadway, one mile south of town center on US 9 (Tel. 584-3461). Seats 100 in two dining areas of a handsome, modern restaurant. Fieldstone fireplace, view of ponds and waterfall. American menu, featuring roast beef, seafood. Cocktail lounge, entertainment. Wine selection. Open dinner only Wednesday through Saturday, after 3 p.m. Sunday. Closed Monday, Tuesday, and from December 15 to March 10.

Moderately expensive

SCHENECTADY — east central section, on New York 5, junction of New York 7, just west of the New York State Thruway, about ten miles northwest of Albany and the same distance from Troy.

Esquire Motel

979 Troy-Schenectady Rd., eight miles east of city center on New York 7 (Tel. 785-5571). Thirty-eight ground-floor rooms, all with color TV, cross ventilation. Landscaped grounds, pool and sun patio. Breakfast available after 7 a.m. Bar.   *Reasonable*

SCHROON LAKE — northeast section, on Schroon Lake and US 9, just east of the New York State Thruway.

Frontier Town Motel

Eight miles north of Schroon Lake on New York 9, Exit 29, New York State Thruway (Tel. 532-9065). Thirty rooms, many with at-door parking, in attractive motel associated with Frontier Town, a re-creation of the Old West. Closed November through April. Landscaped grounds, lake, beach, playground. Restaurant open after 7 a.m. No bar.   *Reasonable*

Restaurant.
Cafe Guy

About two miles south of village center on US 9 (Tel. 532-7988). Seats 125 in a pleasant, chef-owned restaurant. American and French menu, featuring duck, steak, brook trout, homemade bread and pastry. Cocktail lounge, wine selection. Open breakfast and dinner, June 20 through Labor Day. Closed rest of year. *Moderately expensive*

SYRACUSE — north central section, junction of the New York State Thruway and Interstate 81.

Hotel Syracuse Country House

1308 Buckley Rd., six miles north of city center on the New York State Thruway (Tel. 474-6851). Two floors, 150 rooms, some with dressing area, many with parking at door. Attractive motel in landscaped grounds. Guest lobby, meeting rooms. Pool and sun patio. Restaurant open after 7 a.m. Bar. Special family rate.   *Reasonable*

TARRYTOWN — southeast section, on the Hudson River and US 9, about 15 miles north of New York City.

Hilton Inn

455 S. Broadway, one mile south of town center on US 9, Exit 9, New York State Thruway (Tel. 631-5700). Two floors, 204 rooms, some with balcony or terrace. Pleasant, comfortable motor inn. Landscaped grounds, lawns, shade trees. Swimming and wading pools, playground, sun patio. Restaurants open after 7 a.m. Cocktail lounge.
Expensive

TICONDEROGA — northeast section, on Lake Champlain and the Vermont border, junction of New York 9N and New York 22.

Restaurant.
Stone House Restaurant

429 Montcalm St., two blocks north of town center on New York 9N (Tel. 585-7394). Seats 72 in two attractive dining areas, one with fieldstone walls. American menu, Continental specialties like beef burgundy, veal scallopini. Steak, trout, and seafood are featured. Cocktail lounge, wine selection. Open dinner only, closed November through April. Also 16 motel rooms.
Moderately expensive

TUPPER LAKE — northeast section, junction of New York 30 and New York 3, in Adirondack Forest Preserve.

Restaurant.
Riverside Restaurant

Moody Rd., two miles south of town center on New York 30 (Tel. 359-9884). Seats 200 in two dining areas of a pleasant lakeside restaurant, opposite New York State Boat Launching Site. Steak and seafood are featured. Cocktail lounge, wine selection. Open all meals after 8 a.m. in summer, rest of year lunch and dinner only.   *Reasonable*

TUXEDO PARK — southeast section, near the southern border, on New York 17, just west of the New York State Thruway, southwest of Bear Mountain State Park.

Red Apple Motel

Three miles north of town center on New York 17 (Tel. 351-4747). Two floors, 51 rooms, some with balcony or terrace. Attractively decorated motel with fine views of the Ramapo River Valley. Pool and tree-shaded patio, playground. Cafeteria open 24 hours. No bar. Special family rate.
Inexpensive

UTICA – central section, junction of New York 12 and the New York State Thruway, about 50 miles east of Syracuse.

Trinkaus Manor Motor Lodge
Seven miles west of city center on New York 69 (Tel. 736-3355). Two floors, 40 spacious rooms. Handsome motor lodge in four acres of beautifully landscaped grounds, many trees. Guest lobby, meeting rooms. Pool and sun patio, pond, gardens. Excellent restaurant open after 7 a.m. Cocktail lounge.
Moderately expensive

WATERTOWN – northern section, about five miles east of Lake Ontario, junction of New York 37 and New York 12, just east of Interstate 81.

Howard Johnson's Motor Lodge
1190 Arsenal St., two miles west of town center on New York 3, Exit 45, Interstate 81 (Tel. 788-6800). Two floors, 72 spacious rooms, some with balcony or terrace, dressing area. Guest lobby, meeting room, pool and sun patio. Restaurant open after 7 a.m. Cocktail lounge. *Reasonable*

WATKINS GLEN – southwest section, southern end of Seneca Lake, junction of New York 14 and New York 414.

Showboat Motel
Fourteen miles north of town center off New York 14 (Tel. 243-7434). Two floors, 50 rooms, all with balcony or terrace, dressing area, nine with kitchen. Interesting resort motel built out onto Seneca Lake. Private beach, pier; fishing, boating available. Lawn games. Pool and sun patio. Restaurant open after 8 a.m. No bar. *Reasonable*

WHITEHALL – east central section, near the Vermont border, junction of US 4 and New York 22.

Restaurant.
Liberty Eatery
16 N. William St., center of town, just off US 4, on the Champlain Canal (Tel. 499-0301). Seats 50 in an unusual restaurant in a restored canal warehouse, decorated with antiques. Outdoor dining in garden and on deck in season. Yacht moorage and dock, two suites. Limited American menu features ham baked in sherry, Cornish game hen, homemade bread and pastry. No bar.

Nightly entertainment. Open dinner only, closed from mid-October to June 1.
Moderately expensive

WHITE PLAINS – southeast corner, junction of Interstate 287 and New York 22, on the Taconic State Pkwy.

White Plains Executive Hotel
S. Broadway and Lyon Pl., center of town (Tel. 761-8100). Fifteen floors, 218 spacious, attractively decorated rooms, all with dressing area, two double beds. Guest lobby, meeting rooms, barber and beauty shops. Restaurant open lunch, dinner. Cocktail lounge. *Moderately expensive*

Restaurant.
Hunter's Lodge Restaurant
1241 Mamaroneck Ave., two miles south of town center (Tel. 949-6268). Seats 100 in three dining areas of a delightful restaurant decorated in the style of a hunt club. Antique hunting horns, hunt prints, old bottles, and antique wine ‘glasses are displayed. International menu, with emphasis on game in season; Scottish salmon, Dover sole, baby lamb, suckling pig. Cocktail lounge, big wine selection. Open lunch, dinner, closed Monday, three weeks in February, and two weeks in early summer. *Expensive*

WILMINGTON – northeast section, in Adirondack Forest Preserve, on New York 86, about 22 miles northeast of Saranac Lake.

Holiday Motel
One mile west of town center, junction of New York 86 and New York 431 (Tel. 946-2251). Two floors, 28 rooms, some with balcony, in attractive motel near Whiteface Mountain. Guest lobby, meeting and recreation rooms, player piano, table tennis. Extensive, landscaped grounds. Pools, sun patio, playground. Restaurant open breakfast and dinner, featuring Swiss cooking. Lounge, beer and wine. *Reasonable*

Pennsylvania.

ALLENTOWN – east central section, just south of Interstate 78, west of Pennsylvania 309.

Holiday Inn
Six miles west of town center, junction of

US 22 and US 309 (Tel. 395-3731). Three hundred rooms, all with dressing area, most on the ground floor, in modern, attractive motor inn. Guest lobby, meeting rooms, barber, newsstand. Olympic-size pool, sun patio, wading pool, playground. Restaurant open after 6:30 a.m. Cocktail lounge. Special family rate. *Reasonable*

ALTOONA — south central section, on US 220, just north of US 22.

Fountain Motel
2906 Pleasant Valley Blvd., one mile southeast of city center on US 220 (Tel. 944-3555). Twenty-four spacious, attractively decorated rooms with dressing area, all with at-door parking. Guest lobby and meeting rooms. Extensive landscaped grounds, fountain and patio. Restaurant one-quarter mile away, open after 7 a.m. Special family rate. *Inexpensive*

BETHLEHEM — southeast section, near the New Jersey border, sister city of Allentown, south of Interstate 78.

Hotel Bethlehem
437 Main St., center of town on US 191 (Tel. 867-3711). Nine floors, 175 attractively decorated and furnished rooms. Very pleasant and well-maintained hotel. Guest lobby, meeting rooms. Gift and barber shops. Restaurant open after 7 a.m., noted for roast beef buffet. Cocktail lounge. *Inexpensive*

BUCK HILL FALLS — east central section, in the Pocono Mountains, about halfway between Scranton and the New Jersey border, junction of Pennsylvania 447 and Pennsylvania 390.

Buck Hill Inn
One mile northeast of town center off Pennsylvania 191 (Tel. 595-7441). 350 rooms in handsome older hotel, 80 rooms, all with dressing area, in new West Wing. Noted resort in 6,000 acres of wooded grounds. Guest lobby, fireplace, library. Barber and beauty shops, drugstore, recreation room, movies, dancing. Golf, tennis, lawn bowling, horseback riding. Pools, sun patio, playground, children's recreation program. Dining room open after 8 a.m. Coffee shop. Cocktail lounge, wine cellar. American Plan. *Expensive*

BUSHKILL — east central section, in the Poconos, on the New Jersey border and US 209, about 12 miles northeast of Stroudsburg.

Tamiment
Four miles north of town center off US 209 (Tel. 588-6652). Noted Pocono resort, 260 rooms in hotel, 172 in cottages. Many rooms with balcony or terrace, most with dressing area. Several recreation rooms, two night clubs, theater, beauty shop. Over 2,000 acres of wooded and landscaped grounds. Lake swimming, boating, fishing. Golf, tennis, horseback riding. Cultural program. Restaurant open all meals, coffee shop, box lunches. Three cocktail lounges, wine cellar. Season is May through late October. American Plan. *Expensive*

CARLISLE — south central section, between Interstate 76 and Interstate 81 on Pennsylvania 641 and US 11, about 20 miles southwest of Harrisburg.

Quality Motel
1700 Harrisburg Pike, four miles north of town center on US 11, just north of Interstate 81 (Tel. 243-1717). Unusually attractive motel, 123 large, tastefully decorated rooms, all with dressing area, color TV. Guest lobby, meeting room, gift shop. Landscaped grounds, swimming and wading pools, sun patio, playground. Restaurant open after 7 a.m. Cocktail lounge, nightly entertainment. Wine cellar. *Reasonable*

ERIE — on Lake Erie, northwest corner, on US 20, junction of Interstate 79 and US 19.

Howard Johnson's Motor Lodge
7575 Peach St., six miles south of city center on US 19, Exit 6, Interstate 90 (Tel. 864-4811). Four floors, 112 nicely decorated rooms, all with dressing area, balcony or terrace. Guest lobby, meeting rooms, newsstand. Indoor pool and sauna, recreation room, poolside food service. Lawn games. Restaurant open after 6:30 a.m. Cocktail lounge. Special family rate. *Reasonable*

Restaurants.
Barnacle Bill's Eastern Shore
3122 W. Lake Rd., four miles west of city center on Pennsylvania 5A (Tel. 833-6135). Seats 250 in three dining areas decorated in nautical style. Long-established seafood

restaurant specializing in fish, lobster. Service bar. Open dinner only, Sunday after 12 p.m. Closed Monday, and from February 1 through March 15. *Reasonable*

Kontis Restaurant
2212 W. Eighth St., three miles west of city center on Pennsylvania 5A (Tel. 454-0088). Seats 200 in three dining areas of an informal chef-owned restaurant decorated with Early American antiques. Menu features roast beef, steak, chicken. Cocktail lounge, wine selection. Open all meals after 8 a.m., closed Sunday. *Reasonable*

GETTYSBURG — south central section, near the Maryland border, junction of US 140 and US 30.

Holiday Inn
516 Baltimore St., five blocks south of town center on US 140 (Tel. 334-6211). Five floors, 100 rooms, all with dressing area, balcony or terrace. Attractive motel built in Colonial style, next to Gettysburg Tour Center. Guest lobby and meeting rooms, pool and landscaped sun patio. Restaurant open after 7 a.m. Cocktail lounge. Special family rate. *Moderately expensive*

Restaurants.
Dutch Cupboard Restaurant
523 Baltimore St., four blocks south of town center, junction of Pennsylvania 140 and US 15B (Tel. 334-6227). Seats 125 in three dining areas of a pleasant restaurant with Pennsylvania Dutch furniture, antique tinware. Pennsylvania Dutch menu, family style service. Specialties are sauerbraten, chicken, ham, homemade bread. No bar. Open all meals after 8 a.m. Closed last week of December. *Reasonable*

Hickory Bridge Farm Restaurant
Eight miles west of Gettysburg on Pennsylvania 116, then three miles north (Tel. 642-5261). Seats 250 in two dining areas of a delightful restaurant in a 100-year-old barn decorated with American antiques. Hay, pony, and sleigh rides available. Family-style menu features American and Pennsylvania Dutch food. Corn fritters, funny cake, ham, and meat loaf are specialties. No bar. Open lunch, dinner. Closed last week of December. *Reasonable*

HARRISBURG — capital, south central section, junction of US 22 and US 15, on the Delaware River.

Nationwide Inn
525 S. Front St., six blocks south of the capitol on US 322 (Tel. 233-1611). Two floors, 125 rooms, all with color TV, in handsomely decorated motel overlooking the Susquehanna River. Guest lobby, sundries, meeting rooms. Pool and landscaped sun patio. Restaurant open after 6:30 a.m. Cocktail lounge. *Reasonable*

Restaurant.
Inn 22 Restaurant
5390 Jonestown Rd., five miles east of city center on US 22 (Tel. 545-6077). Seats 150 in three dining areas of a charming restaurant decorated with antiques. Fireplace. Gift and antique shops in association. American menu, some French specialties. Noted for roast beef, steak, seafood. Cocktail lounge, wine selection. Open lunch, dinner, closed Sunday. *Moderately expensive*

JOHNSTOWN — southwest section, junction of Pennsylvania 403 and Pennsylvania 53.

Holiday Inn
1540 Scalp Ave., seven miles east of city center on Pennsylvania 56, junction of US 219 (Tel. 266-5851). Two floors, 113 rooms, all with dressing area, in modern motel opposite shopping center. Guest lobby, meeting rooms, sundries. Pool and landscaped sun patio, playground. Restaurant open after 7 a.m., featuring luncheon buffet. Cocktail lounge. Special family rate. *Reasonable*

LANCASTER — southeast section, about 15 miles east of the Susquehanna River, junction of US 222 and US 30.

Host Town Resort Motel
30 Keller Ave., one mile north of town center at junction of US 222 and Pennsylvania 501 (Tel. 393-1551). Three floors, 200 rooms, most with dressing area, over half with balcony or terrace, many with color TV. Well-equipped resort motel, free tennis, golf privileges. Landscaped grounds, two pools, sun patio. Barber and beauty shops, free sauna and whirlpool bath. Health club. Playground. Restaurant open after 6:30 a.m. Cocktail lounge. *Reasonable*

Willows Restaurant

Six miles east of city center on US 30 (Tel. 397-5144). Seats 165 in two dining areas of a pleasant restaurant decorated in Colonial style. Pennsylvania Dutch menu, featuring sauerbraten, steak, turkey, shoofly pie, corn custard. No bar. Open all meals after 7:30 a.m.   *Reasonable*

NEW HOPE — southeast section, on the New Jersey border and the Delaware River, about 20 miles north of Philadelphia, junction of US 202 and Pennsylvania 32.

1740 House

Six miles north of town center on Pennsylvania 32, River Rd., in Lumberville (Tel. 297-5661). Two floors, 24 rooms, all with private balcony or terrace overlooking Delaware River and canal. Quiet, secluded in, tastefully decorated, in wooded grounds. Recreation room, fireplace. Pool and landscaped sun patio. Canoes and rowboats. Free Continental breakfast, lunch available. Several restaurants nearby.   *Expensive*

Restaurant.

Chez Odette Restaurant

River Rd., one-half mile south of town center on Pennsylvania 32 (Tel. 862-2432). Seats 250 in four dining areas, including a dining porch in season, of a pleasant, informal restaurant overlooking the Delaware River and canals. American and French menu, featuring roast beef, steak, snails. Cocktail lounge, wine selection, dancing and entertainment. Open lunch, dinner, closed Sunday.   *Moderately expensive*

PHILADELPHIA — southeast corner, on the Delaware River, junction of Interstate 76 and Interstate 95.

Marriott Motor Hotel

City Line Ave. and Monument Rd., six miles north of city center on US 1 (Tel. 667-0200). Six floors, 435 large, handsomely furnished rooms, all with dressing area, balcony or terrace. Guest lobby, meeting rooms, newsstand, barber and beauty shops. Landscaped grounds, pool, sun patio, ice-skating in winter. Four restaurants. Cocktail lounges.   *Moderately expensive*

Penn Center Inn

Market and 20th streets, near city center

(Tel. 569-3000). Twenty-one floors, 304 rooms, in modern, attractively decorated motor hotel stressing comfort and convenience. Free self-service garage. Guest lobby, meeting rooms, newsstand, sundries. Fifth-floor pool and big sundeck. Wading pool, children's play area. Coffee shop open after 7 a.m., restaurant, cocktail lounge. Children under 21 free.   *Reasonable*

Restaurants.

Barclay Hotel Restaurant

Rittenhouse Square East, center of city (Tel. 545-0300). Seats 120 in several dining areas of an elegant restaurant offering a varied, interesting menu. American, French, and Italian food, featuring lobster Cardinale, beef Wellington, steak Diane, roast beef, cold buffet. Cocktail lounge, excellent wine cellar. Open all meals after 7 a.m., closed Sunday.

Moderately expensive to expensive

Bookbinder's Sea Food House

215 S. 15th St., near city center (Tel. 545-1137). Seats 400 in three dining areas of a famous old seafood restaurant decorated in nautical style. American menu, featuring lobster, crab Imperial, stuffed shrimp, snapper soup. Cocktail lounge, wine selection. Open lunch, dinner. *Moderately expensive*

Kelly's on Mole St. Restaurant

Five S. Mole St., one block from City Hall, downtown (Tel. 567-8398). Seats 180 in two dining areas of an interesting restaurant with a collection of antique oyster plates. American menu, specializing in seafood. Noted for oysters, broiled shad, shore platters. Cocktail lounge, wine selection. Open lunch, dinner, closed Sunday during summer.   *Reasonable*

Old Original Bookbinder's Restaurant

125 Walnut St., one mile east of city center (Tel. 925-7027). Seats 1,000 in seven dining areas. Famous Philadelphia seafood restaurant established in 1865. Menu features lobster, oysters and clams, seafood, steak. Free parking. Cocktail lounge, wine selection. Open lunch, dinner.

Moderately expensive

PITTSBURGH — southwest section, confluence of the Ohio, Monongahela, and Allegheny rivers, junction of Interstate 76 and Interstate 80S.

Pittsburgh Hilton Hotel

Commonwealth Place, downtown, in the Golden Triangle (Tel. 391-4600). Twenty-four floors, 80 nicely decorated outside rooms, many suites. Attractive, modern hotel at northeast edge of Point State Park. Guest lobby and meeting rooms, drugstore, barber and beauty shops. Several dining facilities. Four cocktail lounges. *Expensive*

Restaurants.

Klein's Restaurant

330 Fourth Ave., downtown (Tel. 261-8615). Seats 200 in two dining areas of a pleasant, informal restaurant serving a variety of food. Specialties are seafood, lobster, shell-fish, steak, roast beef. Bar, wine selection. Open lunch, dinner, Saturday dinner only. Closed Sunday, and first two weeks of July. *Moderately expensive*

Red Coach Grill

112 Washington Pl., downtown, in Chatham Center (Tel. 261-0226). Seats 325 in three dining areas of a handsomely decorated restaurant with brick walls, carriage lamps. Menu features steak, lobster, roast beef, seafood. Cocktail lounge, piano music. Wine selection. Open lunch, dinner. *Moderately expensive*

READING — southeast section, junction of US 422 and Pennsylvania 61.

Reading Motor Inn

1040 Park Rd., three miles west of city center off US 422, in Wyomissing (Tel. 372-7811). Handsome motor inn with large, nicely furnished rooms, many with dressing area. Meeting rooms, newsstand, free airport bus. Spacious landscaped grounds, with pool and sun patio, playground. Restaurant open after 7 a.m. Cocktail lounge, dancing. *Moderately expensive*

Restaurants.

Joe's Restaurant

450 S. Seventh St., six blocks south of city center (Tel. 373-6794). Seats 60 in a long-established, chef-owned restaurant decorated with photographs of wild mushrooms, the specialty of the house. Continental menu features filet mignon, beef tenderloin, baked crabmeat, all with wild mushrooms. Unusual fruit desserts. Service bar. Open dinner only, closed Sunday, Monday. *Moderately expensive to expensive*

Stokesay Castle Restaurant

Hill Rd. and Spook Lane, two miles north of city center off US 422 (Tel. 375-4588). Seats 180 in several dining areas, including a large patio in season, of a charming restaurant in a replica of an English castle. Hillside setting, landscaped grounds. American and Continental cooking, featuring steak Diane, lobster, roast beef, frogs' legs. Cocktail lounge, pianist, wine selection. Open lunch, dinner. *Moderately expensive*

SCRANTON — northeast section, junction of US 6, US 611, US 11, and Interstate 81.

Nichols Village Motel

Five miles north of city center on US 6, in Clarks Summit (Tel. 587-1135). Two floors, 50 rooms, all with balcony or terrace, most with dressing area, color TV. Modern, handsome motel in landscaped grounds. Scandinavian Ryah House restaurant, also pancake house, open after 6:30 a.m. Cocktail lounge, wine selection. *Inexpensive*

Restaurant.

Preno's Restaurant

601 Lackawanna Ave., downtown (Tel. 346-2091). Seats 150 in three dining areas of a pleasant restaurant noted for American and Continental cooking. Specialties are veal scallopini, beef tenderloin, filet of sole. Cocktail lounge, wine selection. Open lunch, dinner, closed Sunday in summer. *Moderately expensive*

TITUSVILLE — northwest section, junction of Pennsylvania 27 and Pennsylvania 8, about 40 miles southeast of Erie.

Cross Creek Resort

Five miles south of town center on Pennsylvania 8 (Tel. 825-3201). Two floors, 71 rooms, 40 with balcony or terrace, all with dressing area. Spacious, tastefully decorated rooms. Guest lobby, meeting and recreation rooms. Fishing and hunting available on 400 acres of landscaped, wooded grounds. Noted for championship 18-hole golf course (fee). Buffet service restaurant open after 7 a.m. Cocktail lounge, wine selection. American Plan and golfer's package available. *Reasonable*

WARREN — northwest section, near the New York border, on edge of Allegheny National Forest, junction of US 62 and US 6.

Warren Motel

2240 Pennsylvania Ave., one mile west of town center on US 6-62 (Tel. 723-5550). Thirty-four ground-floor rooms, ten with dressing area, three with kitchen. Comfortable motel with mountain view. Pool, terrace, picnic tables. Free Continental breakfast. *Inexpensive*

WELLSBORO — north central section, about 15 miles south of the New York border, junction of US 6 and Pennsylvania 287.

Sherwood Motel

2 Main St., one block west of town center on US 6 (Tel. 724-3424). Two floors, 30 rooms, some with balcony or terrace, in comfortable motel open from April 1 through December 15. Pool and sun patio, playground. Restaurant and bar one block away, open after 7 a.m. *Inexpensive*

WILLIAMSPORT — central section, junction of US 15 and US 220, about 18 miles north of Interstate 80.

Holiday Inn

1840 E. Third St., two miles northeast of town center on Pennsylvania 220 (Tel. 326-1981). Two floors, 200 rooms, many with dressing area. Modern, attractive motel within walking distance of shopping plaza. Guest lobby, meeting rooms. Spacious landscaped grounds, pool, sun patio, playground. Restaurant open after 6 a.m. Cocktail lounge. Special family rate. *Reasonable*

YORK — south central section, junction of Interstate 83 and US 30, about 15 miles north of the Maryland border.

Howard Johnson's Motor Lodge

About two miles north of town center on Interstate 83, at Arsenal Rd. (Tel. 843-9971). Two floors, 92 rooms, all with dressing area, balcony or terrace. Landscaped grounds, scenic hillside setting. Guest lobby, meeting rooms, pool and sun patio. Restaurant open after 7 a.m. Cocktail lounge. *Reasonable*

New Jersey.

ASBURY PARK — east central part of state, on the Atlantic Ocean, about five miles east of the Garden State Parkway.

Empress Motel

101 Asbury Ave., near center of town, opposite ocean (Tel. 775-0100). Four floors, 100 rooms, all with patio. Guest lobby, all-weather pool, sun patio. Restaurant open after 7 a.m. Cocktail lounge. *Expensive*

Restaurant.
Old Mill Inn

Old Mill Rd., six miles south of Asbury Park between New Jersey 35 and New Jersey 71 (Tel. 449-5370). Seats 250 in several dining areas of a handsome restaurant in a 1720 mill. Dining room and cocktail terrace overlook millrun, bar decorated with antiques. Varied menu, featuring shrimp Creole, chicken Paprika, sauerbraten, frogs' legs. Wine selection. Open lunch, dinner, closed Monday. *Moderately expensive*

ATLANTIC CITY — southeast section, on the Atlantic Ocean, US 30 and US 40-322, five miles east of the Garden State Parkway.

Howard Johnson's Motor Lodge

Arkansas and Pacific avenues, on the ocean, at the end of the Atlantic City Expressway (Tel. 348-4411). Twelve floors, 337 attractively decorated rooms, all with balcony, many with dressing area. Guest lobby, recreation room. Extensive grounds, swimming and wading pools, sun patio. Golf privileges at nearby course. Sauna baths, ice-skating. Restaurant open after 7 a.m. Cocktail lounge, wine selection. *Expensive*

Restaurant.
Flying Dutchman Restaurant

130 S. Chalfonte Ave., center of town, half a block from the Boardwalk (Tel. 345-3285). Seats 160 in a pleasant restaurant decorated in nautical style. Open-hearth charcoal grill. American menu, featuring steak, seafood. Bar, wine selection. Open lunch, dinner, closed from Christmas to mid-Februrary. *Moderately expensive*

CAMDEN — southwest section, on the Pennsylvania border, adjacent to Philadelphia, junction of Interstate 295 and US 130.

Howard Johnson's Motor Lodge

Seven miles east of city center near junction of New Jersey 73 and New Jersey 38, in Maple Shade (Tel. 235-6400). Two floors, 109 rooms, some with dressing area, balcony or terrace, in attractively decorated highway motel. Guest lobby, meeting room. Wooded grounds, playground, swimming and wading pools. Restaurant open after 7 a.m. No bar. Special family rate.

Reasonable

CAPE MAY — southeast tip, end of the Garden State Parkway, on Delaware Bay and the Atlantic Ocean.

Lafayette Inn

Beach Dr., three blocks from town center (Tel. 884-3431). Four floors, 90 rooms in attractive older hotel, 30 motel rooms, all with patio. Pleasant, long-established inn opposite ocean, all rooms with ocean view. Gardened grounds, pool and sun patio. Restaurant open after 8 a.m. Cocktail lounge. Season is Palm Sunday to late November. American Plan available.

Moderately expensive

Restaurant.

Lobster House Restaurant

One mile north of town center off US 9, on Fisherman's Wharf (Tel. 884-8296). Seats 250 in four dining areas of an attractive restaurant decorated in Early American style, overlooking the dock and Cape May Harbor. American menu, featuring lobster tail, crab Imperial, seafood platter. Cocktail lounge on nearby Grand Banks fishing schooner. Open lunch, dinner, closed Monday October through April.

Moderately expensive

MORRISTOWN — north central section, junction of US 202 and New Jersey 24, just west of Interstate 287.

Governor Morris Inn

2 Whippany Rd., one mile east of town center (Tel. 539-7300). Six floors, 200 rooms, 44 with kitchen. Handsome, Colonial-type inn surrounded by wooded, landscaped grounds. Guest lobby, convention facilities. Pool and patio. Barber, health club, sauna. Beef and Bird Restaurant, also coffee shop open after 7 a.m. Cocktail lounge. Special family rate. *Moderately expensive*

NEWARK — northeast section, between the Garden State Parkway and Interstate 95, across the Hudson from Lower Manhattan.

Holiday Inn

430 Broad St., one mile east of town center (Tel. 643-4200). Two floors, 200 rooms, most with dressing area. Attractively decorated and furnished motor inn, big lobby on each floor. Landscaped grounds, pool and sun patio. Restaurant open after 6 a.m. Cocktail lounge, entertainment. Special family rate. *Moderately expensive*

Restaurant.

Brothers Restaurant

42 Commerce St., downtown (Tel. 623-0972). Seats 150 in two dining areas of a pleasant restaurant decorated in Colonial style. American menu features baked stuffed shrimp, roast beef, steak, German specialties. Bar, wine selection. Open lunch, dinner, closed weekends.

Moderately expensive

OCEAN CITY — southeast section, on the Atlantic Ocean and County Route 559, just east of the Garden State Parkway and US 9, ten miles south of Atlantic City.

Forum Motor Inn

Eighth St. and Atlantic Ave., three blocks from center of town (Tel. 399-8700). Three floors, 49 rooms, half with dressing area, all with balcony or terrace. Guest lobby, recreation room. Swimming and wading pools, two sundecks. One block from ocean. Coffee shop open after 8 a.m. No bar. Season is Easter through September, closed rest of year. *Expensive*

Restaurant.

Watson's Restaurant

901 Ocean Ave., two blocks east of town center (Tel. 399-1065). Seats 375 in five dining areas of a pleasant restaurant in an old Colonial mansion. American menu, roast beef, lamb, and seafood are specialties. No bar. Own baking. Open dinner only, Sunday after 12:30 p.m. Closed October 1 to mid-May. *Reasonable*

PRINCETON — west central section, on US 206 and New Jersey 27 about 10 miles northeast of Trenton.

Nassau Inn

Palmer Square, center of town (Tel. 921-7500). Five floors, 120 rooms, four suites. Tastefully decorated and furnished Colonial inn. Public rooms have fireplaces, beamed ceilings. Guest lobby, meeting rooms. Landscaped grounds, pool and sun patio. Restaurant open after 7 a.m. Cocktail lounge, wine celler. Special family rate. *Reasonable*

Restaurant.
King's Court Restaurant
28 Witherspoon St., one block east of town center (Tel. 924-5555). Seats 100 in two dining areas of a delightful old Colonial tavern furnished with antiques, old prints and paintings. Brick floors, beamed ceilings. Menu features brandied duck, herb chicken, crab Chesapeake, homemade desserts. Cocktail lounge, garden terrace. Wine selection. Open lunch, dinner.

Moderately expensive

TRENTON — west central section, on the Pennsylvania border and the Delaware River, junction of US 1 and Interstate 295.

Howard Johnson's Motor Lodge
2991 Brunswick Pike, five miles north of city center on US 1 (Tel. 896-1100). Two floors, 60 rooms, most with dressing area, balcony or terrace. Guest lobby, meeting rooms. Landscaped grounds, pool, playground, sun patio. Restaurant open after 7 a.m. Cocktail lounge. *Reasonable*

Restaurant.
Landwehr's Restaurant
River Rd., seven miles northwest of city center on New Jersey 29 (Tel. 882-0303). Seats 400 in five dining areas and an outdoor terrace. Elegant restaurant, fireplaces, paneled walls. Seven acres of landscaped grounds overlooking the Delaware River. Rose gardens. American menu features steak, capon, roast beef, duckling. Cocktail lounge. Open lunch, dinner, closed Monday, and from June 30 to July 10.

Moderately expensive

WILDWOOD — southeast tip, near the end of Garden State Parkway, on the ocean.

Singapore Motel
Orchid Rd., two miles south of town center, on the ocean (Tel. 522-6961). Three floors, 58 rooms, all with balcony or terrace, 24 kitchen suites. Unusual Oriental-style motel, attractively furnished and decorated. Guest lobby, meeting and recreation rooms. Japanese gardens, swimming and wading pools, playground. Restaurant next door, open after 8 a.m. Season is mid-May to late September. *Moderately expensive*

Restaurant.
Ed Zaberer's Anglesea Inn
400 Spruce Ave., four miles east of town center, Exit 6, Garden State Parkway. (Tel. 522-1423). Seats 1,500 in eight dining areas of a popular, lavishly decorated restaurant with more than 400 Tiffany lamps. American menu, seafood and roast beef featured. Own bake shop. Bar and cocktail lounge, wine selection. Open dinner only, late May to late September, closed rest of year. *Moderately expensive*

Delaware.

DOVER — capital, north central part of state, junction of US 13 and Delaware 8.

Quality Motel—South
222 S. Du Pont Hwy., three blocks east of town center on US 13 (Tel. 674-3300). Two floors, 80 rooms, all with dressing area, in attractively decorated motel well back from highway. Some rooms with sauna, color TV. Guest lobby, meeting rooms. Landscaped grounds, pool, sun patio, playground, picnic area. Restaurant open all meals after 6:30 a.m. Cocktail lounge, entertainment. Special family rate. *Reasonable*

Restaurant.
Dinner Bell Inn
121 S. State St., one block north of town center on US 113A (Tel. 678-1234). Seats 235 in five dining areas of a delightful restaurant in a brick Colonial building. American menu features crab Imperial, stuffed shrimp, steak. Bar, wine selection. Open lunch, dinner, dinner only on Saturday. Closed Sunday. *Reasonable*

GLASGOW — northwest part of state, on US 40, 20 miles southwest of Wilmington.

Restaurant.
Glasgow Arms Restaurant
About 20 miles southwest of Wilmington, junction of US 40 and Delaware 896 (Tel. 368-4729). Seats 300 in six dining areas of an interesting restaurant decorated with the owner's collection of antique firearms. Imaginative menu, some Continental dishes. Crab Imperial, lobster, roast beef, shrimp are specialties. Cocktail lounge, wine selection. Open lunch, dinner, closed Sunday.

Moderately expensive

NEW CASTLE — northeast part of state, a few miles south of Wilmington and of Interstate 295.

Skyways Motor Lodge
Two miles south of Delaware Memorial Bridge on US 13-301, at Greater Wilmington Airport (Tel. 328-6666). Two floors, 100 rooms, half with dressing area, balcony or terrace, all with color TV. Guest lobby, meeting room. Pool and sun patio, wading pool, lawn games. Two restaurants, one open after 6:30 a.m. Cocktail lounge. Special family rate. *Reasonable*

REHOBOTH BEACH — on Delaware 14 and the Atlantic Ocean, southeast part of state.

Henlopen Hotel and Motor Lodge
One mile north of town center at the north end of the boardwalk (Tel. 227-2552). Main hotel, 60 rooms; motel, 28 rooms. All motel rooms with patio, six with dressing area, four with kitchen. Popular, long-established oceanfront hotel. Guest lobby, meeting and recreation rooms. Landscaped grounds, pool and large patio facing ocean. Wading pool, playground. Restaurant open all meals. Cocktail lounge, entertainment, dancing. Modified American Plan. *Expensive*

Restaurant.
Dinner Bell Inn
2 Christian St., one block from town center (Tel. 227-2561). Seats 225 in three dining areas of a pleasant restaurant surrounded by beautiful gardens. American menu, featuring chicken, crab Imperial, fresh vegetables, homemade bread. Bar, wine selection. Open after 8 a.m. Monday through Saturday, Sunday after 1 p.m. Closed mid-October through March. *Reasonable*

WILMINGTON — northeast corner of state, on the Delaware River, Interstate 95, and US 301N.

Holiday Inn of America
4000 Concord Pike, four miles north of city center on US 202 (Tel. 478-2222). Two floors, 142 rooms, all with dressing area, balcony or terrace, many with color TV. Attractive motel built around a pool and grassy sun terrace. Guest lobby, meeting rooms. Wading pool, playground. Dutch Pantry Restaurant open after 6:30 a.m. No bar. Special family rate. *Reasonable*

Maryland.

ANNAPOLIS — capital, east central section, on the Severn River and Maryland 2, just south of US 50-301.

Statler Hilton Inn
Compromise and St. Mary's streets, center of town (Tel. 268-7555). Five floors, 150 rooms, 16 with balcony overlooking the Severn River. Handsome motor inn with spacious rooms. Guest lobby and meeting rooms, pool and sun patio, 250 feet of dock space. Penthouse restaurant overlooking the water open after 7 a.m. Cocktail lounge, entertainment nightly. *Moderately expensive*

Restaurants.
Harbor House Restaurant
City Dock, center of town (Tel. 268-0771). Seats 300 in four dining areas of a pleasant restaurant overlooking the water. American menu, featuring steak, seafood, crab Imperial. Oysters and softshell crab in season. Cocktail lounge, wine selection. Open lunch, dinner. *Moderately expensive*

Maryland Inn
Church Circle, center of town (Tel. 263-2641). Seats 250 in five dining areas of a delightful restaurant in a 100-year-old inn. Several fireplaces, Early American furnishings. Crab dishes a specialty, including crab Imperial and crab soup. Cocktail lounge, wine selection. Open all meals after 7:30 a.m., 8 a.m. Sunday. *Moderately expensive*

BALTIMORE — north central part of state, junction of Interstates 83, 95, and 70N.

Statler Hilton Hotel
101 W. Fayette St., three blocks west of downtown area (Tel. 752-1100). Twenty-three floors, 350 rooms. Handsome new hotel in the heart of Charles Center. Spacious, tastefully decorated rooms, all with outside view. Guest lobby, meeting rooms, convention facilities. Free garage. Pool and sun patio, poolside food service. Coffee shop open after 6 a.m. Miller Bros. Restaurant open lunch, dinner. Cocktail lounge. Special family rate. *Moderately expensive*

Restaurants.
Chesapeake Restaurant
1701 N. Charles St., two miles north of

downtown area, opposite Penn Central station (Tel. 837-7711). Seats 250 in seven dining areas of a popular, long-established restaurant. Wood paneling, old brick trim. Varied menu, some Continental specialties. Steak, roast beef, lobster, fresh fish are featured. Cocktail lounge, piano bar, wine selection. Open lunch, dinner, closed Monday, and two weeks in July or August. Free parking. *Moderately expensive*

Danny's Restaurant

1201 N. Charles St., one mile north of city center (Tel. 539-1393). Seats 175 in five dining areas of an elegant restaurant with mirror walls and crystal chandeliers. Continental service and menu. Lobster and crab dishes are featured, also beef Wellington, steak Diane, Caesar salad, planked shad. Cocktail lounge, wine selection. Open lunch, dinner, dinner only Saturday. Closed Sunday, and first week in August. Free parking.
Moderately expensive

CAMBRIDGE — Eastern Shore, on US 50 and the Choptank River.

Quality Courts

One mile north of town center at junction of US 50 and Maryland 16 (Tel. 228-6900). Two floors, 60 rooms, all with dressing area, balcony or terrace. Attractively decorated and furnished motel near the Choptank River. Guest lobby, meeting and recreation rooms. Pool and sun patio. Restaurant open all meals after 7 a.m. Cocktail lounge. Special family rate. *Reasonable*

CUMBERLAND — western panhandle, junction of US 220 and US 40.

Continental Motel

Seven miles west of town center on US 40 (Tel. 689-8835). Two floors, 33 rooms, some with dressing area, balcony or terrace. Attractively decorated motel. Guest lobby, recreation room, pool and table tennis. Landscaped grounds, pool and sun patio, playground. Newsstand, liquor store. Restaurant open after 7 a.m. Cocktail lounge.
Inexpensive

EASTON — Eastern Shore, just east of US 50, about 15 miles north of Cambridge.

Tidewater Inn

Dover and Harrison streets, center of town

(Tel. 822-1300). Four floors, 125 rooms, 14 suites. Handsome Federal inn. Guest lobby, pool and sun patio. Restaurant, featuring Maryland specialties, open after 7 a.m. Cocktail lounge. Special family rate.
Inexpensive

FREDERICK — north central part of state, junction of US 40 and US 15, Interstates 70N and 70S.

Holiday Inn

999 W. Patrick St., one mile west of city center on US 40 (Tel. 662-5141). Three floors, 100 rooms, all with dressing area, in attractive highway motel. Guest lobby, meeting rooms, pool and landscaped sun patio. Restaurant open after 6 a.m. Cocktail lounge, dancing Thursday through Saturday. Special family rate. *Reasonable*

GEORGETOWN — Eastern Shore, northeast section, on US 213.

Restaurant.
Granary Restaurant

Center of town, just off US 213 (Tel. 275-3771). Seats 300 in four dining areas of an interesting restaurant in an old granary on the Sassafras River. Big picture windows overlook the water. American menu, featuring steak and seafood. Cocktail lounge. Open lunch, dinner. *Moderately expensive*

HAGERSTOWN — near the northern border, junction of Interstates 81 and 70 and US 40.

Venice Motel

431 Dual Hwy., four blocks east of city center on US 40 (Tel. 733-0830). Three floors, 145 large, attractively decorated rooms, many with balcony, most with dressing area. Extensive grounds, Olympic-size swimming pool, sun patio and wading pool. Playground, miniature golf, 9-hole golf course. Barber and beauty shops, liquor store. Restaurant open after 6 a.m. Cocktail lounge. Special family rate. *Inexpensive*

OCEAN CITY — on the Atlantic Ocean and US 50, southern part of state.

Surf and Sands Motel

Boardwalk at 23rd St., two miles north of town center (Tel. 289-7161). Attractive oceanfront motel, three floors, 89 rooms, all with balcony or terrace, front and rear doors. Eight poolside rooms with kitchen. Guest lobby, recreation room. Pool and sun patio, wading pool. Restaurant open after 7 a.m. No bar. Motel open May 1 to September 25, closed rest of year. Three-day minimum stay on summer weekends.

Moderately expensive

Restaurants.
Embers Restaurant
24th St. and Philadelphia Ave., two miles north of town center (Tel. 289-8400). Seats 500 in eight dining areas of an attractive, intimate restaurant with fireplace, Tiffany lamps. American menu, featuring steak, lobster, shrimp. Cocktail lounge, piano bar. Wine selection. Open dinner only from mid-May to late September. Closed rest of year.

Moderately expensive

Ship Cafe
14th St. on the Bay, 14 blocks north of town center (Tel. 289-8171). Seats 750 in five dining areas of a pleasant restaurant with an associated marina. Cocktail deck. Nautical decor, gift shop. Imaginative menu features seafood platters, crab cakes, roast beef; dolphin, sea bass in season. Cocktail lounge, wine selection. Open all meals after 6 a.m., closed October 1 to May 1.

Moderately expensive

SALISBURY — Eastern Shore, southern section, junction of US 50 and US 13, about five miles south of Delaware border.

Howard Johnson's Motor Lodge
Three miles north of town center on US 13 (Tel. 742-5195). Fifty-six ground-floor rooms, all with dressing area, private patio. Pleasant motel in spacious, landscaped grounds. Pool and sun patio, playground. Restaurant open after 7 a.m. Service bar. Special family rate. *Inexpensive*

WALDORF — southwest part of state, junction of US 301 and Maryland 5.

Martha Washington Motel
Two miles north of town center on US 301 (Tel. 645-5656). Fifty ground-floor rooms in attractive, Colonial-style motel. Parking at door. Gardened grounds, picnic and barbecue areas. Pool, playground, sun patio. Restaurant open after 7 a.m. Cocktail lounge. *Reasonable*

District of Columbia.

Hotel America
Massachusetts Ave., at Thomas Circle, a few blocks north of the downtown area (Tel. 783-4600). Nine floors, 345 rooms, 14 suites, a few rooms with balcony, all with dressing area. New, ultramodern motor hotel built around a big indoor-outdoor swimming pool with a domed glass roof. Guest lobby, free valet parking. Complete convention facilities, barber and beauty shops. Beef 'N Bird Restaurant, coffee shop open after 6:30 a.m. Hawaiian-style dining around pool. Haypenny Cocktail Lounge, music, dancing. Wine cellar. Special family rate. *Expensive*

Capitol Hill Hotel
301 First St., N.E., on Capitol Hill (Tel. 546-6800). Six floors, 73 rooms, 16 suites, in completely redecorated, comfortable older hotel. All rooms with color TV, two telephones. Wide range of meeting rooms. Coffee shop open after 6 a.m. Restaurant, noted for steak and seafood, open lunch, dinner. Cocktail lounge, entertainment. Wine cellar. Outdoor dining patio. Special family rate.

Moderately expensive

Hotel Dupont Plaza
1500 New Hampshire Ave., N.W., near center of town at Dupont Circle (Tel. 483-6000). Eight floors, 314 rooms, all with kitchen and dressing area, in modern, comfortable hotel. Large guest lobby. Restaurant open after 7 a.m. Cocktail lounge, entertainment. *Moderately expensive*

Georgetown Inn
1310 Wisconsin Ave., N.W., in center of historic Georgetown (Tel. 333-8900). Six floors, 105 rooms, all with dressing area, ten suites. Modern, handsome motor inn, unusually well furnished and decorated. Guest lobby. Four Georges Restaurant noted for outstanding food served in four distinctive dining rooms. Cocktail lounge, wine cellar. *Expensive*

Holiday Inn Downtown
1615 Rhode Island Ave., N.W., at Scott Circle (Tel. 296-2100). Nine floors, 161 rooms, 33 suites, in a handsome motor inn.

All rooms with refrigerator, some with dressing area. Guest lobby, meeting rooms. Free underground parking. Pool and sun terrace, poolside dining. Old Angus Restaurant open after 7 a.m. Cocktail lounge, dancing and entertainment.   *Moderately expensive*

Madison Hotel
15th and M streets, N.W., a few blocks north of the White House (Tel. 483-6400). Fourteen floors, 363 rooms, 19 suites. All rooms with bathroom phone, icemaker, beautifully decorated in Federal style. Convention facilities, barber and beauty shops. Underground garage. Sauna baths. Montpelier Restaurant, noted for gourmet food, open after 7 a.m. Cocktail lounge.
Expensive

Manger Hay-Adams Hotel
16th and H streets, N.W., center of town (Tel. 638-2260). Eight floors, 200 rooms, some suites, in very attractive, well-maintained, older hotel opposite White House. Guest lobby, meeting rooms, free garage. Restaurant open after 7 a.m., serving notable French and American specialties. Cocktail lounge, wine cellar. Special family rate.   *Expensive*

Mayflower Hotel
1127 Connecticut Ave., N.W., at De Sales St., four blocks from center of town (Tel. 347-3000). Ten floors, 1,000 rooms, in a distinguished, older Washington hotel. Guest lobby, meeting rooms, barber and beauty shops. Rib Room Restaurant features roast beef; La Chatelaine, French food. Cocktail lounge, wine cellar. Special family rate.   *Expensive*

Rock Creek Hotel
1925 Belmont Rd., N.W., off 20th St. (Tel. 462-6007). Three floors, 52 rooms, four with kitchen, in small, attractively decorated new hotel. Guest lobby and meeting room. Restaurant open after 7 a.m., serving breakfast and lunch only. Other restaurants within one block. No bar. Special family rate.
Inexpensive

Shoreham Hotel and Motor Inn
2500 Calvert St., N.W., at Connecticut Ave., two miles northwest of downtown area (Tel. 234-0700). Eight floors, 900 rooms, including nearly 100 suites. Famous older

hotel overlooking wooded Rock Creek Park, in landscaped grounds. Swimming and wading pools, large sun patio, poolside food service. Blue Room Restaurant features terrace dining, top entertainment. Full range of convention facilities, barber and beauty shops. Cocktail lounge, wine cellar. Special family rate.   *Moderately expensive*

Restaurants.
Alhambra Restaurant
1819 M St., N.W., a few blocks from the downtown area (Tel. 223-2125). Intimate, attractive restaurant, with several dining areas decorated in Moorish style. Spanish menu, featuring paella, shrimp Alhambra. Service bar. Guitar music. Open lunch, dinner, closed Sunday.   *Moderately expensive*

Billy Martin's Carriage House
1238 Wisconsin Ave., N.W., in the heart of Georgetown (Tel. 333-5400). Seats 450 in six distinctively decorated dining areas of a handsome, restored Colonial tavern. Varied American menu features steak, seafood. Bar and cocktail lounge, wine selection. Entertainment. Open lunch, dinner.
Moderately expensive

Blackbeard's Restaurant
1801 Connecticut Ave., N.W., several blocks from the White House (Tel. 667-6266). Seats 250 in four dining areas of an attractive restaurant decorated in French and Old English Style. American menu features steak, seafood. Cocktail lounge, music, dancing. Wine cellar.
Moderately expensive

Black Steer Restaurant
730 17th St., N.W., one block from the White House (Tel. 298-7030). Seats 200 in two dining areas of an attractive restaurant decorated in Old West style. Limited American menu, featuring steak and roast beef. Bar and cocktail lounge. Open lunch, dinner, closed Sunday.   *Moderately expensive*

Bonat's Cafe
1022 Vermont Ave., N.W., near center of town (Tel. 737-3373). Seats 475 in eight dining areas of an intimate restaurant with paneled walls, many oil paintings. Sidewalk cafe in season. French-American menu features beef burgundy, frogs' legs, chicken. Cocktail lounge, good wine selection. Open lunch, dinner, closed Sunday.   *Reasonable*

plete recreation and sports facilities, three 18-hole golf courses, 200 miles of riding trails. Indoor and outdoor pools, mineral baths, carriage rides, creative arts colony. Package store, shops. Restaurant, cocktail lounge, wine cellar. Special family rate. American Plan. *Expensive*

Restaurant.
The Greenbrier Restaurant
In the Greenbrier, one-quarter mile west of town center on US 60 (Tel. 536-1110). Seats 700 in four dining areas, including an outdoor patio, of a notable luxury restaurant serving a variety of Continental and American food. Bar and cocktail lounge, dancing, entertainment. All meals. *Expensive*

Virginia

ACCOMAC — on the Eastern Shore, US 13, about one-third of the way down the Virginia section of the peninsula.

Whispering Pines Motel
One mile south of town center on US 13 (Tel. 787-1300). One and two floors, 71 rooms, in attractive, rustic motel set in pine grove, well back from highway. Guest lobby, sundries. Pool and sun patio. Restaurant open all meals after 7 a.m., featuring local seafood. Wine and beer. *Inexpensive*

BEDFORD — south central section of state, junction of US 460 and Virginia 122, about 30 miles east of Roanoke.

Peaks of Otter Lodge
Ten miles west of Bedford on the Blue Ridge Parkway, at the intersection of Virginia 43 (Tel. 586-1081). Two floors, 58 rooms, all with balcony or terrace, in attractively decorated, rustic-style motel run by the National Parks. Season is May through October. No TV or room phones. Guest lobby with fireplace. Extensive, wooded grounds, many hiking trails. On 22-acre lake between two mountains. Restaurant open all meals after 7:30 a.m. Beer and wine. *Reasonable*

BRISTOL — southwestern section, on the Tennessee border and Interstate 81, junction of US 58-241.

Holiday Inn
One mile west of town center at junction of

US 11W, US 58, and US 421 (Tel. 669-7171). Two floors, 141 rooms, all with balcony or terrace, most with kitchen. Modern, attractive motel, guest lobby and meeting rooms. Pool, landscaped sun patio, playground. Restaurant open all meals after 6 a.m., featuring Chinese food, Sunday buffet. Beer, wine. Special family rate. *Moderately expensive*

CHARLOTTESVILLE — east central section, 54 miles northwest of Richmond on Interstate 64.

Boar's Head Inn
Ednam Forest, four miles west of town center on US 250 (Tel. 296-2181). Four floors, 103 rooms, many with balcony or patio. Handsome, English-style country inn, recently enlarged, in 300 acres of landscaped and wooded grounds. Gift shops, tennis, pool and sun patio, wading pool. Par 3 golf, sauna (fees). Two fishing lakes, gardened paths. Restaurant, in a converted gristmill, decorated with antiques, open after 7:30 a.m. Cocktail lounge. *Moderately expensive*

Downtowner Motor Inn
Two miles west of town center at junction of US 29 and US 250, opposite University of Virginia (Tel. 296-8111). Five floors, 116 rooms, all with dressing area, most with balcony. Modern, nicely decorated motel, guest lobby, swimming and wading pools, sun patio. Restaurant open after 6 a.m. Cocktail lounge. Special family rate. *Reasonable*

HAMPTON — southeast corner, on Chesapeake Bay, junction of Interstate 64 and US 258, east of Newport News and north of Norfolk.

Strawberry Banks Motor Inn
Four miles south of town center, Exit 4, Interstate 64 (Tel. 723-6061). One floor, 103 rooms, all with dressing area, at-door parking, eight suites with fireplace. Guest lobby, meeting room, newsstand. Par 3 golf course, 32 acres of gardened grounds overlooking Hampton Roads Harbor. Private beach, boat and fishing docks. Restaurant open after 6 a.m. Service bar. *Reasonable*

LEXINGTON — central section, junction of US 60 and US 11, just west of the Blue Ridge Parkway.

Index.

Pennsylvania.

New Jersey.

Delaware.

Maryland.

District of Columbia.

West Virginia.

Virginia.